CATHOLIC

SEXUAL

THEOLOGY AND

ADOLESCENT

GIRLS

Studies in Women and Religion / Études sur les femmes et la religion

Studies in Women and Religion is a series designed to serve the needs of established scholars in this new area, whose scholarship may not conform to the parameters of more traditional series with respect to content, perspective, and/or methodology. The series will also endeavour to promote scholarship on women and religion by assisting new scholars in developing publishable manuscripts. Studies published in this series will reflect the wide range of disciplines in which the subject of women and religion is currently being studied, as well as the diversity of theoretical and methodological approaches that characterize contemporary women's studies. Books in English are published by Wilfrid Laurier University Press.

Inquiries should be directed to the series coordinator.

Coordinators
Heidi Epstein
St. Thomas More College
University of Saskatchewan

Coordinatrice
Monique Dumais
Université du Québec, Rimouski

CATHOLIC

SEXUAL

THEOLOGY AND

ADOLESCENT

GIRLS

EMBODIED FLOURISHING

Doris M. Kieser

WILFRID LAURIER
UNIVERSITY PRESS

Wilfrid Laurier University Press acknowledges the financial support of the Government of Canada through the Canada Book Fund for our publishing activities. This work is supported by the Research Support Fund.

Library and Archives Canada Cataloguing in Publication

Kieser, Doris, 1964–, author
    Catholic sexual theology and adolescent girls : embodied flourishing / Doris M. Kieser.

(Studies in women and religion)
Includes bibliographical references and index.
Issued in print and electronic formats.
ISBN 978-1-77112-124-8 (pbk.).—ISBN 978-1-77112-079-1 (pdf).—
ISBN 978-1-77112-080-7 (epub)

    1. Sex—Religious aspects—Catholic Church. 2. Teenage girls—Sexual behavior.
3. Feminist theology. I. Title. II. Series: Studies in women and religion (Waterloo, Ont.)

BX1795.S48K53 2015   233'.5   C2015-900225-7
                                               C2015-900226-5

Cover design by David Drummond. Front-cover image from Shutterstock_176400578 (detail). Text design by Daiva Villa, Chris Rowat Design.

This book is printed on FSC® certified paper and is certified Ecologo. It contains post-consumer fibre, is processed chlorine free, and is manufactured using biogas energy.

Printed in Canada

Every reasonable effort has been made to acquire permission for copyright material used in this text, and to acknowledge all such indebtedness accurately. Any errors and omissions called to the publisher's attention will be corrected in future printings.

MIX
Paper from
responsible sources
FSC® C004071

Dedication

For my parents, with gratitude.
~ Laurette and Henry Kieser ~
My compass. My rock. My roots.

CONTENTS

ACKNOWLEDGEMENTS

Thanks to the Canadian Federation for the Humanities and Social Sciences, the Social Sciences and Humanities Research Council of Canada, and the Canada Book Fund of the Government of Canada for granting funds enabling the publication of this book.

Thanks to the kind folks at WLU Press and their colleagues, particularly (in order of appearance) Lisa Quinn, Acquisitions Editor; Leslie Macredie, Website and Marketing Coordinator; Rob Kohlmeier, Managing Editor; Kristen Chew, copy editor; and my anonymous reviewers. You found merit in my thoughts, creatively bound them together, and brought them into daylight. I could not be more grateful.

The Church I love is a jumble of beauty and wisdom, oppression and sin. I owe a great deal to all women of the Church, particularly the feminist theologians and wise women of history, who have suffered for their work and opened the door for the likes of me. These saints and sinners give lively witness to the grace of women's strength and faith in the face of misogyny and sexism, and I am thankful. And for the women and men who will follow—my students and all the bright lights of youth—you are my hope and my inspiration. There is much to do.

The Academy is a quirky space, inhabited by the promise and anxiety of production, teaching, and collegiality. I consider myself fortunate to work among some rather sane, intelligent, and compassionate scholars, who generally enjoy beer. Thank God—if I had to travel this road alone, it would not be nearly so amusing. Thanks to my colleagues at St. Joseph's College, particularly those in the Corridor of Light (Matthews Kostelecky and Hoven, Nathan Kowalsky, Richard Rymarz, and Lorne Zelyck). Thanks also to my colleagues at the Canadian Theological Society for your hospitality, and especially Timothy Harvie, Robert McKeon, and Erin Green for your enthusiastic and gracious support of my scholarship.

I reserve particular space for my extraordinary female colleagues, without whose friendship and humour I would be lost in a sea of crazy. Michelle Rochard, you are an angel of kind and rigorous editing. Donna Meen, you have never failed to facilitate my work through your own, while negotiating the ideologically and financially beleaguered world of the academic library. Indre Cuplinskas, my model of prudence and compassion in a broken world, you have forged a path for us both and for the females yet to occupy this particular ivory tower. I am so very grateful to you all.

Thanks to my colleagues and clients at Insight Psychological, Inc., with whom I have worked for many years. The courage of my clients and the steady caring of my colleagues are ever reminders to me that wellness and grace go hand in hand. I offer special thanks to Cory Hrushka—you steer this particular ship and never cease to amaze.

J. Rowan Scott has for many years been my advocate, supporter, and sounding board. Without your kind wisdoms, I would not be writing these words of thanks, which will never suffice.

To my friends and extended family members who have stood close to me throughout this project, who bring the spicy bean dip to the party and enrich my life, thank you for blessing me with your love: Sandy MacPhail, Margolee Horn, TC Yarema, Michael Liboiron, Kathleen Sullivan, Brendan Leier, Glenn MacDonald, Marilyn Komarnisky, Robert Sheard, Anthony Easton, Bonnie Moser, Yvonne McKinnon, Zinia Pritchard, Jim Parsons, Chris and Susan Kieser, Teresa Bigsby, Sharon Bachand, Alyssa Atkinson, Marion McIntyre, and Claude Prefontaine.

My immediate family does an excellent job helping me to keep my feet on the ground while my head is in the clouds. Elaine and Don Groenenboom; David and Coreen Kieser; Brent and Lori Kieser; Jed, Emily, and Haley Groenenboom; Hank, Ivy, Daniel, and Gabrielle Kieser; and my mother Laurette, ever remind me of whence I come. I love all you weirdos.

Very shortly after I submitted this manuscript to WLU Press, my father, Henry, died rather unexpectedly. He saw neither the cover of the book nor the words in print. I hope he is proud.

In the immortal words of Etta James: At last.

CHAPTER ONE

WHAT'S A GIRL TO DO?
AN INTRODUCTION

INTRODUCTION

What *is* a girl to do? The moral questions facing Western adolescent females today, particularly those regarding sexual expression, are complex and engaging. The diverse cultural influences facing contemporary adolescent females intersect in the concrete lives of actual girls in the throes of teen spirit. La Senza Girl, Pope Francis I, *Maxim*, Girl Guides, Twitter, Miley Cyrus, Instagram, and Mother Teresa exist side by side in the melee of consumer and media messages about what it means to be an adolescent female. Running quietly in parallel to these influences are parents, teachers, coaches, pastors, mentors, siblings, and friends. More immediate personal influences on adolescent females, those quiet influences are living with the reality of adolescence alongside teen girls, often drawing them, hopefully, toward a life of flourishing, integrity, safety, joy, and faith. While external influences encourage girls to spend dollars on constructing external beauty, those close to girls invest hours in fostering their personal self-awareness, intelligence, emotional insight, physical capacity, relational maturity, and life-sustaining spirituality. Adolescent female flourishing is precarious precisely because the girls' engagement with their worlds is so full of ambiguity.

In the thick and thin of both teaching undergraduate theology and providing psychological counselling to adolescent and adult females, few questions touch me more profoundly than those pertaining to gender, sex, sexuality, and sexual experience. Undergraduate students, female and male, are generally keen to approach these questions and their related issues meaningfully when in a safe environment created precisely for such exploration. Conversely, adolescent females tend, generally, to be more hesitant to address sex-related issues, despite acknowledging the pervasive presence of sex in their lives (for better or for worse). These are two different groups of people: examples of the many disparate audiences viewing the current Western spectacle of sex. Yet social messages about the meaning and significance of the person as sexual are fired buckshot into a crowd of differently matured individuals and groups, with little distinction made for appropriateness and/or human flourishing.

Theologians, as much as anyone, are guilty of the wholesale adoption of the buckshot approach to sexual theology. Over two millennia, we theologians have constructed sexual theologies that assume adulthood in their audiences. This assumption is problematic when trying to engage adolescents in meaningful conversation about sexuality. Teens are often distant from the language and the context in which theology has developed, and as a consequence they sit on the margins of the conversation. Meanwhile, religious and theological discourse are becoming more marginalized in the public sphere, and theologians are at risk of becoming dinosaurs as adolescent sexuality and sexual ethics continue to evolve. For these reasons, I address both sexual theologies and empirical data (e.g., psychological, neurological, developmental) in my regard of the realities of adolescent females, and I endeavour to construct a theology that is useful, appropriate, and meaningful to them. My primary question is *What facilitates adolescent female flourishing in the light of Christian faith?*

I elaborate on the concept of human *flourishing* in more depth below, but draw preliminary attention to it here as a central criterion for an appropriate sexual ethic for adolescent females (and others). I locate flourishing within a Christian theological perspective, which assumes beatitude as the ultimate human *telos:* persons flourish in right relationship with God, as is witnessed in their relationships with others, with self, and with creation. To facilitate flourishing in any realm, be it physical, intellectual, emotional, or sexual, persons must ever attend to both practical and spiritual exigencies. A theological articulation of sexual flourishing must always be mindful of the person's relationship with the Divine. In the Christian tradition, this relationship is found in understanding Jesus Christ as the human incarnation of God, whose mediation in the world continues in and through the Holy Spirit. Human sexual flourishing is an embodiment of our relationship with the Divine.

SETTING THE STAGE: ROMAN CATHOLIC THEOLOGICAL TRADITION IN CONTEMPORARY ACADEMIC DISCOURSE

The current state of theoretical discourse regarding anthropology and morality is salient to a meaningful exploration of adolescent female sexual flourishing within the context of theological discourse. The theoretical discourse between Roman Catholic theology and feminist ethical theory, in particular, affects how empirical data is incorporated into theological reflection. I have adopted feminist natural law as the basis for my exploration as a means of responding to the challenges arising from this discourse. To situate this work in the broader academic discourse, I provide a sketch of the landscape within which Roman Catholic theology and feminist theory meet.

Following the death of Pope John Paul II in April 2005, then Cardinal Ratzinger and current Pope Emeritus Benedict XVI spoke strongly against a "dictatorship of relativism that does not recognize anything as definitive and whose ultimate goal consists solely of one's own ego and desires" (Ratzinger, 2005). In numerous homilies and addresses once he assumed the papacy (Benedict XVI, 2006a, 2006b, 2007), Pope Benedict took up the task Pope John Paul II began in his 1993 encyclical *Veritatis splendor* to warn against embracing the winds of change in the contemporary discussion of good and evil, right and wrong. Pope Benedict urged the faithful to see that there are, indeed, natural and sustained truths, of both faith and humanity, upon which persons must build a human and theological morality. In contrast, Pope Francis I has spoken very little about moral relativism, except in the condemnation of social injustices and global wealth disparity, and has moved toward inviting all persons, of faith or not, to reinvigorate a social gospel more explicitly concerned with the poor.

Pope Emeritus Benedict XVI's statements arose in direct response to the emergence of practical and theoretical critiques of the *hegemony of the universal,* exemplified in post-modernist and post-structuralist schools of thought. Recognizing the methodological and procedural difficulties in having exclusive groups positing truths for all of humanity, independent of individual experiences, post-modern theorists have countered such universalism with an assumption of difference among persons. This assumption leads to the difficult conclusion that, in fact, the human community might have nothing to say about normative morality. In such a climate, any ethical theory that posits universal truths about moral action, like one based in natural law, is rejected as an imposition of one culture upon another (or others).

This places Roman Catholic moral theological thinkers in the precarious position of accepting both the constructed and different realities of human experience, along with some ascription to sameness among humans as humans and, therefore, some normative morality. This has been a struggle for theologians through the ages. The Second Vatican Council document *Gaudium et spes* (1965a) beautifully articulates the ambiguity of a faith and morality that lives *already now,* but is *not yet.* Almost fifty years ago, in the light of rapidly changing social realities on a global scale, the Church humbly acknowledged that the human community is "buffeted between hope and anxiety and pressing one another with questions about the present course of events"; we are "burdened down with uneasiness" (1965a, no. 4). The perennial question remains, "What ought we to do?" Ethics and moral theology pertain to how we, humankind, live well together in creation; how we are to be loving, compassionate, just, and faithful to God, self, and others, while recognizing our native capacity for sin. Life is complex and morality is hard.

How do we, Christian people of God, legitimately enter the ethical and moral conversations taking place within the Academy, our own cultures, and human communities more globally? Existing papal statements condemning the "dictatorship of relativism" seem to indicate that an impasse exists between the institutional Church and contemporary post-modernist and post-structuralist discourse: an impasse that threatens to render Catholic theological ethics and morality irrelevant in the broader world. Although Pope Francis I seems to be adopting a more pastoral approach to the moral life than his predecessors, his impact on the institutional Church's dialogue within the Academy remains to be seen, and we remain buffeted between hope and anxiety about our place in contemporary discourse. Into this impasse comes feminist natural law theory.

Why Feminist? Why Natural Law?

In the current scholarly climate featuring discussions of sexuality, sex, and gender, one might well wonder whether a feminist natural law has a place in contemporary discourse or traditional Catholic moral theology. The exchanges pertaining to sex and gender between post-modern/post-structural and traditional Roman Catholic schools of thought have revealed deep tensions between them. Each of these schools of thought is laden with anthropological assumptions and concomitant ethical conclusions.

The crux of the discord within current discussions of sexuality, sex, and gender has to do with the perception of universals and essentials (indeed, of *nature* itself) being in opposition to the perception of particulars and contingents (in the *lack of nature* itself). The general critique of the univer-

salist construction of human nature is that it assumes too much common-
ality among persons. Because universalisms have, historically, been based
on a decidedly hegemonic model of human relationships (e.g., sexisms),
post-structuralist thinkers posit that the resulting oppression of difference among persons has been devastating in human history for groups like
females. This critique extends into issues related to sex, sexuality, and gender. Alternatively, if we assume individual difference, as post-structuralist
thinkers posit, then we have no grounds upon which to base any form of
oppression or hegemony; every normative and ethical stance would be
deserving of equal consideration among various human communities.

In contrast, the Roman Catholic theological and ethical tradition has
always assumed an essential sameness among individual human persons:
we are all born in the image and likeness of God, which binds us together
in solidarity. The strength of this position is its moral imperative to be
responsible to and for one another, and to steward creation with love and
compassion. Unfortunately, history has also shown the vulnerabilities of
an argument for sameness: oppression, violence, and abuse have found
their way into the responses of the Church (and other institutions) to many
types of difference over the centuries, including those pertaining to sexuality and gender.

In contemporary discourse about sex and gender, scholars move along
the continuum between the *sameness* articulation of individual human
sexuality and the *difference* articulation. The sameness proponents, to
varying degrees, espouse a claim to universally normative human sexuality and sexual behaviour. In the official Roman Catholic formulation of
this claim, gender and sex are conflated. Thus, masculine and male, and
feminine and female, are essentially connected and universally discernible.
Acknowledgement of difference is encapsulated within the complementarity of the sexes (see, e.g., *Humanae vitae* [Paul VI, 1968]; *Evangelium vitae*
[John Paul II, 1995a]; *Ordinatio sacerdotalis* [John Paul II, 1994]; *Mulieris dignitatem* [John Paul II, 1988]; Congregation for the Doctrine of the
Faith [CDF], 2004). Males and females, by their very nature, complete one
another in the order of human relationships ordained by God.

Although complementarity of sex and gender are considered essential within official Roman Catholic anthropological teachings, they are
not considered so within feminist and other theological discussions of
sex and gender, for example, Salzman and Lawler (2008). Rather, most
feminist theological positions are predicated upon the assumption that
sex and gender are different human anthropological realities (Coll, 1994),
with the notable exception of the "New Feminist" thinkers in the Roman
Catholic tradition.[1] Typically, however, feminist theologies assume that

masculine and feminine are gender constructions particular to cultural realities, whereas male and female are biological sex realities inherent and meaningful in human experience (e.g., Cahill, 1996, 1997; Coakley, 2002; Farley, 2006; Gudorf, 1994). This feminist articulation walks the middle ground between the sameness and difference schools of thought: the difference schools of thought—like some contemporary feminist theory, for instance—are in polar opposition to the official Roman Catholic anthropological understanding of sameness. Some feminist theory, based heavily on the early, groundbreaking work of Judith Butler (1990/1999), does not posit the conflation of sex and gender in any universal or essential manner; rather, it posits sex and gender as discursive social constructions that, in turn, lead to the performativity of one's sexual, gendered being in society. What it means to be masculine/male, or feminine/female, has everything to do with one's concrete context. In and of itself, biological sex has no meaning. The different anthropological understandings regarding the use of the term "gender" in the United Nations Statement following the 1995 Beijing Conference on Women are notable; Judith Butler outlines these differences in "The End of Sexual Difference?" (2004c).

Current feminist theological ethics engages, in multiple ways, both traditional Roman Catholic theological method and post-modern, poststructural feminist theory (see, e.g., Cahill, 1996 vs. Chopp, 1991). To recognize sameness *and* difference, to walk the ambiguous path between universals *and* particulars, some feminist theologians are rethinking natural law theory methodologically and procedurally to accommodate for difference and sameness. Such natural law is able, substantively, to attend to females' individual and collective experiences. The most comprehensive articulation of feminist natural law to date is Cristina Traina's *Feminist ethics and natural law: The end of anathemas* (1999). Traina's feminist natural law serves as the foundation for my own construction of a theological sexual ethic. In contrast with other contemporary natural law theories, feminist natural law is robust enough to engage both the universal and the particular realities of adolescent females' sexual lives. I will address Traina's (and other theologians') work in more depth in Chapters 2 and 3.

As a feminist Roman Catholic theologian, I am drawn both to some normative account of human nature and experience (a sense of sameness) and to the recognition of concrete differences among individual persons (a sense of difference). This tension is especially apparent for me when I consider adolescent female sexuality. While eager to address individual experiences of sexuality as they are captured in empirical data, I also hope to identify some normative understanding of what facilitates adolescent female sexual and general flourishing. Adolescents are in the precarious between-time of growth from childhood into adult sexuality. They are sexually aware but do not yet possess the sagacity to integrate fully their sexuality. From what we know, developing adolescents require the guidance of adult wisdom, born of experience, to integrate successfully their burgeoning sexuality. Wisdom, however, is hard-won: theologians must attend to adolescent realities in our consideration of values, virtues, and norms, in order to articulate a path to wisdom that is meaningful to adolescents. Only then might we first discern what facilitates adolescent female sexual flourishing, and then encourage its development.

Roman Catholic Theology and Adolescent Females: Sex and Sexuality, Values and Virtues

The enduring worthiness of the values and virtues that inform and shape the Roman Catholic tradition regarding sex, sexuality, and sexual expression merits affirmation. The virtue of *chastity,* for instance, defined in the *Catechism of the Catholic Church* (1995) as "the successful integration of sexuality within the person and thus the inner unity of man [*sic*] in his bodily and spiritual being" (1995, no. 2337), reflects a centuries-old wisdom of the need for human persons not to be driven solely by their sexual desires and impulses. *Self-mastery* and *temperance* as the virtuous means to embody sexual self-respect and dignity are, indeed, both practical and ideological goods serving the long-term well-being of the whole person in relationship with God, others, and self. For the Church to understand human sexuality as both a gift and a responsibility is also for her to recognize both the goodness of the sexual body and the human capacity to sin (e.g., *Catechism,* 1995, nos. 2331–400).

The values that inform relational morality in the Roman Catholic historical tradition also inform the contemporary Christian experience. Our theological understanding of intimate relationships takes as its model the Christian covenant with God in the incarnate Jesus Christ. Christians are called to fidelity, mutuality, respect, honour, commitment, responsibility, maturity, and gift of self to another in the wholeness of loving human relationships. These lofty goals are met through attention to the Holy Spirit and our empowerment to fidelity through a relationship with Christ. The values and virtues embedded within the Roman Catholic moral theological tradition embody respect for human sexuality beyond just its reproductive utility or the random satisfaction of desire. It means that an appropriate expression of sexual intimacy within that tradition requires a loving, committed bond mature enough to withstand the vagaries of human emotion, intellect, and decision-making.

These values and virtues remain steadfast in my consideration of sexual theology and adolescent females' sexualities. What is less satisfactory about the Roman Catholic moral tradition regarding sexuality, however, is its movement from virtues and values to moral norms, or what ought or ought not to be done in any given situation. While other natural law articulations also attempt to provide a systematic application of values to the creation of substantive normative theological content (as I explore in Chapter 2), their lack of procedural attention to a variety of human experiences in their formulation of norms also leaves the resulting content limited, and insufficient for excluded groups, such as adolescent females. The use of feminist natural law in this study, however, allows for a broad consideration of adolescent female realities, in order to move from values to norms. The content of both the official moral teachings of the Church and other methodologically and procedurally limited accounts of natural law are, thus, deficient.

The methodological leap from values and virtues to normative moral prescriptions in traditional (and official) moral theologies circumvents procedural attention to groups historically excluded from the theological enterprise. This methodological leap is also based on a static reading of natural law theory that does not adequately reflect a method, procedure, and content inclusive of females' sexual realities. Consequently, the voices of adolescent females are absent from the formulation of normative content of Roman Catholic theology because the official norms rest on data that excludes their realities. The result is a sexual theology that is inattentive (and, perhaps, inappropriate, inadequate, or irrelevant) to the real sexual experiences of females, and of adolescent females in particular. The content derived from such an inadequate methodology not only suffers diminished moral authority[2] among adolescent females (and others) as a result, but might actually jeopardize their capacity to flourish sexually and as whole persons.

As I note in coming chapters, although the values so deeply ensconced in the Roman Catholic tradition remain entrenched in sexual theological discussion, academic theological discourse has inadequately addressed interpretations of those values among adolescents. It is by no means understood, for instance, that the official articulation of chastity found in the *Catechism* (1995, no. 2352) has been universally adopted among adolescents. Further, there is little theological discussion of the factors that affect, facilitate, or impede the adoption of these values and the development of these virtues among adolescents *in their actual contexts*. How might each person's engagement with his/her own circumstances—social, personal, developmental, financial, familial, educational, or relational—impact the recognition, interpretation, adoption, and manifestation of these values and virtues in his/her own life?

Although empirical data is not the final arbiter of morality and what constitutes a moral life, it is a measure of human flourishing in relationship with others and with God. Theological discourse regarding sexual morality is lacking in attention to empirical data, particularly regarding the sexual realities of adolescent females. Because such data records the stuff of human life—the daily negotiation of sin and grace—it also records human attempts to discern the patterns of God's presence in our world. Moral decisions are made in the ebb and flow of everyday experiences. Theological attention to adolescent life in its sometimes messy reality will, in turn, contribute to the formation of capable moral decision-makers; the faithful will see themselves and their experiences reflected in theology and, perhaps, find it relevant to their flourishing.

The need for self-recognition among the faithful in theological discourse recalls contemporary theoretical discussions of sameness and universality, difference and particularity. If the theological tradition is actually to reflect revelation in human history, then it is necessary to include concrete human experience in our account of ongoing Christian revelation. Yet, it is not sufficient to dismiss the universal values that have been consistently iterated throughout Christian history. It seems reasonable to assume that revelation is neither strictly particular nor strictly universal. The theological task at hand is to discern how best to attend to sameness and difference, and the universal and the particular, regarding sexual theology and adolescent females.

FULL OF GRACE: NOTES ON FLOURISHING

The concept and practical reality of human flourishing looms large in this project. Thus, a brief discussion of the history of the concept of flourishing, and its role as *thick* and central to a sexual theology that adequately accounts for adolescent females, is essential.

The concept and embodiment of human flourishing provides the grounds for synthesis of the bodies of theological and adolescent developmental discourses. Flourishing implies more than merely existing, surviving, or getting by; it means thriving, blossoming, and growing abundantly in order to fulfill our nature as persons. Like all living things, humans require a nurturing atmosphere and a hearty disposition to flourish. Abundant human experience shows that thriving is best facilitated by having basic needs met, living freely and autonomously within loving personal and communal relationships, having dignity respected and protected, living in peace, obtaining useful and edifying knowledge, finding and affording meaning to life, and having self-esteem nurtured. There is no one definitive path to flourishing in the variety of circumstances within the human community, and such diversity of human experience points to the rich possibilities that flourishing holds for both sameness and difference in its articulation.

Flourishing: Concept and Context

Relying on flourishing as a primary ethical criterion is somewhat contentious in contemporary moral and ethical theory (Alkire, 2000; Conly, 1988 vs. Wong, 1988).[3] To posit that we are fulfilling our nature as human persons when we flourish (or live the *good life*), one must also posit that there is a human nature, within which we develop, that is common to all persons. Also, if there is a common nature, then the fulfillment of that nature must include the common development of various positive human capacities and goals: that is, virtues. Such a thesis begs questions: What does it mean to be human? What exactly is the fulfillment of human nature? What are the virtues common among persons, if indeed they do exist? How best does one develop and act upon these virtues? And what does flourishing consist of? One site of controversy regarding flourishing even precedes these questions. Rather than assuming human nature as a starting point for flourishing, some philosophical moral theories suggest that, given the diversity of human experiences, we can assume neither a universal human nature nor a common understanding of virtues and human flourishing (Conly, 1988). This issue is prominent within post-modern ethical and moral theory, which assumes human difference as an anthropological starting point. Here, there can be no telos toward which all persons are oriented. Judith Butler, for example, addresses this issue, particularly regarding sex and gender, in a number of her works, including *Gender trouble* (1990/1999) and *Undoing gender* (2004a). She interrogates the concept and reality of *human nature*, noting the historical tendency of majority groups to exclude, rather than include, persons and groups outside of their constructed, normative perception of *humanity*. In this light, to claim to define virtues and virtuous actions authoritatively, and what might constitute human flourishing, can amount to no more than an imposition of one person's/culture's perception of what is good onto another's.

There is merit in questioning the assumption of universal human nature, virtues, and flourishing that are common to all persons, given the many, blatant examples of exclusion of persons and groups from the realm of *human* in global history through racism, sexism, and homophobia, for example. And yet, Traina's feminist natural law succeeds as a theoretical starting point for my discussion of adolescent female sexual flourishing (see Chapter 3). Insofar as feminist natural law is flexible enough to attend to both the universal and the particular of human experience, it is also capable of understanding human flourishing to be both an individual and a communal endeavour. And so, I do assume a human nature that is the end toward which we move as persons. I also assume that there are virtues that facilitate our attempts to be fully human, and that attending to those virtues in virtuous actions will encourage flourishing. I do not assume that every person's identity is fixed within this common human nature or that there exists a static understanding of virtue that transcends human reflection. Nor do I assume that every person has a fully developed capacity to discern the virtues in every particular situation, or that human persons are equally capable of acting virtuously toward individual flourishing.

As a normative criterion, therefore, human flourishing raises a practical question: How do people flourish in their concrete, day-to-day lives? Numerous historical and contemporary theories address this question with a broad view: Is flourishing best realized in attending to the particulars of each individual human life, or more adequately nurtured by attending to the general patterns of human well-being? Is flourishing more likely to be found within a balance of our individual and communal efforts to live a good life? These questions sit at the core of this work; the foundations of ethical discussion shape its trajectory, methodology, process, and conclusions. I submit that flourishing is best facilitated through an integration of the universal and particular realities of human experiences. Such integration requires a robust theoretical foundation that is dynamic enough to move with the variability of people's actual lives, and is stalwart enough to support a shared ethic.

The same integration is required when focusing on the specific aspect of flourishing that I undertake in this project: namely, the sexual flourishing of adolescent females. Any ethical criteria for such flourishing must not only incorporate norms attentive to general sexual well-being, but experiences specific to actual adolescent females as well. As evidence in the coming chapters will suggest, contemporary Western culture is ambivalent toward adolescent female sexuality. Young females are, by turns, prematurely sexualized and sexually suppressed. The result is a disconnection between what we preach about sexual behaviour and what we practise regarding sexuality. Articulating adolescent female flourishing, therefore, requires careful attention, not only to a general understanding of sexuality and sexual expression but also to the actualization of sexuality in particular social circumstances.

Flourishing: History and Moral Theory

Human flourishing, as a concept, has a rich history within the millennia of Western philosophical thought. The contemporary Western notion of human flourishing is rooted in the Aristotelian understanding of *eudaimonia*, the good (or happy) life or human good.[4] As philosophical thought developed over the course of Western history, virtue ethics fell out of favour at times (notably, from the Enlightenment period on) because of a growing awareness of human diversity and a turn to a more deontological moral philosophy. In the second half of the twentieth century, however, virtue ethics and discussion of human flourishing, the good, or *eudaimonia* resurfaced in moral theory (Hursthouse, 2007). Alasdair MacIntyre's influential work *After virtue* (2007), originally published in 1981, critiques the Enlightenment turn away from the importance of virtuous character in moral action, and recovers the Aristotelian virtues as the basis of a universal ethic. Although the Aristotelian notion of *eudaimonia* and more contemporary notions of the good life have at times parted ways, and virtue ethics themselves have varied in their accounts, it currently enjoys a robust dialogue in moral philosophy.

Artistotle understood *eudaimonia* as an ideal that was practical and compatible with human experience (1985, p. 152). Aristotle's successors are also rooted in human experience in their articulations of the good life, or flourishing. Nussbaum (1988) qualifies Aristotle's thought here: although the practical and theoretical aspects of the virtuous, good life are rooted in Aristotle's understanding of those virtues as non-relative, flourishing via his articulation of the virtues is still relevant and useful in contemporary societies. Contemporary thinkers take a number of different approaches to the notion of human flourishing and its ethical accomplishment. One integrated view posits an understanding of flourishing that is intrinsically linked to human nature, but is not to be confused with strictly self-serving goals and actions. Human flourishing is sought out by individual persons precisely because it is objectively "desirable and choiceworthy" in its inclusion of various human goods and virtues (Rasmussen, 1999, p. 3). And yet, it is not abstract from the lived experience of the person in action: the agent of those goods and virtues. Flourishing is self-directed within the broader social context of the person acting (1999, pp. 3–14). The agent must, however, possess practical wisdom (or prudence) to grow into flourishing:

> *Indeed, practical reason properly used, which is the virtue of practical wisdom, is the intelligent management of one's life so that all the necessary goods and virtues are coherently achieved, maintained, and*

enjoyed in a manner that is appropriate for the individual human being.
(1999, p. 17; italics original)

To realize practical wisdom fully, the agent requires communal living, maturity, personal integrity, intelligence, and self-awareness: the fruits of time and experience. Human persons will find flourishing in varying manifestations and degrees, based upon the confluence of their own capacities and circumstances.

A theoretical understanding of human flourishing independent of the practical circumstances in which the human agent exists (or vice versa) renders it untenable in human experience (MacIntyre, 1981/2007). One must have some intellectual understanding of virtues and good acts in any given situation, but one must also attend to the given situation practically to know what virtues and good acts are appropriate therein. Within this view, human flourishing is both universal and particular, theoretical and practical (Rasmussen, 1999); it is tied to human nature, and assumes a human telos toward flourishing that is neither strictly universal nor strictly relative. Instead, human flourishing is an endeavour that evolves with the developing person in his/her own specific environment, in the broader context of the human community.

Although flourishing might be self-interested (or egoistic), it is not necessarily selfish and disconnected from other human realities (Hunt, 1999). As the ancients understood it, flourishing as a form of self-interest developed alongside equally well-developed perceptions of human virtues (see Annas, 1993; Hunt, 1999). One could not flourish without positioning oneself within a broader human community that placed relational demands upon the individual. In this way, flourishing was not constituted solely by meeting personal desires and wants, but included a focus on others' goods and needs. Virtue and self-interest go hand-in-hand in understanding flourishing (Hunt, 1999). Thus, persons could not and cannot flourish within a simplistic construction of individualistic satisfaction; a relativistic notion of flourishing that defers to personal autonomy, independent of communal responsibility, is untenable. My proposal is not to have individual human satisfaction run socially amok under the guise of unfettered autonomy; rather, individuals will flourish only when they have recognized their responsibilities to and for one another in their ethical choices.

Flourishing and Theology

Theological discourse about human flourishing has developed parallel to and, at times, in concert with Western philosophical traditions. Throughout centuries of theological discourse, ultimate human flourishing—that toward which all persons strive—is thought to exist in right relationship with God: we are tranquil in the heart of the Divine. Scholars of theology, among them Thomas Aquinas, the New Natural Law theorists, and Cristina Traina, suggest that we seek, follow, and respond to the Divine in our imperfect human endeavour to find union with God—the fullness of human flourishing. Theologically speaking, human flourishing is not merely a matter of ensuring that concrete needs and developmental milestones are met; rather, human flourishing also involves engagement with an immanent and transcendent God. Recognizing the teleological nature of flourishing in ancient philosophical anthropology, Christian theological telos takes the human toward the Divine. We seek God as the ultimate good and, thus, virtue consists of our seeking to do the good that is God's will. According to the Christian theological tradition, the development of virtue over time and experience enables us better to choose good and virtuous actions as we endeavour to do God's will. To flourish is to grow more able, over time, not only to know what constitutes the good life and is virtuous, but also to act in such a way as to realize virtues in relation to God, others, and self.

When we grapple with the dynamic tension between our concrete, particular circumstances and our often intangible, shared striving toward the Divine, we manifest human flourishing. In this liminal space, we find the immanent, *incarnate* God in human bodies: we either know God in our bodies, or we do not know God at all. The human sensory experiences of sight, hearing, taste, smell, and touch are located only in the body, which is why the body is how we come to know (and ultimately interpret) the world; our spirits and intellects operate only insofar as our bodies function. If we know God first and foremost in our relationships with others and with creation, then we do so as embodied persons—soul in flesh, flesh in soul. The body is the locus both of our concrete experiences and our striving toward the Divine: our flourishing.

That God chose human embodiment in the world is revelation enough that we are called to nurture the whole person into flourishing. As one might imagine from what has been discussed above, and will be apparent in the various manifestations of natural law outlined below, the historical theological discussion of how we might facilitate flourishing in the human community has been varied and ambivalent. We are at odds over what are good and virtuous acts in general, and what the good and virtuous act might be in certain circumstances, and question the extent to which individual embodied circumstances contribute to right moral decisions. Yet, contemporary popular and academic discussions do position us to reintegrate the goodness of the body within our anthropological and moral dialogues. To flourish as embodied persons requires not only attention to our relationships with the Divine, but also to our relationships with our selves, one another, and the world.

The varied nature of these relationships is no more obvious than in diverse human sexualities. The Christian theological tenet of incarnate goodness in the human sexual body—that we are sexually diverse, and experience the world through self-aware sensualities—marks human embodiment as unique among living creatures. God has given to us the capacity knowingly to experience the world through our senses and bodies. It must be that Divine wisdom intends for the human community to flourish in graceful acknowledgement and wise exercise of sexuality. When embodied sexuality is successfully integrated within individual human persons, we witness a Divine spark of guidance toward flourishing in the presence of God. And, although sexual flourishing is not the whole of the human relationship with God, its realization still points toward ultimate communion.

Sexuality—flesh and spirit in intimate communion with others—highlights our human embodiment. We interact in and through our bodies to experience emotion, thought, sense, spirit, and relationship, which in turn shape sexual meaning in our lives (for better or for worse). Our bodily selves are how we touch the world and how the world touches us. Sexuality, both explicitly and implicitly, expresses what those various touches mean. When we are compassionate, nurturing, and kind or, conversely, callous, neglectful, and mean-spirited, we are not only acting on virtues or vices but also developing a virtuous or vicious character. The development and enactment of virtues and vices pertain acutely to sexuality, as each person and the community at large flourishes or flounders on their own individual and collective sexual perceptions and behaviours. Because each individual experience of human sexuality is unique, we must attend to the particulars of those experiences to understand their meaning in relation to our own flourishing. Yet, because we live in an increasingly global human community, we must also reflect upon the value and meaning of those experiences for humanity in general.

Consider, for instance, sexual pleasure. There is a general social consensus that sexual pleasure is a human good that contributes both to sexual and general flourishing. Western society is happy to inform, educate, and facilitate sexual pleasure in a number of settings, both private and public. Less certain, however, is the extent to which sexual pleasure factors into sexual flourishing. Is it the only, the primary, or the least important aspect of sexual flourishing? We are further socially stymied by how sexual pleasure is achieved by individual persons. There are any number of ways to achieve sexual pleasure that not all persons agree facilitate human flourishing, such as fetishisms and sadomasochism. Thus, what are considered virtues and virtuous acts might vary among individual persons within a common social agreement that sexual pleasure is good. These questions are further complicated by the physiological differences among the sexes. Most females are born with a clitoris, designed exclusively for sexual pleasure, and most males are born with a penis, designed both for sexual activity/pleasure and urination. Both opposite-sex and same-sex couples negotiate the role of sexual pleasure within their relationships, and discover the nuances of sexual pleasure with one another. We are confronted with the complexities of sexual pleasure and sexual flourishing, and must attune ourselves to the moral aspects of individual and communal sexual pleasure (e.g., appropriate contexts or partners), and understand that perceptions of sexual morality will likely differ from place to place and time to time. Here, the questions pertaining to the individual and the universal aspects of sexual pleasure and flourishing—like virtues, vices, and moral behaviours—are all relevant. Each particular experience will contribute to a more general understanding of sexual pleasure in our contemporary context, and this general understanding will, in turn, inform individual experiences.

Attending to both the universal and the particular is the contemporary challenge for theological sexual ethics. Western philosophy has grappled with this tension from its infancy; so, too, has Christian theology. Cristina Traina (1999) presents a feminist natural law that is amenable to both particular and universal human experience. Noting the dissonance between feminist ethics that focus on the particular and traditional theological ethics that focus on the universal, Traina proposes that the articulation of values and norms as "revisable universals" falls well within the scope of a feminist natural law. Her feminist natural law provides a basis for the construction of a sexual ethic attentive to both the concrete particular realities of adolescent females and the more general values and norms that might emerge from a broad study of those realities. In effect, such a theology will attend to the flourishing (sexual and otherwise) of adolescent females in Western cultures. General and sexual human flourishing, and adolescent female sexual flourishing, are robust enough criteria to posit virtues, values, and norms characterizing a theological sexual ethic. In particular, because adolescent females experience considerable sexual development, the facilitation of their sexual flourishing ought to be paramount in articulating what might be appropriate norms for them. Thus, what might *lead to* adult female sexual flourishing is as important a question as what actually *constitutes* adult female sexual flourishing.

HOW TO PROCEED: METHODOLOGICAL
QUESTIONS AND LIMITATIONS

Along with scripture, tradition, and philosophy, human experience is a foundational source of theological reflection and subsequent articulation within the Christian tradition. As noted earlier, attention to the actual experiences of adolescent females in the articulation of sexual moral theology is lacking in Christian thought. Here, I address the dearth of such attention with explicit consideration of empirical data regarding the realities of adolescent females by conducting a secondary analysis of existing theoretical and empirical data and literature regarding adolescent females' developmental and sexual realities; that is, their experiences, perceptions, and influences. I incorporate that data into a feminist natural law construction of a sexual ethic accounting for adolescent females. I have chosen this methodological route to converse among disciplines like developmental psychology, sexuality, and theology, which have previously remained somewhat discrete.

My particular interest here is to address areas of lack in existing sexual theologies. Adolescent females and their experiences are unaccounted for in the Roman Catholic sexual theological tradition; their voices are silent. The lack, in this case, is of theory, empirical data, and experiences of adolescent females' sexual realities. This data is a focus of my study.

As a result, I must, in effect, sideline consideration of other, equally relevant sources of theology, such as direct exegetical and hermeneutical consideration of scripture, for example. To explore scriptural accounts of sex, sexuality, and sexual expression is a worthy undertaking that exceeds this project. In the Roman Catholic tradition, theology relies on scripture as the breakthrough revelation of God in the world that is ongoing and, at times, surprising; it is understood to undergird the Christian theological enterprise. In this light, the revelatory data here is limited to a fairly specific moment in human experience.

An equally obvious omission from this work is explicit consideration of adolescent male experiences and interpretations of sex and sexuality, which is problematic insofar as adolescent females' experiences are inextricably tied to their personal and communal relationships with males. Conclusions I draw regarding sex, sexuality, gender, and sexual experience within adolescent females' lives, and concomitant theological proposals I make, recognize that adolescent male lives are practically, theoretically, and experientially present in the data. This limitation by no means dismisses the concerns that might arise from a study of adolescent males' lives and sexualities; on the contrary, it recognizes the complexity of such a project and the consideration it is due.

Further, the aim of this project is to extend hermeneutical privilege to the lives and experiences of females. Too often our historical accounts of humans have understood females only in relation to, or as an extension or derivative of, males. Although females and males co-exist in practice and are intertwined in multiple spheres, to isolate the experiences of females and spotlight their concerns is to question the theological status quo with regard to social assumptions of gender, sex, and relationship. A hermeneutic of suspicion regarding the necessity of involving male experiences in this project thus facilitates exploration of the constructions that impede, obfuscate, or deny females the possibility of flourishing, and which might otherwise go undetected.

Another limitation of this study has to do with the theoretical questions arising from the consideration of sameness and difference. The empirical data with which I engage in this project reflects the lives of adolescent females primarily in North America and in Western culture more generally. Clearly, the experiences of Western and North American adolescent females, and their interpretations of sex, sexuality, and sexual expression, are not uniform, and can be quite disparate and singular. Some factors, among many, that differentiate among adolescent females include religious, socio-economic, cultural, and racial backgrounds; geographic locations, countries of origin and heritage; gender and sex orientations; family of origin and birth order; and education. It would be inaccurate to suggest that the differentiation of demographic groups among, for instance, Caucasian, African-Canadian/-American, Native, Aboriginal, or Hispanic groups, could adequately capture the nuances of the lived experiences of all adolescent females. However, it would be equally inaccurate to suggest that the data does not capture any significant evidence of similarity. Although empirical data, whether qualitatively or quantitatively collected, is necessarily limited, it does provide some insight into the lives of Western and North American adolescent females. In Chapters 5 and 6, as much as possible, I draw distinctions of difference among the girls as they are captured in the data.

A final limitation of this project is its overall scope and depth. Because I am considering different disciplines in an effort to incorporate empirical data into theological discourse, my consideration of each discipline is focused on points of depth within the discipline rather than a breadth of information. I regret that some explorations are limited to specific points at hand; this is a consequence of doing work across disciplines.

HOW TO PROCEED: SUBSTANTIVE OUTLINE

To construct a sexual theology appropriately mindful of adolescent females, I propose to consider the data of their lives: their experiences and perceptions of sex and sexuality. Following is a skeletal outline of the steps that I take in meeting that task.

First, in Chapter 2, I delve into the Roman Catholic theological tradition and various discussions of natural law theory. Although the tradition is long and heavy with accounts of natural law, I focus first on Thomas Aquinas's definitive scholastic articulation in his *Summa theologica* (1947). Thomas's account of natural law has endured throughout the evolution of Christian theology, particularly within the Roman Catholic tradition, and serves as a starting point for ensuing accounts. Following a discussion of Thomas's natural law, I move to its more contemporary accounts, and the current state of the question both in theological discourse and in broader academic discourse.

In Chapter 3, I ultimately settle on feminist natural law, as articulated by Cristina Traina, as my own theoretical construct for considering the realities of adolescent females in the formulation of sexual theology. I situate Traina's natural law within other feminist introductions to natural law, and in dialogue with other, non-feminist accounts of natural law.

In chapter 4, I present an overview of contemporary Christian feminist sexual theologies to provide insight into the lack of consideration of females in general, and adolescent females in particular, in the Christian theological tradition. In this chapter I also discuss various body theologies operative in contemporary Christian thought, including erotic theologies and Pope John Paul II's theology of the body. In contrast with John Paul's theology of the body, I present feminist ethical theories and theological anthropologies that offer alternatives to that pope's ubiquitous anthropology and theology of the body. In so doing, I consider ways in which anthropology and theology can both impede and facilitate human sexual flourishing.

The second step in this project is to explore developmental theories and empirical data pertaining to adolescent females' sexualities and sexual experiences. In Chapters 5 and 6, I consider multiple factors that influence, and are relevant to, sexual development, including gender development, social heteronormativity, adolescent identity formation and voice, and biological and neural development. I focus extensively on the female pubertal experience of menarche and subsequent experiences of menstruation. First menstruation arguably constitutes a female's experiential introduction to her own reproductive capacity, and is a visible manifestation of female sexuality. Extensive evidence suggests that Western social perceptions of menarche and menstruation serve to colour female experiences and perceptions of their own sexual bodies, and often negatively. In Chapter 6, my consideration of menarche and menstruation provides the central reality and metaphor for the place of female sexuality and sexual experience in Western culture, and in the Roman Catholic theological tradition.

In Chapter 7, I pay close attention to factors that promote or impede adolescent female flourishing, particularly those within a positive perception of adolescent female sexuality that pushes against social heteronormativity and male sexual privilege. Here, I explore in some depth the ambiguity of female sexual desire, its pleasure and its danger, and its manifestations in sexual expression. A discussion of female sexual pleasure in the Catholic theological tradition yields recognition of both social and religious distaste for female experiences of sexual pleasure and the means by which it is achieved; hence, social, personal, religious, and physical danger all factor into female experiences and expressions of desire, along with quests for pleasure. Perceptions of masturbation, particularly in Christian theology, provide the backdrop for the place of pleasure and desire in females' sexual flourishing.

The synthesis of data pertaining to adolescent females and the Christian, Roman Catholic theological tradition is the focus of this work. In Chapter 8, I propose a sexual theology appropriate to adolescent females' flourishing, based within feminist natural law. Cristina Traina's articulation of feminist natural law is open to the integration of discrete discourses and theoretical constructs, and so, theoretical and empirical accounts of development and theology are woven through the normative content I propose for a sexual theology accounting for adolescent females. I acknowledge the moral ambiguity that accompanies the Christian experience of sin and grace, and in the light of this moral ambiguity, I propose both prerequisites and normative content for a sexual theology that adequately addresses the sexualities of adolescent females.

WHO'S THAT GIRL? AN INTRODUCTION

This project hits close to the bone for me, as its author. I am both a Roman Catholic theologian working in the area of morality and ethics, and a psychological counsellor working primarily with adolescent females and women. I am also feminist—the kind of feminist who is invested in the flourishing of females, children, and other vulnerable individuals and groups in society. I like males. I like females. I like children and teens, although I have none of my own. I am committed to females and feminism within Roman

Catholic, Christian communities and within my psychological counselling practice. I hope for mutual love and justice in human relationships, and watch for the movement of Wisdom in the world. I advocate for females. I am curious about the inherent entanglements connecting sex, sexuality, and God. I believe that we encounter the Divine first and foremost in the faces of creation. I am grateful for others' generosity of time and spirit in my times of abundance and need.

All of what I am converges in my love for girls and women in the world. This convergence fuels my teaching, research, and counselling. My family, friends, education, social upbringing, employment, and relationships all play roles in my life. I am fortunate to be surrounded by people who nurture in me strength of character, fortitude, patience for the long view of justice, and reliance on the Holy Spirit. Loved ones have shown me joy and comfort in moments of despair, and ongoing encouragement of my inquiries. I have learned by volunteering that community is the locus of justice and work for human well-being. My work has variously nurtured my growth and expanded my humility. My personal and professional relationships have graced me with a deepening capacity for compassion and forgiveness. Each person in my life has shown me, for better or for worse, some of myself and some of God. When I attend to adolescent females, sexuality, theology, and God, I do so in context, in what is for me a work of love.

My collective life experience necessarily informs my work and introduces biases: the data to which I attend, the questions I consider, my interpretation of existing accounts of the issues I present. I acknowledge such biases and limitations as testament to the tension in the Christian experience found between what we already now know of God, and what is yet to be revealed. God among us in the person of Jesus Christ invited us to a radical new relationship with the Divine. In and through the Holy Spirit, we are called to speak courageously to the meaning of God's presence among us, to trust in the movement of Wisdom in our lives, and to open ourselves, through prayer and reflection, to the will of God. I am already now in relationship with the Divine but I am not yet fully so.

As a theologian, my understanding of the will of God as it is revealed in human history has come to rely heavily on a thick account of human flourishing. In the personal and communal realities of human interaction with the world, God calls us to herself, toward the fullness of humanity. The response to this call can be difficult, filled with ambivalence and the tension of already knowing the presence of God, but not yet knowing that presence fully. Movement in her direction is coloured both with false starts, wrong turns, and hurdles, and compassionate neighbours, insights, and bridges of grace.

This work considers what might facilitate sexual flourishing among adolescent females: for them simply to know that their sexuality is God's own gift to them. It is admittedly a tricky business stewarding this gift well, particularly in the full flush of adolescence. But, we are not without hope in development; we are not without intelligence and prudence. We desire flourishing, not as a destination but as a journey into and with the heart of God: the human person fully alive.

This book is the result of my work in different worlds that are actually quite fruitfully connected. The negotiations inherent to doing work among disciplines open a space for creative dialogue. In the following chapters I explore the tensions among sexuality, gender, theological anthropology, adolescence, development, and sexual theology as a means of considering human sexual flourishing. The connections that I experience among my different worlds are the connections that I hope to expand upon creatively in this work.

CHAPTER TWO

NATURAL LAW IN THE ROMAN CATHOLIC THEOLOGICAL TRADITION

INTRODUCTION

The colourful milieu in which ambivalent and conflicting cultural messages about ourselves as human persons in the world swirl about, arguably, defines our contemporary context. In North America, and likely a good deal of the rest of the world, we are inundated daily with images and information showing us what we need, inviting us continually to buy, and telling us how to live. Amidst the babel of consumerism, consumption, and body perfectionism that colours Western culture resides the Roman Catholic Church, whose moral message is articulated in numerous voices: the official magisterial voice, pastoral voices, and theological voices. The issues that are of particularly pressing concern for the official Church are those pertaining to life and its generation. The value of human life and bodies, our means of procreation (or contraception), and questions regarding gender, sex, and sexuality have been front and centre in a good deal of Roman Catholic moral teaching in the past fifty years. In concert with the voice of the Magisterium are the voices of pastoral ministers and theologians representing a variety of positions on these issues.

The voices most obviously advocating for women in the Church and in the world are those of feminist theologians: women and men who are paying particular attention to the care and well-being of females, children, and other marginalized persons (Tina Beattie, 2003; Lisa Sowle Cahill, 1985; Sarah Coakley, 2002; Mary Daly, 1973, 1968; Margaret Farley, 1993; Ada Maria Isasi-Diaz, 1993; Pui-lan Kwok, 1992; Rosemary Radford Ruether, 1983; Elizabeth Schussler Fiorenza, 1983/1990; Cristina Traina, 1999; Phyllis

Trible, 1978). From differing contexts, perspectives, traditions, and experiences, feminist theologians ask questions about how females live a moral life in contemporary social realities. Mary Daly (1928–2010), considered by many the grandmother of contemporary feminist theology, effectively launched feminist theological inquiry with her 1968 work, *The Church and the second sex*. Since that time, feminist theology has evolved and grown in both content and respectability. No longer on the margins of the Church, feminist theology is now a staple in theological discourse.

Because feminist theology explicitly adopts a non-patriarchal perspective on issues of faith and action, it has often stood in contrast to the Church, although not necessarily over conclusions drawn. While frequently disputing the conclusions of official teachings and traditional theology, there are still times when feminist thought dovetails with magisterial teachings; over interpretations of new reproductive technologies, for example. More frequently, however, contrasts become apparent in the methodology of their theological enterprise; feminist thinkers and the Magisterium generally take very different routes to reach their conclusions. In the midst of shifting world views and theological methods sit the moral questions pertaining to bodies, gender, sex, and sexuality. How we reach moral conclusions has been the subject of significant theological discussion in the Church, particularly since the groundswell of women entering into the discipline of theology following the Second Vatican Council.

The Catholic moral tradition's long-standing commitment to natural law has recently met the post-modern world view head-on; the interrogation of universal abiding truths and objectivity, and of relativism and subjectivism, colour contemporary discourse on what are good and bad, right and wrong behaviours. In this chapter, I explore Roman Catholic theology in terms of the method and substance of the natural law tradition, which has seen numerous iterations over the years. To provide a context for contemporary natural law discussions, I turn to Catholic medieval scholar Thomas Aquinas (ca. 1225–1274),[1] whose succinct treatment of natural law in the scholastic tradition remains the benchmark for natural law thinkers to this day. Thomas's work has been richly mined for insights relevant to contemporary moral and ethical issues, yet not without controversy. Competing interpretations of Thomas's work and other subsequent developments of natural law shape the discussion of method in Catholic moral theology.

Following my brief account of natural law in Thomas's thought, I address two contemporary schools of thought that are especially relevant to Catholic moral theology today, and that provide further context for natural law theory: New Natural Law (NNL) and Revisionism. It is apparent, upon critique, that neither NNL nor Revisionism is adequate to support a feminist sexual ethic accounting for adolescent females, precisely because neither school procedurally incorporates females' realities. In the following chapter, therefore, I will introduce a relatively new consideration: feminist natural law, which has a theoretical foundation that is methodologically and procedurally able to support a feminist sexual ethic accounting specifically for adolescent female realities.

NATURAL LAW AND THEOLOGY

Many contemporary moral theologies within the Roman Catholic tradition proceed from a dynamic development of natural law theory, which finds its most sturdy roots in the work of medieval theologian Thomas Aquinas. Thomas's formulation of natural law is situated within the First Part of the Second Part of his extensive *Summa theologica* (1947), within the broader discussion of law in general. This brief outline of Thomas's thought on natural law, practical moral decision-making, and moral action does not do justice to its nuance and complexity, but it does provide a context for more contemporary natural law theories within the Roman Catholic theological tradition.

Thomas Aquinas and Natural Law

According to Thomas Aquinas, law is "nothing else than an ordinance of reason for the common good, made by him who has care of the community, and promulgated" (I–II, Q. 90, a.4); that is, a public decree declared by a person/group in authority, in order to secure communal well-being. He further qualifies law as having three types: eternal/divine law, natural law, and human/positive law. Most importantly for Thomas, eternal law is that law which is Divine Reason's governance of all things in the universe. Since Divine Reason is not subject to time, the law thereby promulgated must, of necessity, be eternal (I–II, Q. 91, a. 1). Thomas further posits that natural law is the rational creature's (i.e., human's) participation of eternal or divine law (I–II, Q. 91, a. 2).

For Thomas, there is no formulation of the reasonable apprehension of natural law by human persons discrete from the recognition of eternal law. His world view regarding the relationship between faith and reason is such that eternal law and natural law are inseparable: one cannot posit a natural law without reference to its perfection in eternal law. This connection is based on his understanding of union with God as the natural human telos: God is central to Thomas's natural law, as the ultimate end toward which human persons strive. Thomas's formulation is not strictly philosophical— that is, of reason distinct from faith—but rather theological, or of faith elucidated by reason (Hittinger, 1997; Porter, 1999).

Conflating the theological and philosophical when regarding the law is natural for Thomas; however, later manifestations of natural law will propose that its more philosophical character is a means of appealing to a broadly secular, rather than Christian, basis for ethical discussion. Because Thomas sees beatitude as the telos of human persons, he sees natural law and moral goodness as, therefore, oriented toward this end; the lived experience of the human person is, of necessity, inclined toward God. Thomas discusses all goods within the broader understanding of this human telos; thus, the goods are not for themselves, but are a means for the attainment of beatitude. To separate natural law from eternal law in the service of a strictly philosophical natural law would then situate the goods themselves as the human telos, which would have been untenable within Thomas's medieval world view.

Regarding moral action, Thomas's first precept of natural law is "'good is to be done and pursued, and evil is to be avoided.' All other precepts of the natural law are based upon this" (I–II, Q. 94, a.2). Beyond the first precept, he indicates only three further precepts, as they flow from the first:

1. the preservation of one's own being and the avoidance of its obstacles;
2. the inclination of humans in matters as pertain to all animals, "such as sexual intercourse, education of offspring and so forth"; and
3. the inclination to know the truth about God. (I–II, Q. 94, a.2)

Thomas goes no further with the precepts of natural law. His paucity of detail regarding specific precepts has been the source of a good deal of scholarly discussion over the years, as we will see when we consider the New Natural Law theory. Thomas was not inclined to use the natural law as a means of solving moral questions, but rather saw it as a means by which to formulate and address moral questions themselves (Hittinger, 1997).

For Thomas, the means by which we attain the goods and move toward God are the virtues. Thus, he locates his discussion of natural law within his own broader discussion in the *Summa* of human will and action toward obtaining ultimate fulfillment, which is in God (I–II, QQ.1–89). Our actions, virtuous or vicious, are choices in the direction of our passions for absolute and restricted goods or evils. We develop habits, both virtues and vices, by the constitutive nature of our moral (or immoral) actions. For example, the more we choose virtuous actions, the more virtue will become our habit; the more habitual our acts of virtue, the more virtuous we become as persons. Only after Thomas's development of the ultimate human end, human acts, the passions, the habits, and the virtues and vices, does he introduce his Treatise on Law (QQ. 90–108), one question of which pertains to natural law (Q. 94). It is, perhaps, telling that his Treatise on Law is followed directly by his Treatise on Grace, the final section of the First Part of the Second Part of the *Summa*; his is a theological construct that recognizes the unity of reason, nature, and grace as constitutive of the moral person.

The Second Part of the Second Part of the *Summa* pertains to the Christian life (QQ. 1–189). In it, Thomas outlines the various virtues: theological (faith, hope, and charity), intellectual (prudence), and moral (justice, fortitude, and temperance). The final section of the Second Part addresses the gifts of the Spirit, which become manifest in the diversities of life choices (active and contemplative) and the various states in life. By situating his discussion of natural law amidst a broader discussion of human activity and decision-making, and of Christian life in the Spirit, Thomas is framing the moral life as a very human endeavour to act well under complex circumstances while attending to the will of God. Reason and faith work together to discern human participation in the Divine will: not by rote application of precepts and norms but, rather, by development in virtue through the practice of virtuous habits. We act well only by discerning what the good thing to do is, and by practising our capacity to choose rightly. The law is not, for Thomas, the strict articulation of rules for following that effect a quantitative analysis of right or wrong human activity. Rather, the law is the basic structure by which human persons develop qualitatively good habits (virtues) over time, with a good deal of room for error in practical wisdom and, therefore, grace. Virtue is exacting work.

Chief among all human capacities in practical moral reasoning is the virtue of prudence: "Prudence is an intellectual virtue with a practical purpose: it tells us what pertains to the accomplishment of ends...by installing flexible, multivalent, but rigorous reasoning at the center of practical moral reflection" (Traina, 1999, p. 65). Thomas expects that each person will, to varying degrees, be capable of prudent moral reflection in his/her own particular circumstance. He is willing to allow for the uncertainty that might arise from such an open interpretation of inclinations toward the Divine, while clearly understanding that not all moral choices are equally legitimate.

Compounding the ambiguity that ensues from his lack of detail pertaining strictly to natural law is Thomas's recognition of the potential for error in the application of practical reason (I–II, Q. 94, a.4). Thomas makes three points pertaining to natural law. The first is that natural law pertains not only to nature but also to reason; that is, what occurs as natural is not the determiner of morality, without reasonable (prudent, just, and charitable) reflection on its place in each circumstance. For Thomas, what *is* is not necessarily what *ought to be*. The second point is historicity.[2] In recognizing the more detailed the circumstance, the more likelihood of error in practical reasoning, Thomas acknowledges the need for prudence in declaring absolutes, lest we declare necessary that which is circumstantial. In so cautioning for prudence in practical reason, Thomas indicates that historical situational circumstance is a factor in moral judgment. The third point Thomas makes is that there are differences in the human capacity for practical reason and moral judgment. For various reasons, upon which he does not elaborate here in the *Summa theologica* (e.g., maturity, intelligence, information; see also Aquinas, 1986, pp. 99–102), people will know more or less, and thus be more or less prudent in moral decision-making: "As for his estimation of the efficacy of natural law in the human mind, Thomas never wavered from the judgment that only the rudiments (or the *seminalia*, the seeds) are known by the untutored mind" (Hittinger, 1997, p. 7). Practical moral reason takes time, diligence, and maturity, and the point of the moral life is to become a person who pursues virtuous ends "wisely and habitually" (Traina, 1999, p. 77).

> In short, the moral life, in both its natural and its supernatural dimensions, is a process of maturation in virtue requiring diligence and practice. This fact warns us to keep on our toes. But it also forbids us to expect all the acts of the virtues even from a person who has their infused habits and so invites conversation with contemporary theories of moral development that might help us chart and evaluate progress in moral virtue. (Traina, 1999, p. 78)

Traina's identification of developmental theories as particularly useful in understanding the moral life is exactly the line of thinking I will take up in coming chapters. When understanding the moral agent as developing over time through the process of maturation, it is sensible to attend to those aspects of development that nurture or impede moral decision-making. That Thomas recognized the complexity of moral decision-making in the structure of natural law is invitation enough to engage contemporary theories of development, and empirical evidence, in understanding the moral aspects of adolescent female sexualities based upon a natural law foundation.

In the centuries following Thomas's discussion, countless scholars have taken up natural law, which has occupied a privileged place in moral thought in the Roman Catholic theological tradition. It remains foundational in official magisterial moral teachings and has enjoyed a renaissance among Catholic and secular scholars in search of some objective moral order. These various positions, however, are not without contention. In the first place, the position that there is a universally accessible moral understanding of human experience has met with opposition in contemporary scholarship, which I will address in coming chapters. In the second place, interpretations of natural law itself are varied. In the following sections, I address two particularly influential interpretations of natural law in contemporary Roman Catholic thought: New Natural Law (NNL) and Revisionism.

Contemporary Natural Law: New Natural Law

The primary proponents of the New Natural Law (NNL)—also known as the Basic Goods Theory (Salzman, 2003)—are Germain Grisez, Joseph Boyle, John Finnis, and William E. May,[3] based heavily on Germaine Grisez's initial work on natural law (1965). The NNL theorists are interested in the application of natural law in various realms of social and academic discourse, including theology, philosophy, and law. Their aim is to articulate a common, universal, and objective moral order for human activity. Finnis (1980) is recognized particularly for his development of natural law within secular legal theory. NNL theory holds that natural law is accessible by reason to all persons, prior to reference to the eternal law of God (that is, they lift natural law out of Thomas's telos of beatitude), and that Thomas himself did not move sufficiently into the specific precepts of natural law to provide adequate guidance for moral action. They propose basic goods that are based neither in nature (as if what *is* in nature dictates what *ought* to be done) nor telos (as that end toward which all persons tend, such as God). Rather, the basic goods are self-evident to the moral agent operating with unfettered reason; that is, reason free from impediments of bias (Grisez, Boyle, & Finnis, 1987). "Good is to be done and pursued" is the first principle of morality: thus, to fulfill this first principle, one must be morally good. And "to be morally good is precisely to be completely reasonable. *Right reason* is nothing but *unfettered reason*, working throughout deliberation and receiving full attention" (p. 121; emphasis in original).

The NNL theorists outline eight basic goods that are incommensurable (i.e., cannot be weighed against one another in moral decision-making, in either theory or practice), self-evident to all reasonable persons, and that place moral requirements on our behaviours. With both nature and reason operative in their articulation of the goods, they situate the reasonable person's approximation of happiness not in relationship with God (as Thomas does) but in the ideal of "integral human fulfillment"—that is, the fulfillment of the basic goods, which is ultimately unattainable due to human limitations (Grisez, Boyle, & Finnis, 1987, p. 112).

These eight basic goods fall into two categories (May, 2003, pp. 96–97). In one category are three "substantive" basic goods, substantive insofar as they do not include choice in their fulfillment of aspects or dimensions of human persons. May (2003) describes these three basic goods as:

1. human life itself, including health, reproduction, and education;
2. knowledge of truth and beauty, in service of human intelligence; and
3. playful activity and development of skill, in participation in culture. (p. 96)

A second category of human goods is "reflexive" or "existential": "they fulfill persons precisely insofar as they are able to make choices and are thus capable of moral good and evil" (p. 95). These four goods share *harmony* as their theme:

1. self-integration of feelings, choices, and judgments;
2. authentic expression of one's self-integration;
3. just and neighbourly relationships with others; and
4. peace with God in pursuit of meaning and value. (p. 95)

The eighth and final good identified within the NNL is marriage (Grisez, 1993, pp. 567–69). This more recent addition to the basic goods is considered both a reflexive good, because it includes "marital friendship and fidelity," and a substantive good, because its core is the "indissoluble one-flesh unity" and "it is open to the good of human life" (May, 2003, p. 96). Although the reflexive goods do require choice and place moral imperatives upon us, they do not themselves have moral value, because one can choose to participate in the basic goods in immoral ways, even while striving to fulfill them (May, 2003).

Recognizing the lack of moral content in the articulation of the basic goods, NNL theorists further propose the First Principle of Morality (FPM). The function of the FPM is to provide a criterion to distinguish between morally good and morally bad choices in our pursuit of the basic goods. Specifically, the FPM states:

In voluntarily acting for human goods and avoiding what is opposed to them, one ought to choose and otherwise will those and only those possibilities whose willing is compatible with a will toward integral human fulfillment. (Grisez, Boyle, & Finnis, 1987, p. 128)

Along with choosing for basic human goods, one is called not to choose against other basic goods. Because the goods are incommensurable, one cannot choose one over the other without, in some way, willing the destruction of the good not chosen.

In the context of the NNL, integral human fulfillment is that toward which practical reason strives (which is in contrast with Thomas's telos toward beatitude): "integral human fulfillment is not a reason for acting, but an ideal whose attractiveness depends on all the reasons for acting which can appeal to morally good people" (Grisez, Boyle, & Finnis, 1987, p. 132). Persons are able reasonably to attend to basic human goods and direct their wills toward the fulfillment of those goods.

> The will of a person committed to choosing and acting in accord with the requirements of integral human fulfillment is the will of a person inwardly disposed to choose well, to choose in accord with unfettered or "right" reason. In short, it is the ideal community of all human persons richly fulfilled in all human goods, for whose realization a virtuous person wishes; this ideal guides such a person's choices in pursuing particular benefits for particular persons and communities. (May, 2003, p. 101)

To substantiate moral content further, New Natural Law introduces the Modes of Responsibility (MoR). The purpose of the MoR is to specify the First Principle of Morality by excluding as immoral those actions that involve willing in ways that are incompatible with willing integral human fulfillment (May, 2003). These MoR include the entire range of real goods available to human persons and the requirements of prudence in its fullness. As a means of identifying the presence of character within an individual in accord with the MoR, one need only look for their corresponding virtues. The eight Modes of Responsibility and their corresponding virtues are:

1. One ought not to allow inertia to impede acting for intelligible goods (i.e., diligence).
2. One ought not to allow excessive emotion to lead one to act individualistically for an intelligible good (i.e., team spirit).
3. One ought not to act solely to satisfy an emotional desire apart from the pursuit of an intelligible good (i.e., self-control, temperance).
4. One ought not to act solely to satisfy an emotional aversion apart from the avoidance of an intelligible evil (i.e., courage, fortitude).
5. One ought not to act in relation to other persons solely based upon an emotional response to them apart from the pursuit of an intelligible good or avoidance of an intelligible evil (i.e., fairness, justice).

6. One ought not to allow emotions to cloud reflection on the empirical facts related to an intelligible good—or evil (i.e., sincerity, seriousness).
7. One ought not to allow hostility to contribute to one's choice to allow for or cause the destruction or damage of an intelligible good (i.e., patience, forgiveness).
8. One ought not to allow one's motivation toward one intelligible good to lead one to act to destroy or damage another intelligible good (i.e., reverence). (Grisez & Shaw, 1991, pp. 86–98)

The eight MoR and their corresponding virtues provide the NNL with a means of moving from the First Principle of Morality and the basic goods toward specific moral norms.

> The modes of responsibility…are normative principles more specific than the first principle of morality, but they are more general than specific moral norms identifying kinds of human choices as morally good or morally bad. Such specific norms are discovered by considering the ways a proposed human action relates a person's will to basic human goods and by considering such a proposed human action in light of the first principle of morality and its specifications. (May, 2003, p. 105)

In articulating the modes of responsibility and alluding to specific moral norms (which can be either absolute or non-absolute), the proponents of the New Natural Law attempt to flesh out the content of natural law itself in contrast to, for instance, Thomas Aquinas's rather more sparse articulation. Following an outline of the Revisionist formulation of natural law, I will return to critique both NNL and Revisionism as possible frameworks for feminist ethics.

CONTEMPORARY NATURAL LAW: REVISIONISM

Revisionism (also commonly referred to as Proportionalism) is a second school of thought in contemporary natural law discussions. Two primary proponents of Revisionism are Richard A. McCormick and Charles E. Curran (Salzman, 2003), both of whom have engaged in systematic inquiries about moral decision-making and the structure of natural law, often in conversation with proponents of the New Natural Law theory (Curran, 1991; McCormick, 1978). Unlike the NNL, however, there exists no unified, systematic articulation of Revisionism as a theory.

The Revisionist consideration of natural law rests more easily with Thomas Aquinas's ambiguity regarding specific behaviours and moral norms than the NNL. Curran notes that Thomas himself perceived natural law as "a deliberative ethic which arrives at decisions not primarily by the application of laws, but by the deliberation of reason" and that "there is no such thing as *the* natural law as a monolithic philosophical system with an agreed upon body of ethical content existing from the beginning of time" (1991, pp. 253–54). The proponents of the Revisionist school of thought are concerned not so much with articulation of the *content* of natural law as they are concerned with addressing the *method and system* by which natural law operates in moral decision-making.

In a discussion of theological method and moral decision-making, Curran points out the emergence of an historically conscious world view that understands the world as a dynamic reality.[4] He further posits that an inductive moral theological method within such a world view allows for ambiguous options and uncertain moral choices.

> A more historically conscious methodology does not pretend to have or even to aim at absolute certitude. Since time, history, and individual differences are important, they cannot be dismissed as mere accidents which do not affect essential truth. This approach does not emphasize abstract essences, but concrete phenomena. Conclusions are based on the observations and experience gleaned in a more inductive approach. Such an approach can never strive for absolute certitude. (1991, p. 274)

In this same light, McCormick critiques Grisez on the NNL, not for the articulation of basic goods themselves, but for the method of their application; the NNL does not allow for the moral ambiguity that comes with "the complexity of reality," especially in "conflict situations" (1978, p. 34). Hence, Revisionist thinkers are more apt than NNL theorists to recognize the possibility of conflict in moral decision-making (i.e., weighing one choice against another) and to consider in more depth the circumstances within which practical moral decisions are made.

The interchanges between the Revisionists and the New Natural Law theorists delve deeply into both the philosophical and theological aspects of natural law. My intention here is simply to provide context for further discussion of natural law in contemporary moral theology. To that end, the following brief comparison of the two schools of thought is to provide an overview of points of agreement and disagreement.

First, along with the NNL, Revisionism acknowledges the articulation of the basic goods as helpful in moral decision-making (Salzman, 2003).

Furthermore, the Revisionists would agree that, *in theory*, the basic goods are incommensurable. As McCormick (1978) points out, however, *in practice* we do in fact weigh the goods about which we must morally decide when the goods themselves are in conflict. Consequently, the basic goods are not practically incommensurable. From this point arises the Revisionist notion of proportionate good. An inductive methodology that moves from actual human experiences to theoretical propositions (Curran, 1991), the notion of proportionate good leads the Revisionists to conclude that, on specific occasions and in specific circumstances, we must choose between goods. McCormick (1978) further posits that this choice does not necessarily will the destruction of the choice not taken, as the NNL theorists propose in their notion of incommensurability, but rather that this choice wills the proportionate good *in this circumstance*.

Second, the Revisionist thinkers agree with the NNL theorists about the existence and, to a great extent, the content of moral norms. Unlike the NNL (and the Magisterium of the Roman Catholic Church), however, they posit that moral norms pertaining to specific acts are not of themselves absolute (Salzman, 2003). Rather, in accounting for circumstances in the reality of moral decision-making, the Revisionists posit that proportionate reason weighs each act in context, and functions as the norm by which we judge the act to be moral or not (e.g., circumstances can inform the *choice* to use birth control in marriage vs. judging the *act* of using birth control itself as inherently "anti-life"). In particular, Curran suggests that when moral norms and judgments on specific human actions focus disproportionately on the physical nature of the act itself, rather than on "the act in terms of the person placing the act"—like seeing artificial birth control as intrinsically evil, for instance (1991, p. 282)—they fail to account adequately for the moral complexity of personal human circumstance, as when a woman may choose artificial birth control as a means of preserving her health. In this way, Revisionists see moral complexity and the necessity of proportionate decision-making as integral to moral theory and natural law. Curran states that acceptance of ambiguity in moral decision-making is, in fact, built in to Thomas's natural law: "Despite the classical world view of his day, in his system Thomas did leave room for the virtue of prudence and the creativity of the individual" (1991, p. 279). The moral norms are subject to proportionate reason in the particular context of the individual person.

Insofar as both the New Natural Law and Revisionist theories accept that human persons are morally inclined toward basic goods and that we can articulate moral norms stemming from our perception of these goods, the NNL theorists and the Revisionist thinkers co-exist happily in the realm of natural law. When the basic precepts are applied, however, the two theories part ways: the NNL theorists move toward incommensurability and absolute moral norms; the Revisionist thinkers move toward proportionate moral decision-making and non-absolute moral norms. The discussions between the two schools of thought engage the issues in much more depth and precision than have been articulated here, but this basic overview provides enough of a snapshot to understand the ways in which they affect moral conclusions regarding particular actions. If one follows the NNL, one might conclude that moral decisions are merely the correct application of the Modes of Responsibility toward integral human fulfillment as fleshed out in the basic goods. One might further conclude that this application of the MoR ought to be in accordance with specific non-absolute or absolute moral norms, particularly those articulated by the Magisterium of the Roman Catholic Church. If one follows a Revisionist natural law, one might conclude that moral decisions are the practical and proportionate consideration of the basic goods, whereby one applies non-absolute moral norms according to the particular circumstance in which one finds oneself.

Contemporary Natural Law Critiqued
Both New Natural Law and Revisionism are intelligible articulations of natural law in the Roman Catholic intellectual tradition. However, neither theory adequately reflects or accounts for diverse experiences within the human community. Their commitment to existing moral norms means that voices historically excluded from moral theological discourse have no access to the contemporary discourse. In my reading, female voices, particularly those of adolescent females, remain unrepresented in both of these accounts of natural law. Below, I critique New Natural Law and Revisionism from a feminist perspective; and, in that light, I introduce the Feminist Natural Law presented by Cristina Traina (1999) as a viable natural law option and theoretical framework, within which adolescent females' sexual experiences are appropriate data for consideration.

I begin with the New Natural Law. This theory of basic goods is a thorough articulation of human moral tendencies not toward something beyond reasonable intelligibility, but toward self-evident goods that are encapsulated in integral human fulfillment. As Porter (1993) points out, however, it is not at all clear that the basic goods are, in fact, self-evident without some prior commitment to what might constitute *human good*. The content of the basic goods, for example, seems to draw upon Catholic magisterial teaching, and May (2003) acknowledges that the recognition of marriage as the eighth basic good was "primarily because of the teaching of the Church's magisterium on marriage" (p. 96). Porter's concern is further borne out in the NNL theorists' application of the theory to specific moral questions and subsequent moral conclusions. For instance, Grisez (1993) states that contraception, in all circumstances, is contra-life and therefore morally unacceptable. He states this, however, only after noting that Catholics ought to believe this teaching simply because it is promulgated as true by the Magisterium (pp. 506–19). Yet one might conclude, to the contrary, that employing contraceptives to prevent procreation is not tantamount (or morally equivalent) to choosing against the good of procreation in marriage—that is, choosing contra-life. If one did not subscribe to the teachings of the Roman Catholic Church, one might further question the self-evident nature of such a proposal.

In the same vein, Finnis's (1994) discussion of sexual orientation in relation to law and morality is directed toward the public good and the onus of the state to safeguard its citizens against morally evil vices. Here, says Finnis (1994), we must not only deny social rights demanded by homosexual persons, but we must also legislate against allowing morally bad behaviour, like sodomy, to protect social stability in defence of heterosexual marriage and procreation. Ultimately, homosexual acts are unreasonable because they are non-procreative and essentially lacking in mutuality. They also constitute a real threat to the good of society; therefore, homosexual acts are immoral (Finnis, 1994). Like Grisez's assessment of contraception as contra-life, Finnis's conclusions regarding homosexuality also rely upon his commitment to the basic good of marriage and procreation, and its incommensurability with other goods. If, however, one does not accept that marriage and procreation are self-evident basic goods, then one might conclude that Finnis's views are based more on Roman Catholic official teaching than on the philosophical construct he proposes. In any case, these examples question the NNL theorists' assertion that the basic goods and, therefore, the content of natural law, are of themselves known by unfettered reason and only enlightened by faith. One might surmise that marriage as a basic good, as opposed to partnering, mating, or companionship, could be more readily accepted as a matter of faith (Catholic faith, in particular) than as a matter of reason.[5]

The New Natural Law theorists' ascription of natural law to the realm of reason, independent of eternal law, is a shift away from scholastic discussions of natural law, and the NNL theorists generally acknowledge this. The scholastics' understanding of natural law (including Thomas's) is that, although one can ascertain natural law by reason, it is an inherently theological construct, tied necessarily to divine law (Porter, 1999). That is, they assume a relationship between the will of God and human moral action, insofar as we are naturally inclined to meet the goods as a means to seek union with God. Proponents of the NNL posit the goods as reasonably ascertainable by all persons without an inherent connection to any faith-based construct. The difficulty with such a position is not whether the theory begins within an inherently theological construct but, rather, whether, depending on its starting point, the theory ends within a theological construct: that is, whether the content of the theory assumes revelation in its substance. If such an assumption is the case (e.g., marriage as a basic good), the theory must abandon its premise of being based solely in right reason, and only enlightened by faith. This, in turn, would limit its capacity to weigh in on significant social issues from a reasonable, universalist perspective.

For Thomas Aquinas, however, the interconnection of the theological and the philosophical (i.e., faith and reason) was a natural one and clearly apparent in the conclusions he draws from within his specific faith perspective. Further, his theological assumptions provide the direction toward which our moral actions are inclined: that is, God. And, although the conclusions of faith are clearly included in moral reflection, they are also complemented by a great deal of data that is not generated theologically. Thomas's rather sparse discussion and the content of natural law itself provides space for faith and theology to be conversant with other perspectives and traditions regarding moral questions. Given that he assumes natural law's manifestation in actions that are virtuous (or not), Thomas leaves plenty of room for human agency and growth in the Spirit. Perhaps the most enduring aspect of his natural law is its elegant faith in the capacity of reasonable persons to act well in particular circumstances, without articulating specific moral norms. The human capacity for prudence itself directs us toward God.

By contrast, in divorcing themselves from theology in their philosophical formulation of natural law, the NNL theorists, by default, must suspend any reliance on faith perspectives in their construction of its structure. This divorce is unsuccessful because, by virtue of the roots upon which they rely (namely, Thomas Aquinas), natural law is a faith-infused philosophical construct. The New Natural Law's philosophical, reasonable structure attempts to address a multi-faith culture with some account of moral and legal normativity, and conveniently goes a long way toward serving their ultimate, somewhat socially conservative, moral conclusions (e.g., Grisez, 1993). In a Western post-modern era of difference, however, a theory openly based upon a faith perspective ought to be as valid as the next theory that is not; acknowledging a natural law tradition from within a specifically Catholic Christian faith perspective ought not to hinder respectful discourse among other disciplines.

The structure of the NNL theory does not allow sufficient space (in contrast to Thomas's development of habits and virtues) to include the actual data of human experience in its application of natural law. For instance, the incommensurability of the goods (Grisez, Boyle, & Finnis, 1987, p. 110) puts the theory at odds with practice. If the basic goods cannot be measured against one another within practical moral decision-making, then we are left with rather narrow, even non-existent choices. In practice, however, we do make choices of proportionate good on a regular basis (e.g., whether to play or to study), and in making these choices, we do not necessarily will the destruction of other goods.

Another difficulty of the NNL regarding human experience is the place of emotions in moral decision-making. By equating "unfettered reason" with moral goodness, the NNL theorists paint emotions as problematic to integral human fulfillment when not reined in by rational guidance (Grisez, Boyle, & Finnis, 1987; Grisez & Shaw, 1991). While a situation in which emotions run amok can, indeed, lead to poor moral choices, such as acting in anger, the NNL does not account for the possibility that rational thinking run amok might also lead to the suppression of emotions that constitute important data in moral decision-making, such as suppressing discomfort or shame. Finnis's assertion that "reality is known in judgement, not in emotion" (1994, p. 1067) is true only insofar as one does not consider emotion to be a real (and legitimate) factor in adequate moral judgment. The NNL theorists overlook the possibility that feelings might well direct us to positive moral action, as love can direct us toward marriage and procreation, despite reasonable reasons to move toward some other good, like financial stability. The heart truly has reasons that reason does not know. Far from being a negative barrier to morally right action, feelings are a positive and integral part of decision-making. As human experience indicates, we minimize emotions at our own peril. One might speculate, for example, that the current sexual abuse crisis facing the Catholic Church globally is a result not only of the failure to integrate feelings (and sexuality) adequately within concrete persons (most prominently, clerics), but also of the failure to recognize in the first instance that we all experience feelings, which are not good or bad of themselves but are important to overall well-being, and which require our attention. The NNL theorists' narrow perception of emotion in relation to reason does not adequately integrate feelings into moral choices and judgments, although such integration is one of the basic goods of NNL theory.

In their attempt to add content to the natural law to provide guidance (and perhaps moral surety?) to human moral reflection and action, the New Natural Law theorists effectively minimize its messy reality.

Moral decision-making is difficult: the available data may change and the capacity to choose is variably developed among us. The ambiguity of the human moral experience sits precisely within the concrete details of human life, which is, of course, where moral decisions take place. We feel, we think, we believe, and we act, often toward equally good ends that cannot all be met. The NNL, therefore, does not have the capacity to address adequately the data of adolescent female lives. Its methodology—that is, the incommensurable application of goods, values, and norms in moral decision-making—diminishes the complicating circumstances of actual persons' lives.

In contrast to the NNL, Revisionism allows somewhat for the ambiguity of human experience in moral decision-making. However, it also presents limitations in constructing an ethics accounting for the lives of females. Traina (1999), in her discussion of McCormick's work, focuses on his proportionalist interpretation of natural law: although he would not posit absolute moral norms, still he remains methodologically committed to constant norms as they are articulated by the Magisterium. Traina's feminist critique of McCormick is that, although he is open to the circumstantial realities of moral decision-making, his commitment to constant moral norms as articulated by the Magisterium does not allow procedurally for inclusion of the experiences of females. She maintains that an adequate natural law theory would incorporate women's experiences explicitly into the formulation of norms. Because the Magisterium and the theological tradition have historically based positions, teachings, and norms on the experiences and scholarship of males (and, by and large, continue to do so), the norms themselves require revision.

While both of these contemporary natural law theories provide insight into its ongoing evolution, neither seems completely capable of meeting the exigencies of moral decision-making in the light of the particular experiences of females. With regard to the New Natural Law, for instance, a woman might well find herself facing a conflict between the basic good of authentic expression of self-integration and the basic good of marriage. If a woman's marriage is itself an impediment to authentic expression of self-integration, perhaps because of abuse, then the woman is left with her moral hands tied between the incommensurability of the two basic goods. In reality, as the Revisionists suggest, the woman would, in fact, be likely to weigh the goods before her in the light of her own circumstances and decide to act in support of one of the two goods. This would not necessarily mean that she is acting wilfully to destroy the other good; it means rather that she finds one good proportionately more pressing considering the moral choice facing her.

Continuing the inquiry into the practical application of natural law with regard to the Revisionist theory, if the same woman were to ascribe to the magisterial norm of the indissolubility of a sacramental marriage (were the marriage deemed a valid sacrament; see *Catechism,* Part 2, Art. 7, I), the woman's moral agency would further be compromised by the acceptance of the norm itself. Because there is no accounting for female experiences of male spousal abuse in the articulation of the norm, the broad normative application of natural law is compromised by its intrinsic limitation. In this case, the woman's practical agency is also compromised by the virtual absence of her experience within the norm itself. Accordingly, the Revisionist theory, by committing to existing moral norms, forfeits the explicit voices of females in its articulation of natural law.

Further, applying the inquiry into the practical application of natural law consideration of Thomas Aquinas's work reintroduces Curran's discussion of historical consciousness and inductive methodology into the theological enterprise. Thomas's own applications of natural law are bound by the historical context in which he lived, "unquestioningly ordered around the sexual and social hierarchies of the medieval world" (Beattie, 2006, p. 58). Still, his methodology opens a pathway to consider how natural law might incorporate the bodily experiences of females within an understanding of sexuality ordered toward integral human fulfillment in the contextual realities of human lives.

Each of the natural law theories presented above is both helpful and limited in its contribution to a theological discussion of female bodies, sexualities, and experiences. Feminist natural law, however, is able to address the concerns raised by the limitations of the above natural law theories. The following chapter explores feminist natural law in its various iterations.

CHAPTER THREE

FEMINIST NATURAL LAW

INTRODUCTION

Feminist natural law is a contemporary theological rereading of natural law that attends both structurally and substantively to the realities of females in the world, while attempting to discern what is normatively human and ethical. Other historical and contemporary articulations of natural law lack the capacity to address adolescent female sexuality and theology fully, due to limitations regarding either method, procedure, or content. In this chapter, I explore recent discussions and, ultimately, a systematic formulation of feminist natural law that provide a theoretical framework robust enough to support this project. I begin with a brief exploration of some limited feminist theological re-readings and discussions of natural law.

FEMINIST NATURAL LAW: INITIAL VOICES

While exploring Christian sexual ethics by way of the body, sex, and pleasure, Christine Gudorf (1994) briefly articulates a feminist re-vision of natural law. Gudorf identifies the inadequacy of a static understanding of historicity, particularly as regards human evolution. The defining problem with the official Roman Catholic formulation of natural law (and its theoretical sympathizers) as it pertains to sexuality, is that its physicalist understanding of the human person does not provide for evolution in understanding the physiological reality of procreation. Such a static approach to the sexual person leaves the tradition open to an out-of-date and limited perception of morally normative sexual behaviour. In particular, the official teaching is insulated against the real sexual experiences of women. This insulation in turn creates a natural law formulation that is unable adequately to address women's sexual lives, because it is ill-equipped to address historicity and the unfolding of human sexual realities in the first place. For Gudorf, a feminist natural law ethic clearly must embrace both the particular sexual experiences of women and some general understanding of human sexuality (1994, pp. 51–80).

In a Lonerganian approach, Cynthia Crysdale (1995) revisions natural law out of the classicist world view from which it emerged and into an historically conscious world view. She cites Bernard Lonergan (1972, 1957) in noting that the classicist world view would see both nature and reason (the Thomistic components of natural law) as static entities that are best understood by necessary laws. The historically conscious world view, on the contrary, would acknowledge the dynamic unfolding of both nature and reason in the form of statistical probability: that is, not everything that exists can be understood as necessary. Her conclusion regarding natural law in the light of these insights is that human persons live in a situation that calls to both necessary (classical) laws and statistical laws in the unfolding of human reality. Crysdale's point here is that we do not confuse one for the other in our formulation of natural law. Our theological task is to discern between what are necessary (or universal) aspects of creation and what are statistical possibilities (or probabilities) in the unfolding of creation. If we identify as universal that which is merely statistically probable, we become vulnerable to an hegemonic understanding of reason or nature that impedes genuine human flourishing for particular individuals.

Finally, in her consideration of foundations for Christian sexual ethics, Lisa Sowle Cahill lays the groundwork for a feminist natural law that she returns to and addresses in more depth in her later work (1985, pp. 105–22; 1997). Cahill notes that Thomas's openness to particular circumstances in moral reflection makes a feminist reinterpretation of natural law in the light of historicity consistent with (although not identical to) the early formulations of the tradition. And, while it would be anachronistic and false to identify Thomas as a feminist (given his anthropological conclusions, see, e.g., *Summa* I, Q. 92), his general methodological approach to natural law is still rather compatible with a feminist concern for difference. Within a reformulation of natural law, Cahill proposes that feminists can attend to the concern for women's flourishing both particularly and universally.

While each of these scholars considers a feminist rereading of natural law to be important to the work of feminist ethics, none of them attempts a systematic inquiry into what such an ethic would entail. In her articulation of feminist natural law, Cristina Traina (1999) undertakes just such an inquiry in a contemporary context. Her development of a feminist natural law ethic yields a revisable universalism, which in turn creates a useful ethical web in which to weave a sexual theology that is both appropriate for, and adequately reflective of, adolescent female experiences.

PRIMARY VOICE: CRISTINA TRAINA AND THE END OF ANATHEMAS

Cristina Traina's (1999, 1997) thorough consideration of natural law and engagement with feminist theories and concerns makes her an ideal dialogue partner for this project. While her work embodies a strategic essentialism useful in feminist dialogue, it also engages the Catholic theological tradition of natural law in a refreshing and helpful way. In particular, it forwards the evolution of Catholic theology regarding sexual ethics, and provides an open space to engage the realities of adolescent females in relevant and appropriate ways.

Traina succinctly identifies why a feminist natural law ethic is needed in contemporary feminist dialogue: "[F]eminism exists to free women from human oppression and, more broadly, from all forces that prevent their flourishing. In order to accomplish this task, feminism needs some relatively stable point of critical leverage, some point beyond which systems and behaviors are clearly wrong" (1999, p. 5). This need is especially true "in a social context inclined to exploit ambiguity, powerlessness, and reticence" (Traina, 1999, pp. 5–6). Traina walks the path between a universalist natural law tradition, which has oppressed women with its notions of nature and the natural, and the deconstructive post-structuralist feminisms that so protect difference and contingency that they leave us politically paralyzed and unable to act in the face of cultural oppression and harm to women. She espouses a non-deterministic telic and thick anthropology with convictions about goals toward which humans are to strive (1999, pp. 6–7, 12). Such is the basis for Traina's walk on the "line between tentativeness and absolutism" (1999, p. 10).

Traina and Feminist Moral Discourse

Traina (1999) begins her discussion with an engagement of contemporary feminist discourse. Addressing liberal feminism, naturalist feminism, and social constructionism as possible feminist ethical methodologies, she points out that each in its own way places limitations on the moral demands feminists can make on behalf of women. Liberal feminism is based in the ideals of equality, freedom, autonomy and rights, and invests itself in reason and science (over nature) as means of ensuring women's well-being in the world. Attention to equality among human persons is the strength of liberal feminism, particularly in light of the historical subjugation of women. However, given its uncritical confidence in the capacity of reason and science to account for meaning, Traina finds its understanding of human good to be too heavily located in individualism, and thus too thin to sustain feminist ethics (1999, pp. 26–28).

Naturalist feminism stands upon the biological and teleological norms invested in human embodiment. It recognizes the fundamental differences between the sexes but does not construct a hierarchy of merit on those differences. As a response to a skewed anthropology favouring traditionally male and masculine characteristics, naturalist feminism effectively legitimizes traditionally female and feminine characteristics in the realm of universal human truths. The primary difficulty with naturalist feminism, however, is its glossing over of actual, deep differences between and among sexes and genders, leaving it impotent to address the ethical and experiential gaps that must arise from said differences (Traina, 1999, pp. 29–32).

In contrast, social constructionism does not put any stock in natural, innate differences of either gender or sex. Rather, it holds that male/female and masculine/feminine are not stable categories of the human subject at all, but discursively constructed categories. The social constructionist stance allows for the deconstruction of historical and social grand narratives that effectively oppress dynamics of power. Unfortunately, the deconstruction of social difference also leads to moral paralysis, and an inability to act against harmful differences via any common understanding of ethical norms. A constructionist ethic impedes our capacity to speak on behalf of oppressed females in a variety of social settings, and is therefore inadequate as an ethical methodology (Traina, 1999, pp. 32–35).

Ultimately, Traina recognizes that, although each of these feminisms is an inadequate ethical methodology, attention to their primary concerns gives preliminary shape to the feminism she is attempting to articulate:

> It is committed to women's flourishing; to a critical realism that operates within the limitations and goals of human historical existence; to an historical, social, and mutually critical view of nature and reason; to the rights and dignity of individuals; to confident, prophetic transformation of and survival in an imperfect world; to inclusiveness, self-criticism, and humility. (1999, pp. 38–39)

Traina, thus, addresses the epistemological and anthropological claims necessary to her feminist natural law. Her primary epistemological criterion is the privileging of women's well-being: *a preferential option for women* (1999, pp. 39–42). Returning to her discussion of thick anthropology, Traina focuses on the tension between an absolute, fixed human anthropology that recognizes common points in our shared lives, and a tentative, flexible anthropology that recognizes the varied creativities of individuals making their way in the world. Human flourishing, a basic moral criterion for well-being, applies both to individuals and communities in concrete historical circumstances (Traina, 1999, pp. 42–48). She ultimately recognizes the sexed and gendered body as crucial to the anthropological consideration of the individual in the world. While it should not be the only criterion, it must certainly be taken into account (Traina, 1999, p. 47). The insights from a variety of feminist perspectives, therefore, provide nuance in Traina's own approach to Christian ethics; she attends both to contemporary feminist claims and the theological tradition of natural law. For our purposes, Traina's dialogical place within the Roman Catholic tradition facilitates serious engagement with both the tradition and the lives of adolescent females, who currently sit on the margins of sexual ethics.

Traina and the Catholic Ethical Tradition

Traina engages the history of the Catholic moral tradition in depth in a number of ways, from natural law, through casuistry, to personalism. First, she examines the natural law formulation within the hierarchical ecclesiastical realm and includes reflections on both the use of casuistry and the development of personalism in natural law since Thomas Aquinas (1999, pp. 100–139). Casuistry is the use of cases to attend to moral dilemmas lacking the guidance of precedence or the precision of existing principles (Curran, 1999, pp. 164–65). When moral dilemmas lacking any precedent arise, analogous cases are applied to the dilemmas at hand as an inductive means of sorting through the moral similarities (or differences). Casuistry is an especially helpful methodology when social and religious realities face major upheaval and innovation. In such situations, where existing principles or maxims are not sufficient to solve moral dilemmas, casuistry allows for consideration of concrete circumstances (Rudy, 1994). A prominent example of the use of casuistry pertains to usury: the charging of interest, or exorbitant amounts of interest, when loaning money. As the economies of Europe grew during the 1400s and 1500s, they moved away from bartering as an economic base and toward the use of currency. Through increased exploration and trade off of the European continent, business people were looking to insure their investments under somewhat speculative circumstances. Casuistry was a means of circumventing the moral prohibition against usury to allow cargo and trade expeditions to be insured (Keenan, 1999). Over the course of the economic transitions of the fifteenth to seventeenth centuries, when casuist theological scholarship flourished, casuists began to establish standards for moral action in a variety of circumstances.

Eventually, casuistry fell into disrepute as it became more of a deductive application of previously established standards for moral action than the careful attention paid to the concrete circumstances of cases. Casuistry's disrepute was especially pronounced from the seventeenth century on, as it came to be abused in the Roman Catholic practice of confession and penance, and in moral deliberation over circumstances arising from social and religious evolution (Jonsen & Toulmin, 1988). The abuse of casuistry reached its peak "from the eighteenth century until the Second Vatican Council, that is, during the period when moralists wrote manuals to differentiate permitted from sinful activity... existing principles were simply applied deductively to a case and the case was solved. In geometric or manualist casuistry, it is a principle and not the case that is the standard" (Keenan, 1996, pp. 129–30). When casuistry was applied in this way, the subject was nigh removed from moral deliberation and the particulars of the case were merely incidental to the principles applied.

Although it has a chequered history in Roman Catholic ethical thought, casuistry is currently enjoying a revival in our post-modern context. It is a particularly useful methodology for contemporary situations in which moral questions evolve as quickly as knowledge advances; its fit within an inductive methodology increases its usefulness in considering the data of the sexualities of adolescent females. Traina points out the advantage of using casuist theory as a tool to mediate between what is and what ought to be. She also notes, however, that its historical abuse in practice within the tradition indicates that casuistry is vulnerable to devolving into static consideration of moral realities (1999, pp. 102–6). Its historical resistance to attending to the case at hand in plural and diverse circumstances leaves casuistry further open to the vagaries of its users: it is "only as good as its choice of paradigmatic case and therefore is only as good as the chooser, a casuist. A strong self-critical—or even a critical—principle is lacking in most of the Roman Catholic casuistical tradition" (Traina, 1999, p. 106). To work well with casuistry, the casuist must have the ability to undertake prudent moral discernment, and not merely apply pre-existing principles and norms.

Charting the development of personalism in Roman Catholic theology since the early twentieth century, Traina identifies its two most enduring ethical aspects: "the person as integral moral actor and as holistic source of moral norms" (1999, p. 108). The focus of a personalist ethic shifts away from an act-centred morality toward a person-centred morality; that is, persons in relationship with their environment. There is no unified personalist school of thought, however; rather, conclusions based on personalist criteria take shape variably, based upon differences of anthropologies, perceptions of the mutability (or not) of moral norms, and ecclesial commitments. Thus, one of the difficulties of personalism is its moral ambiguity. Precisely to the extent that morality involves a turn to loving subjects as attentive, intelligent, reasonable, and responsible (Himes, 1989), their personal capacities as moral agents are uncertain. One influential contemporary manifestation of personalism counters this ambiguity with the reinforcement of traditional norms: the "personalist Thomism" of Pope John Paul II.

According to Traina, John Paul II's application of personalist criteria serves first to reinforce traditional moral norms as absolute. In particular, personalist criteria bolster the authority of the Magisterium in what Traina terms "magisterial absolutism" (1999, p. 119; 1997). Although the Magisterium recognizes personal moral reflection and individual decision-making, still it holds that any disagreements with the conclusions of the Magisterium are simply wrong. As Traina says, "Anyone may ponder moral questions, but the church hierarchy is the authoritative critic" (1999, p. 121). A second result of this strain of personalism is the diminishment of social and political realities in which individual persons live. While theoretical attention to the personal and particular compensates for what was missing in the casuist tradition, it still oversimplifies the person in the world (Traina, 1999, pp. 106–14, 119–22).

The methodological difficulty with such an interpretation of personalism is that it adopts historical moral conclusions of the natural law tradition without opening itself appropriately to a natural law methodology. The data informing this personalist stance is not the data of contemporary personal circumstances and realities. In effect, hierarchical personalism bypasses the subject's own situation and capacity for moral reasoning—their practical reason or prudence—in favour of pre-existing moral conclusions. In sum, "By accepting the conclusions of traditional natural law reasoning but refusing to permit natural law's methods to operate freely, hierarchical personalism rejects the rich and complex Thomistic understanding of prudence and thus implicitly also denies the holistic anthropology upon which prudence rests" (Traina, 1999, p. 122).

To better examine the moral exigencies of living this life in the here and now, Traina turns to the methodological and procedural developments of liberation theologies toward social justice (1999, pp. 114–19). She points out that the application of Thomas Aquinas's thought regarding virtue, justice, and prudence is most pronounced in a liberationist methodology. Linking the virtues of justice and prudence, liberation theologies aver that any promotion of individuals or groups in the development of law (including formulations of natural law) to the detriment of other individuals or groups can be neither prudent nor just (Traina, 1999, pp. 118–19). Hence, those members of the Church sitting outside of the ecclesiastical hierarchy possess epistemological privilege equal to scholars and clerics, and their experiences are equally as informative in the development of moral theologies as the experiences of their more educated and/or enlightened counterparts. Here, listening is key. This recognition provides an open entry for women into moral dialogue. Traina notes that both the method and procedure of liberationist theology provide for the voices of the oppressed not only to be articulated, but also meaningfully incorporated into Church teaching (1999, 116–19). Hence, if the historical natural law tradition has not incorporated female experience into its understanding of nature and reason, and remains static in that understanding, then it is inadequate to address their moral lives.

Traina: Feminist Ethics and Natural Law

For Traina, a critical synthesis of feminist ethics and natural law is imperative for a feminist theological ethic. She provides what she calls "bases for the conversation between feminist ethics and natural law": legitimate self-interest, anthropology, embodiment, virtue, reason, common good, and ethical reflection as a communal endeavour (1999, pp. 150–58). Most pressing of these shared interests for Traina is anthropology (1999, pp. 151–54), the most prominent point of discord between the two schools of thought. A natural law ethic will clearly propose some constant in the human subject upon which we can build an ethic. Conversely, much of feminist theory will reject this constant in favour of the radical social construction of subjectivity. Traina distinguishes, however, between the method and content of anthropological statements: the fundamental method of natural law allows for a continuous unfolding of how we understand what is human; in contrast, the content of its formulation depends upon which data is engaged in reaching conclusions (in this case, regarding anthropology). For Traina, the flaw in traditional natural law anthropology has more to do with data and content than with method. A reconsideration of anthropology in the light of women's experiences (and of other oppressed people) will yield a more fruitful and robust theological anthropology. In essence, she recommends not throwing the methodological baby out with the inadequate conclusions within the historical bathwater. While the method might indeed be in need of some reconsideration, it is not equivalent to its conclusions.

As Traina points out, this reconsideration is no easy task. The bases for the dialogue between feminist ethics and natural law ultimately leave us in an ambiguous and tenuous moral environment. Even with regard to the fundamental criterion of flourishing, she is deliberately vague:

There is no single ideal of flourishing, no final and authoritative set of moral principles, no unique path to moral wisdom. The task is rather to discern, in each place and age, which ways of life, guidelines, and ways of moral discernment seem best to respect and promote the integral good of particular people. (1999, p. 160)

This ambiguity suggests that the task will require humility and some dexterity in navigating the independently and mutually fruitful schools of thought at hand. In Traina's estimation, however, the task is a requirement for both groups in order to ensure their development in theoretical and practical realms. In summation, Traina turns to a useful, if lengthy, passage from Crysdale (1995) exploring a revised natural law with attention to the particular:

[A] revised natural law is both possible and imperative. It will recognize the conditioned nature of all of existence, and in particular the statistical laws that contribute to world process. It must further locate itself in an analysis of history that is critical and normative, but that grounds its critical stance in the norms constitutive of human intelligence. It will attend to chemical, biological, and zoological schemes of recurrence as conditioning factors in human existence, both within the human subject and between that subject and her environment, without seeking to derive moral norms directly from these natural processes. It will take as an important task, not defining ways in which persons should conform to nature, but clarifying the values implicit in interventions in nature, and stipulating which transformations are ultimately conducive to human flourishing and which are not. (Crysdale, 1995, p. 484)

Having established the necessity of a critical synthesis of feminist ethics and natural law, Traina addresses the question of what such a synthesis might entail. She notes the limitations of both contemporary feminist ethical theory and the Roman Catholic ethical tradition (broadly considered) and identifies a number of guidelines regarding the synthesis of the two.

Traina: Guidelines for a Feminist Natural Law Ethic

Traina advances her natural law ethic with a synthesis of feminist thought within the paradigm of natural law. In so doing, she enacts the theoretical framework for a feminist natural law, including: consideration of method, "the theoretical structure of ethical argument"; procedure, "the practical structure of ethical conversation"; and content, "the norms or guides the ethic develops" (1999, p. 140). Although distinguishable, these aspects of a feminist natural law are interdependent and clearly accommodate its guidelines. The following are six points gleaned from Traina's work regarding the emergent synthesis of feminist thought within natural law.

First, natural law's attention to the theological vision of a natural human telos must, from here on, be based upon a "thick" anthropology. That is, it "must encompass all the concrete goods of which genuine, integral human flourishing consists" (Traina, 1999, p. 306). In a specifically Christian theological context, this requires a "credible connection among Christianity's formal encompassing *telos*, salvation; concrete flourishing; and the moral life" (Traina, 1999, p. 316). Assuming the goodness of the human subject, this connection is established in the synthesis of feminist, Thomist, and liberationist thought (Traina, 1999, p. 316). In attending to Thomas's discussion of virtues such as prudence and justice as means by which we are able to make wise moral decisions and liberationist stress on the common good, the flourishing of females is more "thickly" articulated (Traina, 1999, p. 318).

Consequently, the method of feminist natural law must be unified insofar as it accounts for both the social and particular implications of moral stances and behaviours, with specific regard for females (Traina, 1999, p. 141). To further a "thick" anthropology, in attending to the social and the particular in moral articulations, theological method must also engage modes of reasoning generally marginalized in the Academy. This engagement would include emotion, relational thinking, and some empirical data that has historically been ignored or devalued in theoretical discourses. Applied to my project, disciplines that aim to understand particular aspects of the human experience in depth (e.g., developmental psychology) are not only useful but necessary within an adequate natural law-based sexual theology. If such data is omitted from theological discourse, then the content will be truncated as a result of methodological oversight.

Further, procedurally, to enact engagement with heretofore marginalized groups requires a preferential option for those marginalized and vulnerable. In regards to feminist natural law, solidarity in recognizing the feminist objective of a preferential option for females is a criterion of procedural efficacy in ethical discourse (Traina, 1999, pp. 146–47). Theoretical and practical commitment to female well-being in the world requires broad solicitation of women's wisdom and experiences in order to manifest, explicitly, commitment to female flourishing by bettering the actual day-to-day lives of girls and women. Promulgating theological ethical statements about women, for instance, without procedurally involving diverse groups of them in the discourse, contradicts the possibility of an adequate sexual ethic and almost certainly impedes a thick anthropology.

Traina's second guideline pertains to the understanding of "embodiment" in the context of a feminist natural law ethic (1999, pp. 306–7). Feminist attention to the oppressive anthropology within natural law history (e.g., Coll, 1994; Ruether, 1983) has enhanced our understanding of the fully embodied subject in the world. A feminist account of embodiment will, of necessity, consider sex and gender differences and the moral exigencies stemming from that reality. Traina also notes that the Roman Catholic natural law tradition's historical, systematic exclusion of women's experiences has rendered it virtually void of an account of females' bodies. The confluence of the attention of both Thomas Aquinas and contemporary feminist ethics (e.g., Cahill, 1996; Gudorf, 1994) to embodied subjects in their particular contexts indicates that an adequate feminist natural law ethic must also attend to the goodness of the body and, in particular, the female body.

That actual female bodies have been marginalized in theological anthropology and natural law history is due largely to the procedural exclusion of females from moral discourse. By systematically removing females from formal moral discourse, and offering universal responses to and behaviours within particular circumstances instead, historical magisterial ethical formulations have created under-skilled moral reasoners of women. As such, one of Traina's procedural criteria for a feminist natural law is "the advancement of women's moral agency" (1999, pp. 145–46). If natural law is available to all human persons in the course of right reason and prudential reflection, then moral decision-makers ought to possess equitable capacity to discern communally agreed-upon moral norms. If the method is to function within a particular communal circumstance, all moral reasoners must be procedurally involved in the reflection on and formulation of the ethic itself. In so doing, females' bodies will be more accurately represented in theological formulations.

Third, Traina notes the proportionalist penchant for either/or decision-making (e.g., McCormick, 1978; Salzman, 2003). A feminist recognition of, and tolerance for, the ambiguity of possibilities in moral decision-making enhances revisionist attention to the particular (Traina, 1999, p. 307). Rather than limiting our moral scope to discrete problems in discrete circumstances, attention to the broad contexts of our moral dilemmas, as has been a focus of feminist ethics, would enhance natural law and facilitate the methodological criterion of the flourishing of females. Attention to difference between and among moral thinkers allows for the inclusion in ethical theory of the particular circumstances in which any action takes place.

Such attention to context disrupts the internal logic of a bound system created and perpetuated by and for male thinkers, and facilitates attention to female flourishing beyond discrete actions. As Traina notes, an ethic created by such narrow and stunted method "is almost certainly false. But, more to the point, its practitioners are sinful" (1999, p. 144).

This thought leads to Traina's fourth point: the need for the integral person's particularity to be dynamically intertwined with his/her context. In this light, feminist theology itself is not exempt from critique. Many liberation womanist and feminist theologians with global perspectives (corresponding with a broader post-colonial focus in contemporary scholarship) have critiqued early liberal feminisms for the assumption of sameness in women. More recent feminist and womanist scholarship identifies the numerous differences among women within the matrix of sexual difference, race, socio-economic status, geographical location, and ability, and their place in an integrated theology (e.g., Hayes, 2011, 1996; Isasi-Diaz, 1993; Kwok, 2005, 1992; Williams, 1993). Attentive to these critiques, feminists are mindful of the inadequacies of existing theories: both the New Natural Law and Revisionist proponents' very limited dialogue with oppressed and marginalized groups left those persons with diminished representation in the development of moral theology. This exclusion, in turn, limited the universal status of natural law and its effectiveness in ethical thought (Traina, 1999, pp. 308–9). A feminist natural law framework thus invites a procedure that is open and participatory, and allows for dialogue inclusive of all the voices with a stake in its conclusions. If method is open to a wide range of evidence, then the procedure must facilitate inclusion of a wide range of participants. To the contrary, traditional natural law and subsequent teachings have employed methodological and participatory exclusion. "The procedure of exclusion, backed up by an epistemology of privilege, in turn enforced by an ecclesiology of limited charism, thus incapacitates natural law's methodological openness to new information and eventually profoundly distorts both its content and its conduct" (Traina, 1999, p. 145).

To this point, Traina notes, a key criterion of the content of feminist natural law is that the principles derived from authentic methodological and procedural enterprises must serve the ends for which they are discerned: human persons (1999, pp. 148–49). When stunted method and procedure produce distorted ethical content, natural law ceases to function appropriately in the lives of actual moral decision-makers: an uncritical adherence to principles thwarts genuine moral discernment and human flourishing in the ethical enterprise. Principles are meant not to shape moral realities, but to guide moral decision-making toward fullness of well-being with God.

Considered in the context of female flourishing, this criterion has not been met in the historical tradition of official Roman Catholic ethical teaching.

Traina's fifth point in this critical synthesis addresses the enhancement of feminist ethical theory with natural law's attention to norms, the substantive content of feminist natural law. In the articulation of normative content of natural law, first and foremost, attention must be paid to the complexities of female flourishing and the possibility of thriving and developing (Traina, 1999, p. 147). This element of content is the yardstick by which we measure the success of ethical formulation, which in turn indicates the gravity of ethical attention to females' flourishing.

> This is a question not merely of abstract metaphysics but of practical inquiry into the requirements of women's flourishing in a particular time and place. Neither an abstract liberal criterion of freedom of choice nor a technical measure of the organic functioning of the body is expansive enough to do the job here. A "thick" description of women's contemporary flourishing includes not just the theoretical freedom to do as we please but the prerequisites for truly free choices: healthy bodies, healthy relationships, and a degree of economic and political security. Sexual and reproductive self-possession, as well as a social position secure enough to enable women truly to choose intercourse, childbirth, or parenting, are thus among the prerequisites for women's flourishing. (Traina, 1999, p. 147)

Because of the historical oppression of women (and others) by specific and limited groups articulating "universal" norms that have been detrimental to women's flourishing, feminist thinkers share a general aversion to asserting norms. To discuss sexual norms (for instance) with due attention to females' bodily realities, the pure or reasonable normativity predicated on universal realities begins to break down under the weight of women's lives. When females speak of their bodies as their own, rather than when others speak to them about their bodies, the content of ethical norms is more authentically supportive of their flourishing (Traina, 1999, p. 148). Attention to the bodily realities of females and the concomitant normative social constructs of gender and sex are the stuff of feminist theory; it is, therefore, uniquely positioned to articulate a more authentic content of natural law ethics. Traina further points out that feminist ethics does not so much lack principles, as it lacks a connected articulation of them (1999, pp. 309–10). The articulation and re-articulation of ethical claims in concrete circumstances will, indeed, provide for a feminist gleaning and assertion of norms. Traina proposes that casuistry is the method best suited to this task: within the casuist paradigm, there is room to assert tentative norms that arise from ongoing consideration of particular, concrete circumstances (1999, p. 317).[1]

Finally, Traina suggests that the historical natural law tradition pays little critical attention, even in the liberationist camp, to gender and sex differences and their concomitant ethical requirements (1999, pp. 310–12). To address the injustices wrought upon females (and others) effectively in the light of difference, she suggests that whitewashing the oppression under the guise of "sinful social constructions" obliterates the possibility of addressing and redressing the injustices. Social justice depends, instead, upon clear and critical affirmation of difference and a commitment to exercising justice in its presence. Recognizing the delicate discussion required between these two ethical theories, Traina (1999) addresses the specific requirements for its successful outcome:

> Feminist critical analysis trades on its unique ability to distinguish pure cultural constructions from either just or oppressive cultural interpretations of ineradicable human difference and on its superior capacity to deal justly with difference. Feminism's basic claim is not, therefore, essentialist, romantic, or simplistically naturalist. Feminism need not argue that more divides men and women than unites them; that men and women complement each other or have mutually exclusive skills; that sexual characteristics categorically exclude anyone from just wages, a standard education, or positions of responsibility; or that one sex is superior to another. But it must argue that this almost universal difference in embodied existence is likely to yield differences in experience that affect moral reflection and that these must be explored critically. This is the uniquely important frontier between natural law and feminist thought. It points...to issues crucial to the success of both. (p. 312)

In her guidelines for the synthesis of feminist ethics and natural law ethics, Traina weaves a sturdy, flexible fabric between concrete human experience and universal statements about the human. In particular, she undertakes the groundwork for the articulation of an ethics that meets the exigencies both of feminist attention to the concrete and natural law attention to the universal, by constructing a theoretical framework addressing method, procedure, and content. She concludes:

> Natural law thus models elements that any viable, constructive feminist theological ethic must also possess: above all, an overarching

telos, as well as an inductive method of matching cases and principles; an eschatology and a developmental virtue theory that connect individual and communal ends at both the immediate and ultimate levels; a tradition of social analysis; an argument for self-preservation; and an integral rather than ambivalent reading of human embodiment. But these elements also provide a constructive Christian feminism the rudiments of a coherent theological ethic. (1999, p. 319)

Still recognizing the difficulty of making universal claims in a pluralistic world, Traina proposes "revisable universals" as a means of addressing norms (1999, pp. 320–22). For her, this phrase inherently expresses openness to reconsideration of universals in the light of thoughtful criticisms. Yet Traina does not say that universal claims are impossible; rather, the claims we make to universality must be made "with earnest humility" (1999, p. 320). They are strong hypotheses that we must propose with self-conscious awareness of our own particularity in the world. Thus, she concludes that it is indeed possible to "live in the tension between prophecy and pluralism" (1999, p. 320). A broad cultural respect for difference opens the door for a denominational ethic that can engage fruitfully with other ethics without the façade of neutrality; we can dialogue among a plurality of experiences (Traina, 1999, pp. 321–22).

The combined flexibility and structure of feminist natural law make it a particularly useful theory, not only for my own work but also for other contemporary moral theologies grappling with the tension between universality and particularity. Within this framework, attention to empirical data is imperative and the procedural incorporation of previously marginalized voices yields a robust collection of experiences. In this way, any universal claims are rooted in the diverse lives of the human community and open to the possibility of revision as new data surfaces. Feminist natural law allows for the inclusion of adolescent females' sexualities in the construction of a contemporary theological sexual ethic.

SUMMARY
Roman Catholic theology has a rich history of natural law theory that continues to develop in contemporary theological discourse. Of the various contemporary natural law formulations; that is, New Natural Law, the Revisionist schools of thought, and Feminist Natural Law; the feminist natural law framework of Cristina Traina emerges as the best theoretical option to attend adequately to the realities of adolescent females and the need for a sexual ethic that accounts for them and their experiences. Feminist natural law provides a forum in which to address the dearth of attention to

the actual experiences of adolescent females in Christian sexual theology by explicitly considering empirical data wherein adolescent females' realities are featured. Its methodological, procedural, and substantial flexibility allow for systematic consideration of various types of data in constructing an adequate sexual ethic. It is open to ongoing critique and revision in its dynamic evolution, yet is able to facilitate the proposal of tentative universals and norms in its engagement with the data. To propose such an ethic requires exploration of contemporary theoretical and empirical realities with regard to sex, sexuality, and sexual expression, which I will undertake in Chapters 5 and 6. First, however, I continue in Chapter 4 to explore existing feminist theological discussion of female sexuality as it sits within the Roman Catholic and Christian tradition.

CHAPTER FOUR

FEMALES, SEXUALITY, AND GENDER: THEOLOGICAL ANTHROPOLOGY

INTRODUCTION: ADDRESSING DUALISMS

The Roman Catholic theological tradition has long expressed an awkward distrust of females. Referring to early Church fathers, Clark (1983) plainly states their ambivalence toward women: they "praised and blamed, honored and disparaged the female sex" (p. 15). This ambivalence stems largely from *anthropological dualisms* scattered throughout the evolution of Christian theology, whereby aspects of the human experience have been split into opposing pairs. Each aspect of the pair has been judged more positively or more negatively, and has been attributed either a male/masculine character (more positive) or a female/feminine character (more negative). Some traditional dualisms include soul/body, spiritual/material, and Christ/Church (e.g., Augustine, 1955, 1952; Chrysostom, 1986), in which the former aspect of each pair is considered more male and the latter more female (Coll, 1994). The recognition of these dualisms (also known as *binaries*) has launched considerable debate in theoretical and practical circles alike.

Feminist theologians in particular have taken up the task of addressing and redressing oppressive realities faced by females within (and without) the Christian tradition. Recognizing the denigration of females in the perpetuation of a theological anthropology of opposition, feminist theologians have deconstructed the dualisms as a means of shifting the negative perceptions of females apparent in Christian theology. There are numerous classic feminist theological critiques of the Church's historical and contemporary teachings on, and subsequent treatment of, women.

These works engage biblical, historical, and contemporary texts central to Christian theology (e.g., Daly, 1968, 1973; Ruether, 1983; Schneiders, 1991; Schussler Fiorenza, 1983/1990). The experiences of females, so long omitted from Christian theological discussion, are now required consideration in the theological enterprise; female experiences challenge the historical dualistic thinking so embedded in the theological tradition. To uncover the negative biases against females inherent in these dualisms is to uncover the anthropological underpinnings of an often patriarchal and sexist theology.

Rather than reiterating an extensive overview of the manifestation of dualisms within official and other Roman Catholic theology (see authors above), I propose instead to attend more to contemporary manifestations of sex, gender, and sexuality within the Christian theological tradition. To that end, in this chapter, I address and critique contemporary accounts of the body in sexual theology, including loosely connected personalist accounts of the erotic (e.g., Heyward, 1989; Nelson, 1978) and the more unified theology of the body (e.g., John Paul II, 1997).[1] Contemporary official Catholic teachings, which reflect Pope John Paul II's account of the theology of the body, persist in the promulgation of anthropological dualisms by assuming complementarity of the sexes and genders, power differentials, heteronormativity, and male sexuality. This promulgation relies upon a static reading of natural law that is unable to account adequately for female experiences, generally speaking, and certainly fails to account at all for the sexual experiences of adolescent females. And so, I will also address explicitly feminist sexual theologies that more adequately incorporate female sexualities, feminist theory, and evolving social realities, while attending more obviously to female flourishing. Ultimately, I aim to deconstruct traditional theologies of sexuality *en route* to constructing a sexual theology that adequately accounts for and facilitates adolescent female experiences and flourishing.

Beginning with Pope Paul VI's watershed document *Humanae vitae* (1968), subsequent works by Pope John Paul II (both official, such as *Evangelium vitae* [1995a], and unofficial, like *The Theology of the body* [1997]), and various other official documents, such as *Donum vitae* from the Congregation for the Doctrine of the Faith [CDF] (1987), maintain a dualistic assumption that extends into the roles and meaning of both sex and gender. This assumption is operative in the extension of theological anthropology into sexual ethics and theology; normative behaviour is, therefore, predicated upon what is considered natural to each of the sexes by virtue of their complementary natures.

Feminist theologians and feminist theorists (among others) recognize the omissions and assumptions inherent in the official sexual theology of the Roman Catholic Church. Such a theology is open to critique on a number of levels, three of which I discuss here. The first critique is of the lack of attention given to actual female experiences, which results in an inadequate understanding of women's nature and sexuality. A second critique is of the negative assessment of both females and sexuality based upon the assumption of anthropological dualisms within the teachings (Cahill, 1985, 1996; Gudorf, 1994). A final critique is of the positing in itself of an essential understanding of nature (and natures) that would universalize human realities across place, time, and circumstance. This critique pertains especially to the use of natural law in Church teaching (Traina, 1999). Within each of these critiques, there is not only a focus on the content of the teachings as they pertain to females in particular, but also a focus on the method and procedure from which the content is derived. The following section considers theologies of the body and Eros, the erotic manifestation of love that is motivated by desire for another. These theologies arose in response to traditional sexual theologies that diminished sex and sexuality as manifestations of the lesser aspect of the body/soul dualism. While they are a helpful counter to the imbalance between sense and intellect characteristic of Enlightenment thinking, the body theologies are still practically unsatisfactory, and are themselves open to critique, particularly with regard to the construction of a sexual ethic that adequately accounts for adolescent female sexuality. Consequently, this chapter concludes with an account of feminist theological and feminist theoretical perspectives pertaining to sex, gender, particularity, and universality, mining the insights from each of these perspectives and giving preferential attention to female embodiment and sexuality.

THE BODY, EROS, AND THEOLOGY

Historical discourse about sexual theology has not so much ignored the human body as it has eyed it with suspicion as an impediment to holiness; this attitude is evident in the pervasive dualisms (Cahill, 1996, 1995).[2] To mitigate suspicion of the body and sexuality, contemporary body theologies intending to reclaim the goodness of Eros and to attend to positive human sensual, bodily experiences, question the assumption of the superiority of the intellect over the senses with a focus on embodied Christian faith. Within the Christian context, there are theologies that take decidedly different approaches to the body: the loosely kindred erotic/body theologies, and the more unified theology of the body.

Erotic/Body Theologies and Critiques

To temper ambivalence toward the body and sexuality, body theologies that recognize the potential goodness of Eros attend first to positive human erotic experiences and predicate sexual norms upon this recognition (e.g., Lorde, 1994). In affirming the body as equally constitutive of person-hood as the mind and spirit, erotic/body theologies refute the ahistorical Enlightenment location of morality and thought outside of the body in its particular context (Heyward, 1989; Nelson, 1978), suggesting instead that "embodiedness is constitutive of human consciousness" (Cahill, 1996, p. 73). Responding to a theoretical split in the human person that would have the mind in opposition, and superior, to the body, embodiment theologies aim to reclaim the goodness of the body as created in the image of God.

Theologically speaking, insofar as human bodies are good and tend toward fulfillment in union with God, human sexuality must be too. Embodiment theologies aim to reconnect the spiritual and the sexual in the human body, in the human drive toward the sacred (Cahill, 1995).

> Theologically, we believe that human sexuality, while includ-ing God's gift of the procreative capacity, is most fundamentally the divine invitation to find our destinies not in loneliness but in deep connection. To the degree that it is free from the distortions of unjust and abusive power relations, we experience our sexuality as the basic *eros* of our humanness that urges, invites, and lures us out of our loneliness into intimate communication and communion with God and the world. It is instructive to remember that the word "sexuality" itself comes from the Latin *sexus*, probably akin to the Latin *secare*, meaning to cut or divide—suggesting incompleteness seeking wholeness and connection that reaches through and beyond our differences and divisions. Sexuality, in sum, is the physiological and emotional grounding of our capacities to love. (Nelson & Long-fellow, 1994, p. xiv)

Inductive methodology informs embodiment theologies that begin with human sexual experience in constructing sexual theology, rather than with theological conclusions applied to sexual experience, to deter-mine moral goodness (Nelson, 1992). In this light, embodiment theologies can more readily accommodate diverse experiences of human sexuality. Unlike contemporary non-religious theoretical discourse on sex and gen-der, most Christian embodiment theologies continue to posit a telos, an end toward which human sexuality is directed: that is, union with God. This telos is also understood to be constitutive of human sexuality (a universal human reality), which is a disputed point in some contemporary theoretical discourse.

In response to theologies that reflect the Enlightenment mind/body split, body theologies aim to bolster positive perceptions of the body in the human endeavour to flourish, rather than accept negative perceptions of the body as an impediment to relationship with God. True to the Christian theological tenet of God's Incarnation in the person of Jesus Christ, contemporary embodiment theologies point to the presence of God in human flesh and sexuality. Through our sexualities, God continues to be revealed to us in the flesh, in our bodies. Because God chose to become completely human while remaining completely divine, human bodily sexuality is graced by divine presence in the sexual person. People find God in the many and various physical realities of human existence, including (but not exclusively) sexual expression; human sexuality is potentially revelatory of God. This revelation takes place not only personally, to the individual, but also communally, to all of creation (Cahill, 1995). Thus, "our sexuality invites us to intimacy not only with the beloved person but also with all creation. It is intimacy marked by right relationships, mutual power, and justice in our social structures" (Nelson & Longfellow, 1994, p. xv).

Feminist Episcopalian theologian Carter Heyward's early text on erotic/body theology, *Touching our strength: The erotic as power and the love of God* (1989), remains a benchmark in explicitly feminist discussions of theology and the body. For Heyward, the dualisms operative in the Christian tradition have been particularly harmful to women. Social and individual sexual injustices against women are predicated on the assumption of female inferiority to males. By reclaiming the goodness of the body, Heyward suggests we are also able to move toward more just relational experiences among males and females; the erotic yearning for mutuality moves justice beyond the individual sexual/personal level to the social level. Any abusive relationship, therefore, is a "distortion" of true mutuality that breaks off "right relation" with injustice in a "power over" relationship, in contrast to a "power with" relationship (Heyward, 1989, pp. 187–95). For Heyward, moral normativity is situated in the constructed sexual reality of the individual with regard to her/his embodied experiences; she rejects sexual normativity as something that exists outside of subjective experience.

Personalism

The body theologies, including those of James Nelson and Carter Heyward, reflect the theological turn to personalism beginning in the early twentieth century: "Personalism is a characteristically modern phenomenon in that it stresses the priority and the experience of the human subject.

Intersubjective values become pre-eminently important in moral think-ing" (Cahill, 1996, p. 194). Locating moral thought regarding sexuality and sexual expression more explicitly in the realm of the concrete and personal, rather than in the realm of the abstract and universal, works well as a means to recognize the complexity of moral circumstances (as the Revisionists purport in their account of natural law). Criticisms of rigid essentialist articulations of sexual morality focus on the inflexibility of a universal ethics, and its inability to integrate contextual experience adequately into moral thinking. Personalism places the subject's experience at the centre of moral deliberation, allowing the subject to accommodate for diversity in complex situations.

Yet, there are significant critiques of embodiment theologies stemming from personalism that require consideration. One difficulty in espous-ing a strictly personalist embodiment is the moral ambiguity that might arise among actual decision-makers. Although moral decision-making is always ambiguous, it can be more or less so depending upon the history and capacities of the moral agent. For example, the perception that abusive sexual situations are merely a distortion of the true mutuality inherent in the erotic minimizes, if not dismisses, the very real negative sexual expe-riences that many people endure. It is necessary to attune to the good-ness of the body as created in the image of God, but in the face of sexual violation a victim's or survivor's subjective sexual normativity could be more harmful than helpful in particular situations. When violation is a person's subjective norm, the goodness of the body is not easily discerned. A person requires mature and healthy developmental capacities to real-ize, safely, a positive perception of sexual normativity. If a person's history and/or current reality does not reflect such development, it is unlikely that a purely subjective normativity will serve to protect her ensuing vulner-abilities. Such a theology of the body runs headlong into the need to define what exactly "true erotic mutuality" might be—which, given the variables above, is a task that proves to be difficult.

While it is true that attention to each bodily person and context is a necessary aspect of moral reflection, any overly idealized notion of the erotic subject as automatically being able to return to the essence of Eros-as-good bypasses the difficulties of moral decision-making in any par-ticular context. It is helpful here to recall Thomas Aquinas's observation that the capacity of people for decision-making is variable, and that the more detailed the reality, the more prone we are to error. The erotic is not, in every manifestation, good. Nor is its goodness always easy to discern; human sexuality requires time and experience to understand and act well upon. Some normative and contextual understanding of how to respond well to sexuality serves those persons whose lack of time and experience (or healthy experience) is an impediment to prudence.

Theology of the body

Pope John Paul II takes a different tack toward personalism in his theology of the body. Long before he became pope in 1978, John Paul (then Karol Wojtyla) began to develop his theology of the body in *Love and responsibility* (1981; originally published in Polish in 1960). The more extensive *Theology of the body: Human love in the divine plan* (1997) is a collection of his Wednesday addresses given between September 1979, shortly after he assumed the papacy, and November 1984. Neither of these works belongs to official magisterial teaching of the Church, but their substance is reflected in many of John Paul's subsequent official papal teachings (*Evangelium vitae*, 1995a; *Familiaris consortio*, 1981; *Mulieris dignitatem*, 1988; *Ordinatio sacerdotalis*, 1994; and *Veritatis splendor*, 1993). A good deal of the substance of the contemporary *Catechism of the Catholic Church* (initially published in 1994, with subsequent editions) also bears the hallmark of John Paul's thinking. The so-called *Personalist Thomism* he adopted in the theology of the body looms largely in contemporary Roman Catholic thought on sex, sexuality, gender, and relationships.

Following a presentation of Pope John Paul II's theology of the body and those theologies stemming from it, I offer some critique of this school of thought, particularly regarding adolescent female sexualities. I contend that John Paul's articulation of body theology is unsuccessful insofar as it is generally inattentive to actual human sexual experience, and particularly void of an account of adolescent female sexual experiences. Such a void renders the theology of the body a problematic theological starting point for constructing a sexual ethic accounting for adolescent females. Prior to my critique, however, I offer an account of Pope John Paul II's theology of the body.

Pope John Paul II's theology of the body: An account

Not unlike the personalism of other body theologies, John Paul II's personalism envisions physically, spiritually, cognitively, and socially integrated persons. His theology of the body centres on the human, acting person in relationship with God. Most importantly, John Paul interprets the authentic meaning of the body as God has intended for humans, a reflection of the theological anthropology of *complementarity of the sexes* within Pope Paul VI's encyclical *Humanae vitae* (1968). This interpretation focuses on the sexual nature of the human person and the ways in which our actions reflect or deny the will of God. Because John Paul's theology of the body is so influential in contemporary Roman Catholic official teaching and theology, I spend time here developing a number of its more potent concepts, which are significant in theological discourse on sexuality. In exploring John Paul's understanding of these concepts, I also explore how heavily laden his theology of the body is with anthropological assumptions that are, at best, inattentive to experiential and empirical realities and, at worst, harmful to females.

Pope John Paul II employs the biblical creation accounts from Genesis (Gen. 1, 2 [New Revised Standard Version: Catholic Edition])[3] and the subsequent account of the fall of humanity (Gen. 3) as a basis for authentic human sexuality and anthropology (John Paul II, 1997, pp. 25–102, re: "Original unity of man and woman: Catechesis on the Book of Genesis"). He develops what he terms the *nuptial* meaning of the body, which points to the communion of persons within the covenant and sacrament of marriage, as outlined in Genesis 2. He refers to the *complementarity* of Adam and Eve and the gift of the body that the man gives to the woman (and vice versa) in both the unitive and procreative functions of sexual intercourse.[4] In sexual intimacy, we give the *total gift of self* to one another. This gift of self, he proposes, is the original manifestation of males and females as human bodies (John Paul II, 1997). The following is an overview of John Paul's thought on the nuptial body.

> Seeing each other, as if through the mystery of creation, man and woman see each other even more fully and distinctly than through the sense of sight itself, that is, through the eyes of the body. They see and know each other with all the peace of the interior gaze, which creates precisely the fullness of the intimacy of persons.... Shame brings with it a specific limitation in seeing with the eyes of the body. This takes place above all because personal intimacy is disturbed and almost threatened by this sight. According to Genesis 2:25, the man and the woman were not ashamed seeing and knowing each other in all the peace and tranquility of the interior gaze. They communicate in the fullness of humanity, which is manifested in them as reciprocal complementarity precisely because they are "male" and "female." At the same time, they communicate on the basis of that communion of persons in which, through femininity and masculinity, they become a gift for each other. In this way they reach in reciprocity a special understanding of the meaning of their own body. (John Paul II, 1997, p. 57ff)

In developing the nuptial meaning of the body, John Paul points not only to the necessary complementarity of male and female as willed by

God, but also to the sexual *self-donation* or *gift of self* that must accompany what he terms *authentic* sexual interaction between a married male and female. To accomplish this self-gift, one must first accomplish self-mastery, for if one is not fully in possession of oneself, then the gift of self to another cannot be free and authentic (John Paul II, 1997, pp. 60–66). For John Paul, only in self-mastery can one find freedom to do the will of God. The gift of self to another must be total, and is only possible in the divinely ordained sacrament of marriage. Drawing on the notions of complementarity, self-gift, authenticity, and the physical reality of male and female bodies, John Paul concludes that the natural end of the nuptial meaning of the body is procreation (1997, pp. 62–63). If procreation is the telos of the sexual person, then any contraceptive act between spouses is a violation of the nuptial gift of self. The capacity to achieve self-mastery with regard to one's sexual expression is a cornerstone in John Paul's development of marital sexual relationships as bodily expressions:

> According to the criterion of this truth [i.e., the inseparable aspects of marital sexual intercourse as articulated in *Humanae vitae*], which should be expressed in the language of the body, the conjugal act signi-fies not only love, but also potential fecundity. Therefore it cannot be deprived of its full and adequate significance by artificial means. In the conjugal act it is not licit to separate the unitive aspect from the procre-ative aspect, because both the one and the other pertain to the intimate truth of the conjugal act. The one is activated together with the other and in a certain sense the one by means of the other. This is what the encyclical teaches (cf. *HV* 12). Therefore, in such a case the conjugal act, deprived of its interior truth because it is artificially deprived of its procreative capacity, ceases also to be an act of love. (1997, p. 398)

In a final analysis, the nuptial meaning of the body points unwaveringly to the full union of the spouses and their openness to procreation. John Paul maintains that God created humanity male and female as an expression of the nuptial meaning of the body and, in this creation, are inherent roles and responsibilities proper to each of the sexes (e.g., "Man and woman: A gift for each other" [pp. 69–72] and "The mystery of woman is revealed in mother-hood" [pp. 80–83], both in John Paul II, 1997; reiterated in CDF, 2004).

Pope John Paul II's theology of the body: A critique

Pope John Paul's II's theology of the body has faced a mixed reception. Its supporters tend also to be supportive of the teachings regarding birth con-trol in *Humanae vitae* (1968) and, indeed, of most magisterial teachings.

They embrace John Paul II's reiteration of the unchanging norms of the Catholic tradition regarding sexual ethics on the one hand, and his personalist approach on the other. Glick states, for example, that "[t]he Pope set out to make a strong theological and personalistic defense of *Humanae vitae*, and painstakingly laid considerable groundwork in order to do so.... Certainly John Paul II is answering his own call... for a fuller development of the personalistic reasons behind the received teaching" (1986, p. 24; see also Rousseau, 2000; Shivanandan, 2001; West, 2005, 2004, 2003, 1998).[5] Perhaps the most enticing aspect of John Paul's theology of the body, however, is its personalistic appeal to the relational experiences of contemporary Catholics. For instance, Cloutier (2006) notes that John Paul's theology of the body seems to speak to young people in that it opposes a culture of sexual *selfishness* and the *instrumentalization* of relationships, and leads them toward loving in a "truly self-giving way." He also suggests that the theology of the body

> generally appeals to two sorts of people: people disaffected by the past emptiness of their sexual experience (often men?) and people with very little experience of relationships (often women?). Both of these groups find in the Theology of the Body a support for their own idealism about love and relationships, about the immense possibilities offered by human relationships. (p. 203, no. 34)

As West notes in his Prologue to *Theology of the body explained* (2003), John Paul believed it imperative that the teachings of *Humanae vitae* (1968) be brought to life in a personalistic ethic: one that could speak to the lives of faithful Catholics the world over. For John Paul, the whole of our perception of human life is tied up in the teachings promulgated therein.

While West and others are unreservedly enthusiastic about Pope John Paul II's theology of the body, it still has detractors. Critiques of the theology of the body cover a range of objections. Feminist objections focus on the repercussions of John Paul's adherence to the anthropological notion of essential complementarity of the sexes (Cahill, 1996; Kaveny, 2003). A particular critique here is that, despite the personalist approach to body theology, John Paul manages to sustain magisterial norms that are largely devoid of attention to actual female sexual experiences. Further, the roles iterated regarding the complementary nature of males and females reinforce gender stereotypes of masculinity and femininity (Kaveny, 2003). From a feminist perspective, the notion that women's special genius is tied almost exclusively to the role of nurturing mother is belied by the experiences of many contemporary females. The New Feminists, like Allen

(2006), Lemmons (2002), and Sweeny (2006), refute this claim. Also, the implications of a complementary nature of the sexes move beyond hetero-sexual normativity into the condemnation of same-sex behaviours as dis-ordered expressions of the nuptial meaning of the body (Ross, 2001). While clearly problematic for females, the theology of the body also further mar-ginalizes non-heterosexuals in accordance with traditional moral norms.[6]

Another critique of John Paul II's theology of the body is that, despite its professed personalism, "it represents a mode of theology that has little to say to ordinary people because it shows so little awareness of ordinary life" (Johnson, 2001, p. 12). In his overview and critique of the theology of the body, Johnson takes issue with John Paul's lack of attention to the empiri-cal bodily realities of human persons, both sexually and non-sexually, and wonders at a perception of revelation on human bodiliness that ends in the scriptural accounts of creation and redemption (Johnson, 2001).[7] This critique is echoed by Modras (1988), and by Traina (2006) in her con-sideration of discipleship and sexual morality in the "real world." John Paul's unique reading of the scriptural accounts of pre-lapsarian human-ity, and the sexual normativity arising from it, is problematic in the light of contemporary biblical scholarship. His perception that undertaking anything less than a total self-gift to one's spouse is selfish ignores contem-porary psychological data that questions whether total self-giving love is even possible (or wise/prudent). And his suggestion that persons will find freedom only in self-mastery over the passions negates the possibility of other authentic forms of sexual interaction or goodness in the sometimes spontaneous emotional, playful, and loving acts persons show toward a committed other (Modras, 1988).

Perhaps the most problematic aspect of Pope John Paul II's theology of the body is the reading of natural law and the method by which he con-structs his conclusions. Because John Paul locates the true, nuptial mean-ing of the body in pre-lapsarian humanity, he must then locate lust, when one sees the other as the "object of one's own desire" ... "at the cost of a real and full communion of persons" (1997, p. 123) and other sexual sins in post-lapsarian humanity. This reading creates the anthropological conun-drum of positing, as normative, a morality based upon the absence of sin in the human condition, rather than a normative morality based upon actual human experience of sinfulness and grace. Hence, the *real and full communion of persons* that manifests the nuptial meaning of the body sits beyond our capacity as post-lapsarian humans. John Paul proposes that the natural, authentic, and normative state of human sexuality lies in the creation of Adam and Eve, prior to the introduction of original sin into our human reality.

For John Paul, "original sin marks precisely the subjective loss or obscuring of the nuptial meaning of the body" (West, 2003, p. 99). Because the nuptial meaning of the body is the basis for sexual normativity, we are called to live a sexual morality that is based on the ideal state of human sexual relationships. We accomplish this morality through relationship with Christ (West, 2004, pp. 19–20). This position contrasts with the Roman Catholic natural law tradition, which holds that "grace completes nature rather than contradicting it" (Traina, 2006, p. 87). That is, the grace we encounter in relationship with God works in the context of concomitant human realities of essential goodness and the capacity to sin. In effect, John Paul is proposing that what is ideal is, in fact, normative, and that we are called to live outside of original sin. As a general critique, because his personalism is without reference to empirical data about the lived realities of human persons, his call to a pre-lapsarian norm seems methodologically faulty as a personalist Thomism. What is ideal (i.e., the lack of original sin) or prior to the actual reality of humans (i.e., the capacity to sin and to access grace) cannot be natural to us; the norm of the nuptial meaning of the body sits outside of the methodological requirements of natural law.

The deficiency of the theology of the body in accounting for experience leaves it wanting as a theological sexual ethic. A more specific critique is that, like previous understandings of normative human sexuality, the experiences of females (and others) are substantively absent. Traina's (1999) feminist natural law could remedy the absence of female voices in the content of sexual normativity: because she commits methodologically and procedurally to accounting for the experiences of females in feminist natural law, the resulting content is more likely to integrate females appropriately into moral thought. In particular, Traina's method and procedure is able to accommodate adolescent female experiences of sexuality into the data of natural law.

The theology of the body does not seem to consider actual experiences of sexuality, and certainly does not explicitly consider female experiences of sexuality; however, feminist voices regarding the body, theology, sexuality, and gender do. Traina's feminist natural law provides the method and procedure to do exactly this work. Along with feminism's overarching commitment to female well-being, which requires feminists from all disciplines to attend first to supports of, and impediments to, female flourishing, feminist natural law facilitates the incorporation of missing data into theologies of sexuality. The following sections address contemporary feminist thought and the evolution of theological sexual normativity.

Feminist Sexual Ethics: Of Bodies, Sex, and Gender

From the previous discussions of natural law and embodiment theologies arise contemporary questions regarding notions of universality and normativity, sex and gender. From traditional natural law through contemporary accounts of natural law, we arrive at feminist natural law as a theoretical framework within which to address theological anthropology and sexual ethics. Alongside contemporary natural law theories are contemporary feminist theories about the person, identity, sexuality, gender, and the body. Feminist natural law works well within this contemporary theoretical landscape because it accommodates females' experiences both methodologically and procedurally, while remaining committed to some normative account of sexual ethics. It is flexible enough to attend to female flourishing (and its obstructions), and solid enough to make claims for moral action. To situate this ongoing discussion, I first chart feminist theological considerations of sex, sexuality, sexual expression, and normativity. Second, I consider nontheological discourses in response to traditional theoretical and practical formulations of human sexual morality. Contemporary feminist theory contributes well to feminist theology pertaining to the body, sex, and gender, and to subjectivity and universality.

Theological perspectives

Many body theologies are explicitly feminist in orientation. Because dualisms associated the body with females and both were disparaged, feminists take special interest in redeeming the body and females in theology. A hallmark of feminist theological ethics is the explicit attention paid to women's experiences and women's flourishing. Grounded in the interrogation of anthropological dualisms informing the Christian theological tradition, feminist sexual ethics have critiqued the limitations of historical accounts of the human. Noting that females have, at times, been characterized as deficient males, feminist theological anthropologies seek, within numerous theoretical stances, to reformulate a Christian account of human experience (Coakley, 2002; Coll, 1994; Fulkerson, 1997; Jones, 1997; Ruether, 1983). Feminist theologians point out that the negative construction of supposedly female characteristics in dualistic thought has perpetuated the oppression of females in all spheres. Most notably, this oppression includes violence against women (Lebacqz, 1994; Thistlethwaite, 1989), which clearly renders essentialist dualism an untenable theological and social construct.

Perpetuation of a general power differential between males and females leaves women in a precarious relational position. The ambiguity and variety of female sexual experience highlights the pitfalls of any theology that romanticizes the experience of male/female relationships (Lebacqz, 1994). The reality of a history and ongoing pattern of male violence against females, particularly in intimate sexual relationships, leads Lebacqz to conclude that when inviting women into male/female partnerships, we are in effect asking women to "love their enemies" (1994, p. 244).[8] Her point is to "attend to the realities of the links between violence and sexuality in the experiences of women" in order to recognize what is at stake for women in male/female relationships (1994, p. 244).

> To recognize the one whom one loves as "enemy" is to accept the implications of the social construction of sexuality and to understand that the task is not simply to create a private haven into which one can retreat, but is to work for a new social construction of sexuality that will undo the injustices that permeate the present culture. (1994, p. 257)

Lebacqz's concerns highlight the limitations of a theological anthropology and sexual theology that essentializes the sexes as complementary. Although Pope John Paul II rightly states that violence and abuse is a sign of human sinfulness (1997, p. 456–57), he does not adequately account for its reality in his construction of human sexuality. Further, he discounts the possibility that the kind of nuptial relationships willed by God between heterosexual married partners could exist within a same-sex relationship (or any other of the multi-variant manifestations of human sexuality). Lebacqz's work addresses the realities of human sexuality and sexual interaction that are cause for reflection on what an authentic body theology might entail, beyond complementarity of the sexes. When considering the contextual realities in which female sexualities have historically been situated (such as the historical ownership of females by males, the disenfranchisement of females as "non-persons," and the official Roman Catholic rejection of divorce), women's agency about their own relational well-being has been rather restricted (Gudorf, 1994).

Some feminists have also noted the inability of the Church's promulgation of complementarity to capture adequately the realities of gender and sex. Numerous official documents have posited, based on the biblical accounts of creation in Genesis (Gen. 1–2), that God ordained the complementarity of the sexes as the natural order of intimate relationship (see, e.g., CDF, 2004; CDF, 1986). While attention to sexual difference is theologically tenable, still the predication of specific gender roles on that basis is a social construction (Cahill, 1985; Coll, 1994; Gudorf, 1994). Contemporary feminist sexual theologies explicitly incorporate female sexual experience, both to counter an androcentric, heteronormative history of

Christian sexual theology and to challenge the assumptions about females inherent in the dualisms.

The most pointed example of androcentric heteronormativity in the Catholic theological tradition is that sex and sexuality are focused on male orgasm (on ejaculation, to be precise) and human reproduction. The Church does not address actual female experiences beyond childbearing, either in its consideration of sexual pleasure or in its understanding of the female (Gudorf, 1994). Rather, women appear confined to roles most prominently personified in the person of Mary: Mother of God and perpetual virgin (see, e.g., CDF, 2004; John Paul II, 1988). In contrast to the official theology, feminist theology gives explicit consideration of and privilege to female sexual experience (Andolsen, 1996) and female sexual pleasure (Jung, 2000) as positive contributions to theological reflection. Both Andolsen and Jung note that, without such consideration, contemporary sexual theology is destined to perpetuate an androcentric theology that is unfriendly to females. And, the privileging of female sexual pleasure must always be accompanied by attention to justice within the social circumstances in which females live. Without such attention, female sexual pleasure itself is vulnerable to a biased construction within an elite population (Jantzen, 2002; Jung, 2002).

Traditional discussions of theological anthropology and sexuality are based on substantively inadequate experiential data. To address female sexualities successfully, feminist theology must meet two specific methodological challenges. The first challenge is to re-vision Roman Catholic methodology and procedure in such a way that it is able to incorporate the substantive content of females' experiences into its understanding of sexual ethics, while positing some normative account of human sexual ethics. This challenge will be addressed only in the light of the second challenge: to respond adequately to the post-modern—and specifically post-structuralist—feminist deconstruction of the categories of sex, gender, and universality. As noted above, feminist theorists across disciplines have raised serious and important questions about the assumptions inherent to modern thought regarding sex, gender, subjectivity, and universality (Butler, 1990/1999; Irigaray, 1993; Kristeva & Clement, 2001; Nussbaum, 2000). These questions are particularly important to this project, which considers issues of sex and gender, assumes an ontological, embodied subject prior to social construction, and suggests some normative ethical understanding of sexuality.

Feminist theory: Sex, gender, subjectivity, universality

Feminist theory of the late twentieth and early twenty-first centuries offers important challenges to theoretical constructs of the human that are based upon notions of universality, objectivity, and normativity. These challenges

are rightly concerned with the manifestations of theory in oppressive practices toward persons sitting outside the prescribed norms of *human*. As the
previous discussions suggest, females have historically been but one group
of non-normative humans (along with, for example, aboriginals and non-
heterosexuals), based upon traditional dualistic anthropologies. Feminist
theologians are now tangling with the dialectic of particulars and universals
regarding anthropologies: To what extent does each of the particular circumstances and the universal human tendencies shape our thought about
human morality? This dialectic then leads to questions regarding the ethics
of relationships. To what extent do sameness and difference pertain to our
anthropological formulations? What are scholars able to say ethically when
faced with profound cultural differences of values among equally human
persons? Here feminist theologians must engage with, and be informed by,
the work of feminists in other disciplines in order to construct a framework
for an adequate feminist ethic for sexual theology.

Judith Butler

Judith Butler is a prominent feminist philosopher/theorist currently
addressing questions of sex, gender, subjectivity, and universals. Butler
struggled with being identified in a particular sexual category that informed
her early scholarship with regard to sexual identity (1991/2004b). Although
she self-identified as lesbian, she was reluctant to do so because the category
of "lesbian" was problematized in the political realm, and carried with it
normatively expected behaviour in feminist theory and feminist theoretical
circles alike. Hence, Butler became one of the early proponents of so-called
Queer theory, the theoretical destabilization of the subject through the interrogation of the categories of sex, gender, and identity (Butler, 1990/1999).
In her first major work, *Gender trouble* (1990/1999)[9] and subsequent other
works, Butler developed a post-structuralist feminist deconstruction of
gender and sex, and concomitant notions of performativity and identity.

  In *Gender trouble* (1990/1999), Butler takes previous feminisms to task
for their dualistic (or binary) formulations of human sexualities in male
and female, and introduces her understanding of the discursive social construction not only of gender, but also of sex. In positing that both gender
and sex are socially constructed, Butler questions the body as a site of social
hegemony. As a social construct, the body is contested in its discursive construction in the same way that gender is: what it means to be masculine/
male or feminine/female has everything to do with one's concrete context.
While Butler (1993) does not dispute the materiality of the physical body,
she does propose that, in and of itself, biological sex has no meaning. Sexual identification is manifest in the notions of performativity and parody,

and the meanings of gender and sex are wholly constructed through the repetition, reiteration, and regulation of acts, which at times transgress hegemonic social constructions, such as heteronormativity. The body is the locus of such performative, constructive acts (Butler, 1990/1999, 1993, 1997, 1991/2004b).

In *Gender trouble* (1990/1999), Butler also questions the subject's very ontology. Characteristic of Queer theory, she posits the fluid nature of the sexual subject, intentionally aims to disturb the notion that philosophical terms and categories are stable and fixed, and troubles the idea that there is an ontological subject at the helm of the ethical agent. She also questions the possibility of universal claims with regard to human experience and, particularly, sexual experience. By disturbing the notion of a universal human subjectivity, Butler is echoing the broader post-modern critique of hegemonic understandings of the human person. Recognizing the methodological and procedural difficulties of having elite groups (e.g., philosophers, intellectuals, males) positing truths for all of humanity, independent of individual experiences, post-modern theorists like Butler assume difference among persons. Hence, Butler concludes that scholars may actually have nothing to say about universal, normative morality.

Butler's philosophical move away from universal normativity is most pronounced in her earlier works (e.g., Butler, 1990/1999, 1993). In her later work, she seems to step away from an outright denial of the universal to suggest an unfolding and fluid perception of universals and norms in service of the transformation of human society (e.g., Butler, 2004a, pp. 174–203). While Butler continues to posit the deconstruction of existing identity categories, she also proposes that universals do not so much exist, *de facto*, as become ever more adequately articulated by those historically excluded in the categories of human: the *different*.

Post-modernity and post-structuralism: En route to an adequate feminist sexual theology

In the light of post-modern, and particularly post-structuralist, feminist critiques of sex, gender, subjectivity, and universality, an adequate feminist sexual theology must address the reality of difference among persons. It must also address the concomitant understanding that highlights experience as the primary, normative account of women's lives and moralities. If women's experiences vary infinitely from one culture to the next, from one individual to the next, then none of us have any business making normative, universal moral claims. The difficulty with such an understanding, however, is that if this is the case, then we do not have any business claiming universal rights, either. If we have no way of understanding females collectively, then we are left in a quandary about how best to advocate for females in the world.

An adequate feminist sexual theology must also account for the theological tradition in which it sits. It must account for the human realities of sin and grace; for the history of oppression of vulnerable individuals and groups; and for hope in personal and social conversion. Most importantly, it must also account for the incarnational nature of the Christian faith. Because we are all created in the image of God, we have a shared inheritance of human dignity and a resulting responsibility to and for one another in our interconnectedness. An adequate Christian sexual theology must maintain sight of the human body created by a loving God. As a result of this faith claim, we must be able to articulate (or at least begin to articulate) what supports or diminishes human bodily dignity and flourishing in the world, both individually and socially.

To this end, feminist theologians from a number of stances are addressing the concerns raised in post-modern and post-structuralist theories. Serene Jones (2000), who works within a Protestant feminist theology, and Donna Teevan (2003), who works within a Roman Catholic feminist theology, both recognize the importance of engaging feminist theoretical claims seriously in the development of feminist theologies. Teevan identifies a number of insights for feminist theology stemming from post-structuralist feminism, yet, along with Serene Jones, opts for *strategic essentialism* in feminist theologies (similar to Traina's *revisable universals*). This position holds that, although the human subject is historically conditioned, it is not entirely socially constructed. While attending to the particular and collective experiences of females in their historical circumstances, they would still posit universal status for human rights based on dignity and flourishing. Tina Beattie (2006) also engages contemporary post-structuralist theory from within the Roman Catholic tradition, and does so more explicitly in her interrogation of traditional and neo-orthodox theological anthropologies. Beattie is particularly concerned with the rise of anthropologies that support historical gender stereotypes that are often oppressive to women. Beattie (2006) discusses Hans Urs von Balthasar at length, for example, whose theological anthropology informed that of Pope John Paul II. She effectively engages contemporary feminist theory in developing a feminist theological anthropology in tune with women's particular experiences. Finally, working from within the Anglican tradition, Sarah Coakley also engages contemporary feminist theory, in continual dialogue with historical theological formulations of similar questions (Coakley, 2002; see also Bynum, 1995).

Roman Catholic theologian Margaret Farley considers feminism and universal morality from a specifically ethical perspective (1993), ultimately proposing a framework for Christian sexual ethics (2006). Farley makes the case for the precarious balance of universal norms, articulated to advance human flourishing, with particular accounts of women's experiences, which uncover oppressive realities that ensue from social constructions. For Farley, any abstraction that declares one particular facet of the human experience as universally normative, and which, by default, jeopardizes another's well-being, is morally untenable. However, to dismiss the possibility of an ethic that recognizes the interconnectedness of the human community and our concomitant responsibility to one another by virtue of the radical social construction of the human subject, which can leave us morally paralyzed in the face of difference, is also morally untenable. In this light, Farley outlines broad norms articulating what might constitute "Just Sex" (2006, pp. 215–32): norms that are "bottom-line requirements," that "admit of degrees," "that are not mutually exclusive," and that require "respect for an embodied as well as inspirited" human reality (2006, pp. 215–16). Unlike the New Natural Law's claim of the incommensurability of the Basic Goods, Farley recognizes the sometimes overlapping (even conflicting) goods addressed in moral decision-making.

SUMMARY

A contemporary feminist sexual ethic is one that is situated within the context of post-modern and post-structural feminist thought. Given feminist concerns for the particular circumstances of individual females, an adequate sexual theology must re-vision Roman Catholic methodology and procedures in such a way as to incorporate the substantive content of females' experiences into its understanding of sexual ethics, and to posit some normative sexual ethic. There are inadequacies in the traditional and official formulations of human anthropology and sexuality based upon particular readings of the natural law tradition. Contemporary formulations of natural law are inadequate to account for females' realities, and contemporary feminist theory regarding sex, gender, and universals provides no normative account of sexual ethics.

Given the limitations above, the task at hand is to construct, from the wisdoms of each previous possibility, a theological sexual ethic that is able to account for adolescent female experiences. Integrating an ethical theory based on essentials and universals with one based on contingencies and particulars is a delicate business; however, within a feminist natural law and theology, there is a basis for the construction of a robust and fruitful theological sexual ethic.

CHAPTER FIVE

ADOLESCENT FEMALES IN A CONTEMPORARY CONTEXT: SEX, GENDER, AND DEVELOPMENT

INTRODUCTION

As an adult Roman Catholic female, I undertake this work mindful of my own adolescence. While fashion, technology, society, and even theological discourse have changed, Roman Catholic teachings have not; these teachings remain, in essence, the same today as they were in my own adolescence, despite monumental growth in our understanding of human sexuality, gender, and development. Do today's adolescent females experience Church teachings any differently than those of previous generations, given the different contexts? It is safe to conclude, because the teachings have remained unchanged, that contemporary adolescent females' voices remain unrepresented in their content. Methodologically, no mechanism exists to incorporate those voices into contemporary teachings.

The methodology and procedure of feminist natural law are open to the inclusion of empirical data that speaks to the flourishing of adolescent females, and adequately attend to their sexual realities. The content of such a sexual theology must reflect not only its roots in the theological tradition, but the substance that it draws from girls' lives. To that end, I turn to the empirical data from which this ethic will be constructed. I explicitly address adolescent females and their sexuality because theirs is a silent voice in the history of sexual theology. The irony of this silence lies in that a good deal of our energy with regard to sexual morality within Christian churches is directed toward adolescents, and what they ought or ought not to do. In keeping with the methodological and procedural criteria of feminist natural law theory, I aim to incorporate these female voices into sexual theologies, and to weave empirical evidence into theological constructions of human sexuality.

Some of the salient aspects of female adolescent development that contribute to sexual flourishing and an adequate sexual theology include, for example, gender development, heteronormativity, moral development, identity development (which I address in this chapter), and physical development (which I address in Chapter 6). Although not exhaustive, this account of the sexual realities of adolescent females provides sufficient substance to embark upon a synthesis of data within feminist natural law and sexual theology. Because contemporary adolescent development is fraught with the ambivalence of competing social messages, identity formation, and personal realities, the construction of such a sexual ethic requires attention to both personal and social factors.

One significant social factor in the lives of contemporary adolescent females is the moral voices emanating from various Christian churches, and the authoritative voice of the Roman Catholic Church in particular. To consider adolescent female sexuality in the context of Roman Catholic sexual theology is to walk a rather sparsely trodden path. In the history and tradition of Roman Catholic teaching and discussion, theologians have generally assumed adulthood in both our audiences and our subjects. Beyond anecdotal accounts, theological substance reflects limited explicit engagement with empirical evidence and, for the vast majority of official magisterial formulations, the realities of females are absent: this is no more obviously so than in the area of sexual theologies. Not only is there a dearth of reflection on female personal, social, and spiritual realities, but so, too, is there a dearth of reflection on developmental realities in human sexualities.

In a contemporary context, such inattention to adolescent females' realities will not do. To privilege girls' sexual realities in the construction of a sexual theology requires attention to the stories, experiences, and perceptions of the diverse lives of girls in contemporary Western societies.

While counselling adolescent females, I have observed a decided ambivalence among many of them not only toward sex and sexuality, but toward themselves as sexual persons. Despite the continual barrage of sexual messages and images they face in their immediate environments,[1] it seems that many girls have limited meaningful discussions of sexuality, and few concrete and useful values or norms to guide them in their decision-making. Because the realities of adolescent sexualities are generally far removed from the construction of theological sexual ethics, I engage existing empirical data as a means of evaluating the appropriateness of current theologies of sexuality for supporting adolescent female flourishing.

In this chapter, I explore adolescent females' realities with regard to the more contextual influences on development, sex and gender, sexuality, and relationships, in the light of current empirical data. I explore primarily psychological (both theoretical and empirical) studies of adolescent females' experiences and perceptions in contemporary Western societies in order to initiate dialogue between those voices and Roman Catholic theology. I begin with theoretical accounts of factors contributing to adolescent development.

DEVELOPMENTAL FACTORS IN ADOLESCENCE

Adolescence itself is generally understood to be "a prolonged transition period between childhood and adulthood that prepares the young person for occupation, marriage, and mature social roles" (Muuss, 1996, p. 366). Although this transition is a biologically universal experience among males and females, cultural contexts still shape what we make of it and the extent to which we flourish throughout. Various psychoanalytic, anthropological, cognitive-developmental, and social theories account for aspects of this transition and reflect specific concerns relevant to adolescent development, such as individuation into adulthood, cultural normativity, development of cognitive capacities, and social integration, respectively. I understand adolescence to be a time of multi-faceted transition, during which an individual experiences physical, cognitive, affective, relational, spiritual, and social development. The individual, along with his/her social context, contributes to the experience of adolescence, which is woven inextricably within this individual's own physical reality. Development does not hinge solely on one factor—be it genetic inheritance, nurturing, or social support—but on the unique interactions of these variables in the life of each person.

The role of human development is largely unaccounted for in the traditional theological discourse pertaining to sexuality, despite its salience to adolescent experience. In psychological theory and practice, accounts of human development offer insight into how we interact as persons over our lifespans. Examining different stages of development provides insight into how persons differ from infancy through childhood, adolescence, and adulthood. Insights gained, in turn, provide data that can inform theological and ethical reflections regarding sexuality. To flesh out the realities of adolescent development, I pay explicit attention to the body and address the roles of biological and physical development in relation to sex, gender, socialization, identity, and neurological development. Although I discuss them as discrete areas of human development, the experiential interaction of the various aspects of development in persons' lives is complex and intertwined. Because no one aspect of development is untouched by the

others, the conceptualization I present is merely that: a conceptualization. Further, the plethora of theoretical and empirical data around human
development is not fully represented here. Some theories and studies are
left out, and my own biases necessarily colour my choices, perceptions, and
interpretations of the data.

Identity, Gender, and Gender Development Theory

Gender development theory

Initiating this exploration of adolescent development with an account of
gender development is an acknowledgement of gender construction as a crucial aspect of contemporary human experience, and of adolescent sexuality
and flourishing in particular. We are, for the most part, unaware of how
gender affects us in our daily lives, and yet it has a profound significance
in our developmental lives. Gender development theories[2] aim to account
for the various aspects and manifestations of gender among adolescents
and to offer a context within which adolescent females' experiences are
better understood.

Bussey and Bandura's (1999) *social cognitive theory* (SCT) attempts to
integrate multiple factors of gender development, and the authors posit
that a gender development theory that does not account for multiple factors in adolescent development is insufficient.[3] Considering psychoanalytic, cognitive-developmental, gender schema, biological, and sociological
theories regarding the development of gender, Bussey and Bandura propose social cognitive theory as an integrative theory that accounts for a
variety of human capacities, like capacities for symbolization, observa-
tional learning, self-regulation, reflection, and information processing
(1999, p. 683f). They note, however, that these potentialities are not necessarily behavioural dictates; persons are malleable and prone to change over
time in gender identification, understanding, and manifestation (Bussey &
Bandura, 1999, p. 684). Social cognitive theory states that "gender development is neither totally shaped and regulated by environmental forces
nor by socially non-situated intrapsychic processes. Rather, gender development is explained in terms of triadic reciprocal causation" (Bussey &
Bandura, 1999, p. 684): personal, behavioural, and environmental factors
interact in people's lives to facilitate fluid gender development.

Bussey and Bandura (1999) assume that the category of sex, consist-
ing primarily of the female and male, sets each person on a multi-faceted
course of gender development that takes place via numerous influences,
such as modelling of gender by others, interpreting others' responses to our
own gendered behaviours, and direct learning from others about gender

conceptualizations (pp. 685–89). We learn what constitutes "appropriate" gender conduct from others' behaviours and teachings, and by how they respond to our own behaviours. Bussey and Bandura also propose that gender conduct and role behaviour is closely regulated by social sanctions, self-sanctions, and individual and collected perceptions of self-efficacy according to gender (1999, pp. 689–94). For example, a boy might be sanctioned for wearing nail polish because males "do not" wear nail polish, and a girl might perceive herself as less able to undertake welding as a profession because females "do not" do heavy manual labour. Hence, males and females are socialized in multiple ways toward roles and behaviours stereotypically attributed to each of the sexes.

In their social cognitive analysis of gender role development and functioning, Bussey and Bandura (1999, pp. 694–704) identify a number of influences at work in the development of gender over the course of a lifespan:

- pre-gender identity regulation of gender conduct (i.e., gender regulation of children prior to their own recognition of gender);
- self-categorization and acquisition of gender role knowledge (i.e., recognition of personal sex category and concomitant gender role prescriptions);
- movement from social sanctions to self-sanctions (i.e., internalization of social prescriptions regarding gender);
- movement from gender categorization to gender role learning (i.e., moving from understanding one's sex category to the "appropriate" performance of prescribed gender roles);
- parental impact on subsequent gender development; impact of peers on gender development; media representations of gender roles; impact of educational practices on gender development (i.e., educational practices that often reveal a hidden gender curriculum);
- gendered practices of occupational systems (i.e., constructs of employment for females and males); and
- interdependence of gender socializing subsystems (i.e., ways in which the above influences work in concert to create and reinforce gender identification, roles, behaviours, and structures).

Gender development theory helps in understanding the experiences of males and females within particular contexts, as witnessed in Egan and Perry's (2001) *multi-dimensional analysis* of gender identity regarding psychosocial adjustment. Within their study, the more pressure both male and female adolescents felt for gender conformity, and the more they perceived themselves as gender nonconforming, the lower their psychosocial adjustment to gender identity. And although both males and females reported having felt pressure to adopt gender-typed roles and behaviours (to be more feminine, if female, and more masculine if male), females fared worse in terms of psychosocial adjustment to gender atypicality. Egan and Perry (2001) surmised two reasons for this disparity in adjustment: first, that girls are more likely to internalize the perceptions of others regarding appropriate gender type; and second, that male-typed traits, occupations, and academic pursuits are generally more highly valued socially than female-typed traits.

> If felt pressure causes children to veer away from cross-sex activities and traits, then girls who are high in felt pressure will be discouraged from developing the instrumental male-typed competencies that bring prestige and promote effectual coping. For boys, on the other hand, felt pressure is more likely to support than to undermine the acquisition of socially valued and adaptive male-typed characteristics.
> [G]irls who perceive themselves to be competent in male-typed activities and agentic traits are advantaged in terms of self-esteem yet are disliked by female peers. This contradiction may create conflict for girls. (p. 460)

It is quite possible that the double bind in which girls find themselves could be alleviated by social reconsideration of gender types, roles, and behaviours. Gender development is highly socialized and contextual, and the ways in which adolescents perceive their gender typicality are affected by various social contexts; social and peer acceptance mediates the self-worth of gender nonconforming adolescents (Smith & Leaper, 2005). Avoiding the contradiction indicated above by Egan and Perry (2001), the adolescents in Smith and Leaper's study who were not ostracized by their peers for gender atypical manifestations adjusted much better to their own gender identity. A small longitudinal study by Ewing Lee and Troop-Gordon (2011) investigated atypical gender identity adjustment further, by looking closely not only at the effect of peer harassment on gender adjustment, but also at the types of friendships children share. The authors found that gender atypical boys who experienced gender-related peer harassment would adjust their gender atypical characteristics depending upon their friendship affiliations (i.e., same-sex or cross-sex friendships). Boys with more same-sex friends would adjust toward conforming to expected gender behaviours, while boys (more so than girls) with more opposite-sex friends would adjust to exhibit more atypical gender behaviours. They did not obtain the same results for the girls. Rather, negative peer treatment had no effect on girls' gender atypical behaviours when in predominantly same-sex friendships, while cross-sex friendships tended to elicit slightly more gender atypical behaviour. The results of this study suggest that specific contexts and friendship affiliations could add another layer of influence to gender development, along with felt pressure to conform to gender expectations (Ewing Lee & Troop-Gordon, 2011).

With specific regard for females dealing with conventional constructions of femininity, a study by Tolman, Impett, Tracy, and Michael (2006) indicates that "early adolescent girls who internalize conventional femininity ideologies, particularly regarding body objectification, have lower self-esteem and higher depressed mood" (p. 91). When girls embrace social constructions of gender typicality, they are prone to mental health issues. Contemporary Western social constructions of femininity generally embody gender prescriptions that may themselves be harmful to girls and women; for girls, negotiating their own gender development and identity is a somewhat precarious path.

Basow (2006) points out that the social context of gender development weighs heavily on the psychological well-being of adolescent females. She defines gender as a socially constructed phenomenon and gender identity as fluid and malleable, rather than fixed and static. Basow notes that contemporary studies suggest that "those individuals who possess both the stereotypical masculine traits of instrumentality and assertiveness, as well as the stereotypical feminine traits of nurturance and expressiveness (that is, gender aschematic individuals), seem to have the most behavioural flexibility in both work and interpersonal relationships" (2006, p. 247). By broadening our notions of gender, Basow suggests, we could create a society in which all persons "can truly flourish and achieve their maximal psychological health" (2006, p. 250).

Tolman, Striepe, and Harmon (2003) take gender identity and development more explicitly into the construction of a model of adolescent sexual health. They contend that previous models of adolescent sexual health have not sufficiently explored the role of gender (as a social construction) in factors pertaining to the sexual health of females and males. Their study included both females and males in its consideration, not just of the negative effects of adolescent sexual behaviours, such as unplanned pregnancy, STIs, and abuse, but of positive manifestations of adolescent sexuality as well. Their application of a *web of theories*,[4] that is, a multi-dimensional theoretical framework including feminist theory and its critique of compulsory heterosexuality and social injustices regarding gender; social construction theory and phenomenology; relational theory regarding adolescent development; and ecological development theory (2003, pp. 7–9), and a narrative analysis approach to their Listening Guide strategy yielded what they term a theory of *gender complementarity* (2003, p. 10).[5]

> Gender complementarity is meant as a meaningful alternative to arguments about gender difference versus sameness. It means that ideologies of masculinity and femininity, which infuse constructions of adolescent male and female sexuality, fit together to reproduce particular and limited forms of sexuality that are deemed to be "normal," all in the service of reproducing and sustaining compulsory heterosexuality. (Tolman, Striepe, & Harmon, 2003, p. 10)

They conclude that to attend appropriately to the sexual health needs of adolescents (both in their positive and negative manifestations), we must attend explicitly to socially constructed notions of gender that inhibit or impede their capacity to achieve sexual health. For girls, this attention includes noting social barriers to their acknowledgement of "sexual desire, feeling sexually empowered and having access to contraception and condoms," all "'punishable offences' under compulsory heterosexuality" (Tolman, Striepe, & Harmon, 2003, p. 11). For boys, this attention includes the option of experiencing and expressing emotions with regard to sex and sexuality, support in choosing not to objectify females and sex, and access to role models who do not promote sexuality as a means of predation (Tolman, Striepe, & Harmon, 2003, p. 11). This exploration of the impact of gender identity and development on adolescent sexual health recognizes the complex interaction of multiple influences in gendered models of adolescent sexual health.

Theories attentive to sex and gender difference are supported by data suggesting that the sexual experiences of adolescent males and females differ (although less so recently), as do their perceptions of these experiences (Brooks-Gunn, 1992; Cuffee, Hallfors, & Waller, 2007; Fine, 1988; Guggino & Ponzetti, 1997; Moreau-Gruet, Ferron, Jeannin, & Dubois-Arber, 1996; Petersen & Hyde, 2010; Phillips, 2000; Tolman, 2002a; Tolman, 2002b). Girls seem both to expect and to have more negative experiences than do boys in the expression of their sexuality (Silverman, Raj, & Clements, 2004; Thompson, 1990), and they seem to interpret their sexual experiences more negatively than boys do (Guggino & Ponzetti, 1997; Thompson, 1990). Such information is crucial when examining the question of adolescent female sexual flourishing. If the expectations and realities of early sexual experiences for teen females is negative, then long-term social perceptions of female sexualities must be deconstructed and rebuilt so that young females can flourish both as adolescents and adults.

Heteronormativity

Implicit in Western discussions pertaining to gender is a heteronormative sexuality: a social assumption of heterosexuality regarding sex and sexuality that further assumes sex categories of male and female. While the latter assumption is an interesting and important issue to explore (i.e., the relative social invisibility of transsexuality, intersexuality, or transgender), the scope of this project does not allow its consideration in depth. Rather, I turn to the assumption of heterosexuality and its related issues for adolescent females. This assumption renders the possibility and reality of other sexualities among adolescent females invisible and, to a certain extent, dangerous. Lesbian and bisexual girls must navigate heterosexual social constructions to remain safe in their sexual identities and expressions (Tolman, 2002a).

Such navigation is not new in Western culture. What is relatively new, however, is the recognition that such an assumption might have a negative impact upon non-heterosexual girls. Despite a media culture of lesbian chic, the reality for females is less romantic (Hyde & Jaffee, 2000). Tolman (2002a) notes Adrienne Rich's identification of *compulsory heterosexuality* as a Western social construction that effectively establishes heterosexuality as natural and renders other sexualities non-natural (pp. 16–19). This construction creates a normative expectation for heterosexual desire and expression that ignores or even vilifies other sexualities, forcing them into hiding (Tolman, 2002a).

Heterosexual expectation does little to explore, beyond male-female coitus, what sexual expression might include. A timely example of heterosexual assumptions can be found in the relatively recent exploration of oral sexual activities in academic literature. When media reports began to surface about occurrence rates of oral sex among teens (e.g., Lewin, 1997), it became clear that there was little reliable research to substantiate or repudiate the media reports (Reirden et al., 2007; Remez, 2000), as the predominant research focus previously had been heterosexual intercourse. In the past fifteen years, however, investigation into oral sex as an element of adolescent sexual repertoires has expanded, yielding ambiguous results (Backstrom, Armstrong, & Puentes, 2012; DeRosa et al., 2010; Halpern-Felsher, 2008). On the one hand, we know that oral sex is not uncommon among adolescents;[6] that perceptions of oral sexual activity differ among individuals and groups;[7] that occurrences of oral sex and vaginal intercourse correlate regarding initiation and frequency;[8] that, like other sexual behaviours, oral sex correlates with alcohol use, particularly among females;[9] that as adolescents age they become more likely to engage in oral sex;[10] and, finally, that studies tend either to focus on opposite-sex oral sex[11] or not to differentiate the occurrence of opposite-sex and same-sex oral sex.[12]

On the other hand, what the studies leave unclear about oral sex among teens is equally striking. For instance, while some studies show that males and females are giving and receiving oral sex at about the same rate (Council of Ministers of Education, Canada, 2003; Dake, Price, Ward, & Welch, 2011; Lindberg, Jones, & Santelli, 2008), others suggest that females are more often giving than receiving oral sex (Chambers, 2007; Newcomer & Udry, 1985). Also unclear is whether there are racial and ethnic associations with oral sexual activity. The 2011 National Health Statistics Report on sexual behaviour, identity, and attraction in the United States (Chandra, Mosher, Copen, & Sionean)[13] indicates that oral sexual behaviour is slightly more common among white, educated adult populations than any other ethnic, racial, or socio-economic population (see also Lindberg, Jones, & Santelli, 2008). Most studies specifically of adolescents, however, tend to investigate relatively homogeneous populations (i.e., race, education, gender, socio-economic status) and thus yield limited results (Dake, Price, Ward, & Welch, 2011; DeRosa et al., 2010; Halpern-Felsher, Cornell, Kropp, & Tshann, 2005; Markham et al., 2009). Also unclear is the direction of correlation between oral sex and heterosexual vaginal intercourse. Some studies suggest that oral sex is typically initiated simultaneous with or shortly following vaginal intercourse (Brewster & Tillman, 2008; Markham et al., 2009), while others suggest the opposite: that vaginal sex typically occurs simultaneous with or shortly following oral sex (Cornell & Halpern-Felsher, 2006; Halpern-Felsher, Cornell, Kropp, & Tshann, 2005; Song & Halpern-Felsher, 2011). The ambiguity of results means that it is difficult to determine adolescents' reasons for engaging in oral sex: birth control, pleasure, safety, or pressure, for instance? This question yields multi-faceted responses, which in turn uncovers the complexity of sexual interactions among adolescents.

Compounding the complexity of motivations for adolescents' particular sexual behaviours, such as oral sex, is the variety of interpretations of *sex*, *abstinence*, and *virginity* among both adolescents and researchers (Remez, 2000). In Carpenter's (2005) study of sixty-one participants' perceptions of their first sexual experiences, she encountered no unequivocal definition of virginity, of what sexual activities maintained or disrupted virginity, what sexual activities were considered sex, and what sexual activities one could undertake while maintaining abstinence. And, while oral sex featured quite heavily in the discussions among participants of various sexual orientations, there was no clear consensus on whether it fractured virginity (see pp. 44–56, in particular).

The underlying assumption here regarding sexual activity is that penile–vaginal intercourse is "real" sex, and everything else is foreplay. Regarding adolescent female sexuality, girls engaging in same-sex sexual activities are virtually invisible in a heteronormative context incapable of accounting for same-sex female flourishing. This invisibility is mirrored by the lacuna of research accounts specifically addressing cunnilingus in scholarly discourse, which tends to focus more on fellatio. Aside from a passing citation from Deborah Tolman in Remez's article (2000, p. 299), cunnilingus hardly features in the discussion. And, as Alterman (1999) wryly points out in his commentary on the media's fixation with oral sex and teens, it is the girls who are considered "at risk" in this behaviour, not the boys. Only recently have small, qualitative studies exploring females' experiences and perceptions of cunnilingus surfaced (Backstrom, Armstrong, & Puentes, 2012; Bay-Cheng & Fava, 2011), a testament to the fledgling state of the study of female sexual pleasure.

The example provided by oral sex as perceived and experienced suggests that male heteronormative sexual construction practically renders female (and non-heterosexual) sexuality and pleasure insignificant. To bring further attention to female sexual pleasure, the social construction and practice of masturbation bears exploration. Sexual pleasure through masturbation is considered a key component of sexual health (Coleman, 2002) and for females in particular (Hogarth & Ingham, 2009; Kaestle & Allen, 2011). And yet, the achievement of female sexual pleasure remains somewhat incidental in a male heteronormative sexual construction. Wade, Kremer, and Brown (2005) found that female participants in their study of the relationship between clitoral knowledge and sexual pleasure were more likely to experience pleasure and orgasm when their own knowledge was experiential (i.e., through self-exploration), rather than intellectual. They also noted, however, that females were more likely to achieve orgasm through masturbation than within partnered heterosexual intercourse. One might surmise from these results that the narrow, heteronormative construction of sexual experience privileges male sexual pleasure (and orgasm) over that of the female.

Studies further suggest that positive childhood communication about sexuality (particularly with mothers) correlates with rewarding and pleasurable experiences of masturbation, and positive sexual self-perceptions among young adult females (Hogarth & Ingham, 2009). However, social views and practices of masturbation remain gendered. Males consistently report higher rates and frequency of masturbation (Pinkerton, Bogart, Cecil, & Abramson, 2002), particularly as a substitute for vaginal intercourse (Gerressu et al., 2008). Females are more likely not only to abstain from masturbation as a means of self-pleasuring, but also to forego consideration of their own sexual pleasure in heterosexual relationships (Hogarth & Ingham, 2009;

Wade, Kremer, & Brown, 2005). Although cultural perceptions of masturbation and sexual pleasure have changed over time and place (see Laqueur,
2003; Patton, 1985), and the evidence that a positive social construction of
female sexual pleasure facilitates sexual health, female sexual pleasure remains
eclipsed by a narrow heteronormative social script.

Heteronormative assumptions have created a field of data that focuses
disproportionately on the possible negative outcomes of adolescent heterosexual behaviours (Bay-Cheng, 2003). This data points to negative
outcomes for girls in particular: violence, unintended and/or unwanted
pregnancy, sexually transmitted infections, social labelling, religious condemnation, and negative personal affect (Biddlecom, 2004; Council of
Ministers of Education, Canada, 2003; Oswalt, Cameron, & Koob, 2005;
and Whitaker, Miller, May, & Levin, 1999). Judith Levine (2002) offers
a journalistic account of how our negative social construction of sex and
sexuality as it pertains to children and adolescents, and the ensuing abstinence-only education policies at various levels of government within the
United States, might, in fact, be more harmful to minors than helpful. It is
perhaps because we focus on adolescent sexual behaviours and their consequences as negative, that discussions of the positive possibilities stemming
from sexual interaction go underground (Fine, 1988). Tolman's exploration
of adolescent girls' sexual desires (2002a, 2002b) points to the confusion
girls face when positively desiring and experiencing their own sexuality
in a social context of negative evaluation. Such ambivalence between personal experience and social expectation can lead to dissociation from the
body, denial or repression of sexuality, vulnerability in sexual situations,
or myriad negative sexual experiences. Thompson (1990) found that girls
most comfortable with and aware of their own sexuality (physically, psychologically, emotionally) were best able to make positive sexual choices
for themselves, including abstinence, protected intercourse, delayed intercourse, and sexual activity expressing their sexual orientation.

Heteronormativity as developed within a patriarchal society has perpetuated the structure of male sexual privilege. A focus on the negative
outcomes of sexual behaviour assumes that it is the females who must take
responsibility for avoiding such outcomes, as in the question of female
sexual assertiveness as a means of self-protection: are females assertive
enough (Rickert, Sanghvi, & Wiemann, 2002)? It is important, of course,
that adolescent girls and adult women possess a sense of agency regarding
their own sexuality. It is naive, however, to suggest that girls and women
alone can effect such agency. Rather, the complex web of factors woven
within sexual choices points to the social reality of patriarchal heteronormativity: females do not independently control their sexual experiences
(Abma, Driscoll, & Moore, 1998).

To facilitate adolescent female sexual flourishing, therefore, the assumption of heteronormativity and the male sexual privilege it engenders must be challenged. Female sexual pleasure, a positive construction of adolescent sexual development, and the deconstruction of male, heterosexual privilege must be integrated within social consciousness and relational patterns.

Gender, moral development, and voice

The sexed and gendered realities of adolescent females have met with ambivalence in Western culture. The formulation of gender roles and realities based upon a heteronormative sexual social construction creates problematic choices for adolescent girls and adult women. In particular, this social matrix confounds efforts at moral decision-making and female flourishing. This reality is the basis of Carol Gilligan's application of gender as a lens through which to examine the lives of adolescent girls and women in her influential work (1982/1993). Gilligan's early work explored the ways in which gender/sex influenced both the theory and practice of moral development. Her exploration of female development stood her in contrast both with her mentor, Lawrence Kohlberg, and Jean Piaget, Kohlberg's own mentor. Based upon his theory of cognitive development, Piaget posited that moral autonomy, a characteristic of adolescence, was the highest stage of moral development. Kohlberg developed Piaget's cognitive development theory further to construct a theory of moral development. For Kohlberg, the person who was the most morally developed would make decisions based upon universal principles that transcend (although might still be congruent with) the law (Kohlberg, 1976; Muuss, 1996, pp. 176–85). Gilligan noted that the theories proposed by both Piaget and Kohlberg were predicated on a male construction of justice in moral decision-making, which omitted females' moral constructs. Because Kohlberg's subjects were all male, a number of biases coloured his work: there was a philosophical bias of the equation of "male" with "human"; and there was a practical bias to the experiences and perceptions of males. In effect, males were considered higher-level moral decision-makers than females.

Gilligan countered Kohlberg's theory of what she termed "justice-oriented moral development" with what she identified as a decidedly female moral construct: an ethic of care and relationship (Gilligan, 1982/1993). In so doing, she launched a diverse and contentious theoretical discussion of difference in development (moral or otherwise) and experience, and the extent to which these differences are affected by social gender construction.[14] Due to social constructions of gender-appropriate roles for males and females, Gilligan theorized moral orientations developed in support of the gendered realities of males and females: females were socialized for relationship, nurturance, and care; males were socialized for autonomy, individualism, and justice.

In the decades since the initial publication of her work, Gilligan's theory has been tested empirically and critiqued. Her assertion that justice and care are two modes of moral reasoning has found general acceptance; however, her assertion that these two moral orientations are strongly associated with socialized gender are statistically unsupported in empirical studies (Jaffee & Hyde, 2000). The importance of her work, however, has not diminished. Perhaps the most striking contribution of Gilligan's work regarding moral orientation is recognition that "if psychological theories of human development intend to represent lived experience, then they must be constructed with the diversity of such experience in mind" (Jaffee & Hyde, 2000, p. 721). This would include gender and sex differences.

In Gilligan's later work, she and colleague Lyn Mikel Brown move toward a discussion of women's psychology and girls' development, and away from the specific discussion of moral development (Brown & Gilligan, 1992). Following a four-year study of almost one hundred girls (primarily white and socio-economically advantaged) between the ages of seven and eighteen, Brown and Gilligan report a loss of voice and relationship during female adolescence: "girls struggle to stay in connection with themselves and with others, to voice their feelings and thoughts and experiences in relationships" (1992, p. 4). They observed that, in the course of moving from childhood, through adolescence, and into adulthood, females' lives became highly politicized, directing the girls away from their authentic selves into socially acceptable selves as females.

The 1998 study by Harter et al. investigated the loss of voice claims among adolescent females and males, and whether such a loss of voice, if identifiable, was indeed global or context-specific. They found that reported loss of voice in adolescence showed no particular gender bias. Further, they noted that there were mitigating factors around lack of voice and expression that rendered it rather more contextual than global. In particular, they found that external support for vocal expression, gender orientation (i.e., stereotypically masculine or feminine) in private or public contexts, and relational context were all factors affecting adolescents' perceived level of voice.

Harter et al. also "documented the strong relationship between level of voice and relational self-worth within each interpersonal context" (1998, p. 900). If an individual reported a low level of voice in a particular context, he or she correspondingly reported a low level of self-worth. Although the researchers noted an incomplete understanding of the directionality of the relationship between these two factors, they proposed that the impact of the factors is reciprocal. At any rate, their findings that loss of voice is a developmental and functional liability for adolescents correlate with similar perceptions by Gilligan, and specifically regarding adolescent females. In particular, Harter et al. (1998) point to the role that loss and/or lack of voice plays in the suppression of the authentic self and individual identity, which in turn is a barrier to flourishing.

Who Am I? Self-identity

Harter's work on self and identity (2003, 1999) explores and documents the implications of adolescent development on perceptions of self. Harter notes the differences between "self-representations" (how one describes oneself) and "self-evaluations" (references to one's positive or negative attributes); she also notes the important differentiation between global self-evaluations (i.e., "self-esteem") and domain-specific self-evaluations (i.e., "self-concept") (2003, pp. 611–12). The construction of self is both a cognitive and a social process whereby, over our developmental lifespan, we become (under typical circumstances) more able to integrate both the subjective and objective perceptions of the self into a coherent whole. Important for our purposes is Harter's assertion that it is not until late adolescence or early adulthood that the potential to construct a coherent understanding of self emerges. Indeed, Harter distinguishes among stages and capacities within the context of adolescence:

- early adolescence (approximately 12 to 14 years: potential for differentiation of abstract characteristics of the self, with little awareness of seeming contradictions: e.g., intelligence vs. airhead);
- middle adolescence (approximately 15 to 16: potential for "mapping" abstract characteristics of the self, with awareness of seeming contradictions, which causes "considerable intrapsychic conflict, confusion, and distress"; Harter, 2003, p. 622); and
- late adolescence (potential for both mapping and inter-coordinating single abstractions to construct an integrated understanding of self, with awareness and acceptance of seeming contradictions; see Harter, 2003, pp. 622–24; see also Harter, 1999).

The importance of the list of developmental tasks above lies in each individual's success in meeting the challenges along the developmental path, and her or his functional self-perceptions and self-evaluations concomitant to successes or failures. With regard to the overarching well-being of each individual, Harter proposes that self-evaluations are important aspects for measuring mental health, such as self-esteem, depression, and suicidal ideation. The critical factors affecting self-evaluation and resulting self-esteem are two-fold:

1. *The individual's perceived competence in domains that he or she also perceives to be important, for example, high marks and scholastic achievement.* Harter's (2003) findings suggest that if an individual perceives him or herself to be unsuccessful in an important domain (as opposed to one considered unimportant to him or her), then that individual will manifest lower self-esteem than others who perceive themselves as successful in similarly perceived domains of importance. In a situation where one's self-perception in an important domain is low, then one's global self-perception also suffers. Hence, low self-esteem contributes to global identity of the individual and perceived capacity for success.

2. *The individual's perceived support from others that she or he deems important in a specific domain.* Harter notes that both children and adolescents incorporate significant others' appraisals of them into their own perception of self-worth, rendering appropriate positive appraisal crucial in their construction of positive self-worth.[15] Construction of self-identity is, thus, a developmental cognitive and social task that is a cornerstone for the attainment of adult capacities in personal and social functioning. Along with the development of gender and voice, adolescent female identity development in the construction of self constitutes a crucial aspect of self-perception and self-esteem. Such construction obviously takes place within a particular context for each individual person, yet is more generally located within each person's broader setting.

SUMMARY

The various developmental influences explored above correspond with general physical development that occurs throughout adolescence. Together, these aspects of development carry children through their teen years and into adulthood. No one factor has an independent impact upon any given person; instead, each factor interacts and combines gradually to shape the person into adulthood. In the following chapter, I explore the multi-faceted physical developments typical in adolescence, and their integration with social, personal, and psychological developmental factors.

CHAPTER SIX

ADOLESCENT FEMALES IN A CONTEMPORARY CONTEXT: PHYSICAL/BIOLOGICAL DEVELOPMENT

INTRODUCTION

One general reality common to adolescents is their biological and physical development, which is located within myriad social contexts. Female adolescent pubertal development, and the experience of menarche and its concomitant realities in particular, are developmental moments that contribute in significant ways to adolescent female sexual flourishing. Embedded in social constructions of gender, heteronormativity, pleasure, and voice, adolescent females grow into their sexual bodies in both particular and universal ways. The impact of social context on their physical development and perceptions contributes to, or detracts from, their potential for sexual flourishing. In this chapter, I explore the ways in which adolescent females develop physically, and some social responses to those developments.

Developing Bodies: Gender and Socialization

Likely, the most obvious facet of development in adolescence is biological and physical development; for both females and males, the advent of adolescence is marked by the onset of puberty (Dahl, 2004; Rathus et al., 2005). Hormonal and neural triggers set the physical maturation of the individual in motion, starting from approximately eight and nine years of age, for females and males respectively. The recognition of the immense biological changes brought about by hormonal triggers led early biogenetic theorist G. Stanley Hall (1844–1924) to posit adolescence as a universal time of storm and stress (*Sturm und drang*). "Hall assumed that development is brought about by physiological changes. He further assumed that these physiological factors are genetically determined, that internal maturational forces predominantly control and direct development, growth, and behavior. There was little room in this theory for the influence of environmental forces" (Muuss, 1996, pp. 15–16). With a nod to the sporadic and extreme mood fluctuations of some adolescents, along with their propensity toward idealism, passion, and social rebellion, Hall perceived genetic influence as the predominant factor in a turbulent adolescent transition.

Hall's genetic influence theory has encountered opposition. The evolution of psychological understandings of adolescent development has made clear that the complexities of adolescent development go beyond biology. Elements such as cognition or socialization, as important parts of that development, pose complications for Hall's theory. Arnett (1999), in his reconsideration of Hall's theory, has fleshed out some of the research pointing to the inadequacies of Hall's account of adolescence. Arnett concludes that, although there are undeniable biological factors in adolescent development, these factors work in concert with other developmental factors throughout adolescence. Thus, while adolescent storm and stress may indeed be a reality for some adolescents, it is neither necessarily universal, nor mutually exclusive from a time of "exuberant growth" (Arnett, 1999, p. 324).

While the sequence of physical development is relatively constant among adolescents, there can be a great deal of variation regarding the actual age of onset and pace of development. Factors such as the individual's genetic and biological heritage, specific life-events, socio-economic situation, health and diet, and body fat percentage all contribute to the course and timing of puberty (American Psychological Association [APA], 2002, pp. 7–10). The general course of adolescence finds its conclusion around the ages of 17 to 19 for girls, and 20 for boys. Although the developmental category of adolescence is marked by the onset of physical puberty, its conclusion lacks any definitive physical markers. A rather more social marker is the transition of the individual into the capacity to "take on adult responsibilities" (Rathus et al., 2005, p. 237).

Males and females encounter similar physical changes over the course of puberty and adolescence, the most obvious being the development of secondary sex characteristics, such as skeletal growth spurts, the appearance of body hair, the achievement of fertility, and the concomitant shift in their bodies to support fertility (APA, 2002; Rathus et al., 2005). "For boys, the onset of puberty involves enlargement of the testes at around age 11 or 12 and first ejaculation, which typically occurs between the ages of

12 and 14" (APA, 2002, p. 7). Later in puberty, males will also experience their voices dropping. For females, the shift involves breast budding (the initial growth of female breasts), beginning as early as ages eight or nine, and menarche (first menstruation), typically around ages 12 to 13 (APA, 2002, p. 7; Rathus et al., 2005).

Even while adolescent males and females both mature biologically, there are obvious physical differences in their respective transitions. There is also evidence to suggest that the specifics regarding individual perceptions and social constructions of pubertal development and transition differ significantly between males and females (and also among them). In the following section, I deal more closely with female pubertal development, with a focused consideration of menarche as a pivotal moment, both private and public, in adolescent female development and sexual flourishing. Although menarcheal and menstrual realities are experienced individually among girls, all females' experiences are shaped by the culture in which they occur (Stein & Kim, 2009; White, 2013). To facilitate girls' sexual flourishing, therefore, requires attention be paid to the context in which adolescent female perceptions of their menstruating, sexual body-selves develop.

Menarche

Menarche (first menstruation) is my focal point in discussing adolescent female biological development, both because it is a physical marker of puberty and adolescence and because it bears a good deal of weight in social constructions of girls' sexual development and ensuing sexual behaviour (Fingerson, 2006). To focus on female initiation into reproductive capacities in a discussion of female sexuality is to run the risk of identifying their sexuality solely with its capacity for baby-making. Such is not my intention. Given my preceding exploration of female sexual pleasure and orgasm, it should be clear that my current focus on menarche and menstruation is on but one aspect of female sexuality. Further, in constructing an embodied sexual theology that takes seriously the Christian doctrine of the Incarnation, the female bleeding body (so long disparaged in theological discussion) takes on profound significance. The bodies and blood of females historically have been constructed very differently from those of males, even though they share equally in the image of God (Beattie, 2003). The reciprocal influence of the Christian theological tradition and Western social constructions has resulted in an understanding of menstruation that disparages its power as life-giving. Female bodies and blood, far from the redemptive nature of Christ's body and blood, are framed as polluted and uncontrollable. My consideration of menarche in the course of female adolescent sexual development deliberately explores the implications of such an attitude toward menstruation in both the lived experiences of adolescent females and the evolving construction of sexual theology.

In this section, I address multidisciplinary literature concerning the nature of menarche in contemporary Western culture, with an eye to those popular and educational representations aimed explicitly at adolescent females.[1] I also explore a number of themes dominant in the literature pertaining to menarche and adolescent females' experiences thereof. Menarche holds particular significance in the gendered sexual development of girls, primarily as a result of its lack of recognition in the broader social context. This invisibility likely affects the capacity of adolescent females to flourish sexually.

Menarche is one of a number of physical changes that pubertal girls experience, including "accelerated growth in height and weight, an increase in the percentage of overall body fat, and the emergence of secondary sexual characteristics," such as breast buds and pubic hair growth (Dell, 2000, p. 136; see also Golub, 1992). The average ages of menarche in the United States are 12.6 years and 12.1 years for girls of European American ancestry and African American ancestry, respectively (Bordini & Rosenfield, 2011). The normal range is considered to be between the ages of 10 and 14 years. Age at menarche generally decreased in the first half of the twentieth century, while the second half saw a relative stabilization; age at pubertal onset continues to decline (Posner, 2006). Current speculation is that the initial decrease was due in part to increased health and nutrition (Brooks-Gunn, 1992; Dell, 2000, pp. 134–38; Posner, 2006).

As much as menarche is a biological event, however, it is also a psychological and social event (e.g., Diorio & Munro, 2000; Golub, 1992; Merskin, 1999; Moore, 1995; Williams & Currie, 2000). As an occasion of transition from girlhood to womanhood, menarche has a unique place in the understanding of what it means to be female in any given society. Dell (2000), for instance, points to extensive mention of, and ritual demand around, menstruation in the Hebrew Scriptures (e.g., Lam. 1:8–9; Ez. 16:1–9; Lv. 12–15; Lv. 17–26), an indication that menstruation was likely negatively constructed within the purity guidelines and Holiness Code of the Hebrew community (Dell, 2000, pp. 129–34). Menstruating females were considered unclean and to be physically separated from males. To a certain extent, menstrual uncleanliness was associated with contagious illness; a man who was sexually intimate with a menstruating woman was to be "expelled from the people of Israel to maintain cultic purity" (Dell, 2000, p. 132). This historical social construction of menstruation experienced by menarcheal girls of the time, likely shaped both its contemporary females' and our own current understanding of menarche, menstruation, and womanhood.

These biblical messages, explicit and implicit, accurately or inaccurately derived from Scripture and the authority of religious institutions, and handed down through faith communities over the centuries have influenced western civilization's approach to the development of young females both directly through churches and indirectly through wider cultural means. (Dell, 2000, p. 134)

Given the embedded nature of Judeo-Christian social and moral norms in Western cultures, the historical context of menstruation, derived in part from strict Jewish codes of purity and behaviour, is fraught with judgments regarding cleanliness and womanhood.

In our contemporary context, menarcheal girls are the targets of advertising aiming for menstrual product loyalty from the start of menstruation through to menopause (Brumberg, 1997; Erchull, Chrisler, Gorman, & Johnston-Robledo, 2002; Moore, 1995; Simes & Berg, 2001). Adolescent females are also socialized through learning about menstruation and reproduction in sexual education programs in schools (Diorio & Munro, 2000; Swensen, Foster, & Asay, 1995). Extensive evidence suggests that the broader social construction of menarche and menstruation has an impact on adolescent females' own perceptions and constructions of the meaning of menstrual and menarcheal experiences, both as individuals and as a group (Chrisler & Zittel, 1998; Golub, 1992; Koff & Rierdan, 1996, 1995; Koff, Rierdan, & Jacobson, 1981; Moore, 1995; Orringer & Gahagan, 2010; Williams & Currie, 2000).

While the literature seems to indicate general agreement about the reality that menarche is an important event in the lives of adolescent girls, there is less agreement about *what* impact that event has on girls' lives. Next, I explore four recurring themes encountered in the literature as a means to discern how puberty and menarche affect adolescent girls:

1. affective ambiguity and experiential ambivalence;
2. preparation, secrecy, and hiding;
3. bodies and sexuality; and
4. messages and discussion.

These four themes point to the interconnection of biological and physical development of adolescent females and the social context in which these experiences take place. In particular, they point to the social construction of gender and the ways in which gender develops alongside biology. As the introductory moment into female sexuality, menarche plays an important role in shaping female sexuality through adolescence and adulthood.

First theme: Affective ambiguity and experiential ambivalence

Ambiguity and ambivalence seem pervasive in girls' affective, somatic, and cognitive experiences of menarche and menstruation (Golub, 1992; White, 2013). These themes have been strikingly and consistently present in studies conducted over recent decades. At least as early as 1981, girls' ambivalence (in fact, an imbalance leaning toward negative perceptions) regarding menarche was clearly recognized in the literature (Koff, Rierdan, & Jacobson, 1981). In a 1983 overview of menarcheal studies, Brooks-Gunn and Ruble identified the phenomenon of "pubertal amnesia," wherein girls were reluctant to describe the significance of their experiences of menarche. "Girls, when asked about their pubertal experiences, were likely to say that puberty and menarche had little impact upon them, but also recounted vignettes suggesting a profound effect of such experiences" (p. 157). College-aged women seemed to forget events specific to their experiences of puberty, while they remembered details of experiences prior to and following puberty.

In her later study of sixth-grade Australian girls, Moore (1995) uncovered a distinct ambivalence in the majority of self-reported attitudes toward menstruation within both interviews and questionnaires. Over half of the respondents indicated that they recognized the advantage in growing up that was implicit in menarche and menstruation, yet the majority was unsure of "the idea of a first period being a great event in their lives" (Moore, 1995, p. 96). Most girls expressed feelings of "embarrassment, discomfort, and ambivalence" about growing up in general, and "shame, embarrassment, and anxiety" about menstruation in particular (Moore, 1995, p. 102). In her qualitative, interview-based, study of adolescent experiences of puberty, sexuality, and the self, Martin (1996) also encountered ambivalence about puberty and linked that ambivalence to two factors: a lack of subjective knowledge about their bodies; and the association of puberty to adult female sexuality (pp. 20–21). Chrisler and Zittel (1998) interviewed college women from four different cultures (Lithuanian, American, Malaysian, and Sudanese) about their menarcheal experiences, and found in the stories recounted that the most common emotion mentioned by the Americans was embarrassment, at a much higher rate than the other cultural groups, distantly followed by pride, anxiety, and elation (p. 308).[2] What is the impact of such a storm of mixed emotions and perceptions surrounding this pivotal maturational event in the lives of adolescent females? If girls (and women) are consistently ambivalent about this experience, what do they do with its immanence or presence in their own or others' lives? And what is the impact of this experience on their sexual development through adolescence and into adulthood?

Second theme: Preparation, secrecy, and hiding

Preparation for menarche is best facilitated with cognitive (informational) and subjective (experiential) knowledge of menstruation (Brooks-Gunn & Ruble, 1983; Koff & Rierdan, 1995; Martin, 1996). An interesting phenomenon in the formal education of North American girls regarding impending menarche is that much of the information is provided both directly (via educational materials to schools and agencies) and indirectly (via advertising) by companies producing menstrual *hygiene* products (Brumberg, 1997; Merskin, 1999; Simes & Berg, 2001). Brumberg (1997) suggests that the move toward the wholesale social adoption of commercially produced menstrual products has actually shifted menarche from a *maturational event* to an *hygienic crisis* (see also Havens & Swenson, 1988). Previous concerns about educating girls about their developing reproductive capacities have become a preoccupation with concealing the reality of menstruation, and therefore menarche, with the use of the appropriate products. This has become so much the case that fertility awareness education for females, although a positive predictor for female sexual health (American Academy of Pediatrics & American College of Obstetricians and Gynecologists, 2006; Vigil, Ceric, Cortes, & Klaus, 2006), seems marginal to contemporary discourse on sexuality education. Contrary to an adolescent female focus on positive bodily, sexual awareness, Moore (1995) found, in projective testing regarding attitudes toward menstruation, that "deception" was the most common theme portrayed. However, these attitudes excluded mothers: "The importance of secrecy surrounding menstruation was stressed, including keeping the fact of one's period a secret from fathers, friends, and especially boys in general. Mothers were usually excluded from the need for secrecy" (Moore, 1995, p. 97).

The need for secrecy regarding menstruation is likely warranted in its contemporary Western social construction. A small study testing reactions to perceived knowledge of the menstrual status of a female peer found that participants responded negatively to a female who accidentally dropped a tampon (as opposed to a hair clip) from her bag (Roberts, Goldenberg, Power, & Pyszczynski, 2002). While the study is limited by small size, homogeneity of participants, and control for initial perceptions of tampons and hair clips in general, the results (i.e., lower evaluation of the female's competence, lower evaluation of her likeableness, greater physical distancing from her, and greater overall objectification of women) still point to broad, negative perceptions of menstruating women, and women in general, by both males and females. The results regarding the general objectification of women did not hold true, however, for less gender-stereotyped participants (i.e., undifferentiated or androgynous gender). In their final discussion, the authors note: "These findings suggest that the great lengths to which many women go to avoid revelation of menstrual status and discussion of related issues may indeed be well founded, for reminders of menstruation do appear to lead to negative judgments of women" (Roberts et al., 2002, p. 138). The need for secrecy regarding menarcheal and menstrual status among adolescents is consistent with a broader social attitude that constructs a negative perception of female menstrual bleeding.

Advertisements for menstrual products facilitate the need for secrecy regarding menstruation by suggesting that the use of the wrong product will likely lead to the very "embarrassment" and "shame" linked to girls' ambivalence around menstruation (Simes & Berg, 2001). In fact, menstrual product advertisements heighten the insecurities of girls, reflect negative social attitudes, and both perpetuate and maintain silence and shame regarding menstruation (Simes & Berg, 2001). Erchull, Chrisler, Gorman, and Johnson-Robledo (2002) report slightly less negative findings in their examination of commercially produced booklets about menstruation. While they note that the booklets contain anatomical inconsistencies, no information about the subjective experience of menstruation, a narrow portrayal of the diverse users of the products, little contextual understanding of menarche within puberty, and maintenance of the culture of secrecy regarding menstruation, they still do not promote menstruation as a hygiene crisis.[3]

Merskin (1999) found more positive developments in her investigation of menstrual products aimed at adolescents. While admitting that menstruation still is not portrayed positively in girls' lives, her study posits that advertisements for feminine hygiene products are evolving by suggesting "ways for girls to feel more secure in light of the social system in which they live" (1999, p. 955). Unfortunately, Merskin offers little substantial critique of a social system that would make girls feel insecure about a universally occurring female biological event in a way that would lead to secrecy and concealment.

An unexpected and interesting finding from a study of early adolescent females' responses to menarche was one unrelated to the explicit data collected: the resistance of parents to allow their daughters to participate in the study (McGrory, 1990). Almost half of the parents approached declined their daughters' participation because they themselves were uncomfortable and embarrassed by the subject matter. It was "a much too personal topic" (McGrory, 1990, p. 268).

On the other hand, Diorio and Munro (2000) question the efficacy of teaching menarche and menstruation as a matter of course in co-ed schools and classrooms within a culture that remains biased to the male experience. They point out the disparity of social messages passed on to boys and girls regarding sexual development, and contend that to teach menstruation and menarche openly in an environment that characterizes female bleeding as disgusting, and female bodies as being desirous to boys, is to leave girls vulnerable to a power-over relationship with boys. While boys and girls are taught that puberty signals strength and power for boys in muscle growth, they are also taught that menstruation signals sexuality and uncleanliness for girls.[4] Thus, girls embody the ambiguity of puberty and choose concealment as a means of surviving menarche and subsequent menstruation. Diorio and Munro (2000) conclude:

> The material which girls encounter proclaims the need for secrecy and helps construct their acceptance of the concealment of menstruation as positive. Girls are thus inducted into complicity in their own control through a cultural charade in which everyone knows that virtually all women between puberty and menopause menstruate, but everyone pretends that no specific woman is menstruating at any given time. (p. 361)

They ultimately suggest that, until we "address the personal uncertainties and social meaning with which girls must come to terms in the process of their own pubertal development," we will continue to fail to prepare girls adequately for the reality of menstruation (Diorio & Munro, 2000, p. 362).

Research consistently suggests that the task of preparation for menarche lies squarely with mothers; they are the primary purveyors of education about, and preparation for, menarche to adolescent girls (Brooks-Gunn, 1992; Chang, Hayter, & Wu, 2010; Koff & Rierdan, 1995; Koff, Rierdan, & Jacobson, 1981; Lee, 2008; Teitelman, 2004). In their study of adolescent females' recommendations regarding how to prepare for menstruation, Koff and Rierdan (1995) noted that daughters perceive mothers' roles as important and delicate in their preparation for menarche. Mothers should be tactful, poised, and knowledgeable, and provide information (including regarding hygiene), emotional support, understanding, encouragement, sensitivity, and comfort. Mothers should also be comfortable themselves with discussing menstruation and menarche, and be careful not to embarrass their daughters. Girls rely on their mothers to normalize the reality of menstruation, and to stress that it is not necessarily something to be hidden (see also Lee, 2008; Teitelman, 2004).

The involvement of mothers seems to be a cross-cultural phenomenon. (In the absence of a mother in the home, another menstruating female typically steps in: e.g., a grandmother, older sister, or aunt.) In one US study, Orringer and Gahagan (2010) found mothers' roles central to African

American, Mexican American, Arab American, and European American girls' experiences of menarche, although Arab American girls were, overall, the least prepared group. Outside of North America, Chrisler and Zittel's (1998) cross-cultural study found that, with the exception of Malaysian women, all were prepared for menarche primarily by their mothers and, across the board, their mothers were overwhelmingly the first persons they told about their menarche. Moore (1995) also found mothers exempt from the secrecy surrounding menarche and menstruation in her study of Australian girls. Skandhan, Pandya, Skandhan, and Mehta (1988) found Indian girls to be most interested in receiving more preparatory information about menstruation from their mothers, a preference "rooted in the 'holy' relationship between mother and daughter" (p. 152). In contrast, girls generally found very little place for their fathers' involvement in preparing for menstruation, and indicated a general sense of embarrassment and discomfort in discussing menstruation with them (Kalman, 2003a & 2003b; Koff & Rierdan, 1995).

Menarche and menstruation seem almost as precarious a business for mothers and other adults engaged in preparation of adolescent females as it is for the girls themselves (e.g., Lee, 2008). Moreover, as a society we are generally slow to support girls in this respect: they are openly targeted with marginally helpful information by menstrual product companies with dubious intentions, and they are silently co-opted into ongoing social secrecy with regard to the reality of menarche and menstruation (White, 2013). Their welcome to sexuality is the tacit perpetuation of an understanding that females' pubertal and maturing sexual bodies place them at risk in their capacity to make healthy choices for themselves. Adolescent females need better. Any sense of shame or humiliation that comes with poor preparation for or lack of support at menarche can be eased with emotionally attuned mothers and other supportive adult females: "maternal support is important for helping girls navigate a culture that denigrates the feminine…emotionally engaged mothers may be able to buffer the worst forms of misogyny associated with menarche" (Lee, 2008, p. 1345; see also Teitelman, 2004).

Third theme: Bodies and sexuality

In 2007 the American Psychological Association [APA] published the report of its Task Force on the Sexualization of Girls. Confronting the myriad ways in which girls are sexualized in contemporary Western culture (e.g., toy manufacturing and marketing, advertising, television programming, Internet sites) the Task Force aimed to define sexualization, examine the prevalence and examples of sexualization of girls, examine evidence suggesting that sexualization has a negative impact on girls, and describe positive ways to counter pervasive sexualization of girls (2007, p. 2). Sexualization occurs when:

> a person's value comes only from his or her sexual appeal or behavior, to the exclusion of other characteristics; a person is held to a standard that equates physical attractiveness (narrowly defined) with being sexy; a person is sexually objectified—that is, made into a thing for others' sexual use, rather than seen as a person with the capacity for independent action and decision making; and/or sexuality is inappropriately imposed upon a person. (APA, 2007, p. 2)

While the presence of any one of these characteristics would indicate sexualization (as opposed to healthy sexuality), the fourth characteristic—sexuality inappropriately imposed on a person—is especially important to children. In this light, the findings are grim. The report points to factors such as compulsory heterosexuality and heterosexual attraction, the proliferation of plastic surgery both for adults and non-adults, the impact of various media in developing and reflecting social attitudes regarding sexualization, the entertainment industry's perpetuation of a particular body image and particular gender roles, the design and marketing of inappropriate (e.g., sexualized or violent) toys to children, and the promotion of adult-appropriate clothing and cosmetics for children, as ways in which girls are sexualized in contemporary Western society (APA, 2007). The phenomenon of the sexualization of girls, however, has an historical, social, and consumer context. The gradual emergence of the *tween* (a person between childhood and adolescence) is a cultural development that cannot be understood apart from market forces and the rise of consumerism in Western culture (Cook & Kaiser, 2004). Consumerism and marketing are directly tied to the sexualization of girls and our interpretations of pre-pubertal, pubertal, and post-pubertal girls' bodies.

It is helpful to frame menarche further within the social perceptions of female bodies and sexualities. "In a world where the female body is sexualized so early and the stakes are so high, it now seems obvious that it is not enough to teach girls how to be clean and dainty" (Brumberg, 1997, p. 55). Brumberg's critique of the shift in focus regarding menarche and menstruation from its developmental and maturational significance to its external hygienic significance highlights the implications for girls' perceptions of their own sexualities and bodies. By sanitizing menarche and menstruation away from their sexual meanings and responsibilities, we reinforce cultural messages about what constitutes an acceptable body and "set the stage for obsessive over-attention to other aspects of the changing body, such as size and shape" (Brumberg, 1997, p. 55).

Brumberg's hypothesis is borne out in the literature (Brooks-Gunn, 1992; Golub, 1992; Martin, 1996; Moore, 1995; Prendergast, 1995; Williams & Currie, 2000). The cultural standards around ideal body size are far more influential for girls than for boys (Brooks-Gunn, 1992). The normal weight gain that accompanies puberty and sexual development is met with disdain: for females, the ideal is a "linear lean, almost pre-pubertal body" (p.99). The increase in size that pushes girls out of their pre-pubertal bodies can trigger body image crises that manifest as ambivalence regarding sexual development. Williams and Currie (2000) found that any pubertal development that occurred outside of the "normal" time frame triggered reports from adolescent girls of being "too fat," in the case of the early maturers, and "too thin," in the case of the late maturers (p. 143; see also Golub, 1992; Striegel-Moore & Cachelin, 1999). Also, when coupled with heterosexual social activities (the study does not mention whether homosexual social activities incited similar issues), menarcheal timing profoundly affects girls' tendencies to diet and their propensities toward disordered eating (Abraham et al., 2009). Changes (or lack thereof) in body size directly connected to puberty, and hence menarche, incited negative evaluations of body size and poor body image in girls (Cauffman & Steinberg, 1996).

One exploration of this possibility, from the critical gender analysis perspective, posits that girls' experiences are evaluated more negatively and framed more problematically at puberty than boys' experiences (Prendergast, 1995). This problematic framing, in turn, leads to a more negative evaluation of the maturing (and mature) female body in general, and of the menstruating body in particular.

> One might speculate that at adolescence girls are poised between the experience of bodily shock, fragmentation and disorder that seems to accompany menstrual experience in the West, and a pervasive sense that in fact this is their body at its best, its most ideal. From this time on, from the immanence of this fragile and contradictory arrival, a young woman has much to lose: to grow up, to mature, to become adult and enter childbearing can only move her away from this childlike body. There are clear connections here with what has been described as the current epidemic of eating disorders in young women: the attempt to freeze adolescence, to hold on to a childlike body, and to control it rigidly through diet. Perhaps significantly, one consequence of anorexia and bulimia is that menstruation itself ceases. (Prendergast, 1995, p. 208)

Such attention to the body, both by adolescent girls themselves and by those around them (i.e., peers, family, boys, adults), leads to self-objectification of the body as a means of controlling not only appearance, but the appearance of sexuality as well (Martin, 1996). Throughout puberty, girls are under scrutiny about their bodies and concomitantly scrutinize themselves. They develop an understanding of the body-self as an object to be manipulated, controlled, and shaped into an acceptable form. Martin (1996) further proposes two results of girls' objectification of their bodies. "One, girls treat their bodies like distinct others, or two, they psychologically piece apart their bodies and work on them until their body becomes their accomplishment. Both indicate an alienation of the self from body, although the first is most extreme" (pp. 40–41).

Because the body is the locus for sexual experience, any distancing of self from the body is potentially problematic in any personal decision-making and evaluation regarding sexuality and sexual activity. This distancing serves partially to explain why pubertal timing is so important in understanding sexual activity among adolescent females (Golub, 1992; Miller, Norton, Fan, & Christopherson, 1998). The earlier puberty occurs, the earlier girls internalize perceptions of their bodies and, thereby, disembody themselves. Tolman (2002a) proposes that such disembodiment is, in fact, dissociation from the adolescent female sexual self. In disembodying themselves this way, girls compromise their capacity to discern desire and pleasure (and, conversely, displeasure and pain) in their sexual experiences. This can lead them, at times, to make choices that, in turn, compromise their own well-being.

Objectification theory. Objectification theory is useful in exploring the destructive tendencies of some adolescent females regarding their own and others' bodies. Fredrickson and Roberts (1997) propose that the socio-cultural context of sexual objectification that females encounter routinely illuminates the experiences and mental health of girls and women. "Sexual objectification occurs whenever a woman's body, body parts, or sexual functions are separated out from her person, reduced to the status of mere instruments, or regarded as if they were capable of representing her." That is, "women are treated *as bodies*—and in particular, as bodies that exist for the use and pleasure of others" (Fredrickson & Roberts, 1997, p. 175). The theory more pointedly states that objectification by others leads females to adopt a self-perception and self-treatment as objects of social scrutiny. When a female internalizes social objectification, it becomes self-objectification, a means of determining how she will be perceived socially (Fredrickson & Roberts, 1997, pp. 177–80).

The impact of female self-objectification is immense. Fredrickson and Roberts (1997) propose objectification theory as a means by which to understand girls' and women's psychological experiences of shame and anxiety, peak motivational states, and internal bodily awareness. They conclude that self-objectification negatively influences women's experiences of each of the above by triggering perpetual and rigorous body monitoring. Body self-monitoring, in turn, triggers higher incidence of depression, sexual dysfunction, and eating disorders (Fredrickson & Roberts, 1997, pp. 181–92). With pubescent girls in particular, the confluence of factors affecting adolescent females' development requires integrative thinking about the etiology of mental health disorders. If an adolescent girl recognizes upon puberty that her body is the subject of constant scrutiny, then she learns that her body belongs less to her and more to others; at puberty, girls' bodies seem to become "public domain" (Fredrickson & Roberts, 1997, p. 193).

> [E]arly experiences of sexual objectification, whether actual or anticipated, in turn trigger (a) the self-conscious body monitoring that results from internalizing an observer's perspective on self; (b) a range of deleterious subjective experiences, including excesses of shame and anxiety, fewer peak motivational states and numbness to internal bodily states; which may culminate to explain (c) increased risks for several poor mental health outcomes. (Fredrickson & Roberts, 1997, p. 194)

The greater focus on self that is characteristic of adolescent development makes adolescent females particularly vulnerable to the fallout of self-objectification. Slater and Tiggeman's (2002) comparison study of adolescent female ballet dancers and non-dancers found no significant difference between the two groups regarding bodily shame and eating disorders. Body objectification, self-monitoring, body shame, and appearance anxiety, however, were all pathways to disordered eating among girls as young as twelve and thirteen (2002); their hypothesis that body objectification theory was applicable to adolescent girls was affirmed. Grabe, Hyde, and Lindberg (2007) corroborate this hypothesis in their study of the roles of gender, shame, and rumination in body objectification and depression among adolescents. Although they found that adolescent boys experience some body objectification, it did not correlate with depression as it did with girls. Gender, bodily shame and, in particular, rumination were all found to be determiners of depression among girls as young as eleven years of age.

Finally, in a specific application of objectification theory to women's perceptions of menstruation, Roberts and Waters (2004) suggest that female internalization of sexual objectification "produces ambivalent attitudes and attributions toward normal female body and reproductive functions (viz., menarche and menstruation)" (p. 18; see also Roberts, Goldenberg, Power, & Pyszczynski, 2002). And when the internalization results in self-objectification, "the experience of the menstruating body is viewed even more negatively, and is characterized by self-loathing, disgust, and flight or dissociation from their corporeal selves" (Roberts & Waters, 2004, p. 18). Finally, some correlation exists between these phenomena and "the rise of depression and disordered eating during adolescence" (Roberts & Waters, 2004, p. 18). Objectification theory is, thus, capable not only of identifying the outcomes of sexual objectification and self-objectification, but also of identifying the mechanisms by which these processes work.

As a society, we have walked pubertal, adolescent girls to the precipice of negative self-perception and concomitant responses to the world. While the menarcheal girl embodies female creativity at its most primal, she simultaneously embodies the social perceptions of gender, menstruation, and developing maturity. The messages emphasized regarding developing sexuality at the onset of menstruation colour the ways in which girls interpret their own menarche and sexual subjectivity, either positively or negatively (Teitelman, 2004). It is little wonder that ambivalence regarding menarche is a common experience among girls. To balance the onset of physical maturity with a culture of secrecy regarding menstruation and a culture of control regarding their developing bodies is shaky, at best. Again, it is no surprise that there exists a "growing body of data suggesting that menarche is perceived and experienced by young adolescent girls in a primarily negative light" (Koff, Rierdan, & Jacobson, 1981, p. 157; see also Brumberg, 1997). It is unclear how such an objectifying and negative introduction to their own sexuality could prepare females for its subjective integration into their whole persons.

Fourth theme: Messages and discussion

In 1970, Judy Blume published *Are you there God? It's me, Margaret*, an adolescent novel about a young girl's impressions of puberty. Blume explored the anxieties, hopes, expectations, and experiences of Margaret and her friends as they anticipated their first menstruation, the growth of their breasts, and their transition into womanhood. This novel remains in the canon of adolescent girls' literature today as a frank, funny, and poignant fictional account of menarche in North America. Some forty years later, adolescent girls continue to face the reality of menarche in much the same way as Margaret did—with curiosity, ambivalence, secrecy, and, even at times, with humour.

In the National Film Board of Canada's *Under wraps: A film about going with the flow* (Wheelwright & MacInnes, 1996), Judy Blume recounts her experiences after writing *Are you there God? It's me, Margaret.* There had been mixed reactions to the book upon its initial release, and some libraries had refused to carry it because of its subject matter. In recalling her subsequent experiences with readers of the book, Blume wept: so many of them had said to her that they had never had the chance to speak openly about menstruation in general, or their own menarche in particular. If this is the case more generally, what messages are adolescent females receiving about menarche, menstruation, development, and sexuality? More to the point, perhaps, what social messages are being sent to menarcheal adolescent girls in a culture focused on bodily perfection, hygiene, and manipulation? Social ambivalence toward menstruation, and the need for its concealment, effect a confounding menarcheal silence.

> We live in a greeting-card culture where, for twenty-five cents [four dollars today], we can purchase socially approved statements about childbirth, marriage, or death. But Hallmark manufactures no cards that say, "Best Wishes on Becoming a Woman." Rather than celebrate the coming-of-age in America, we hide the fact of the menarche, just as we are advised to deodorize, sanitize, and remove the evidence. (Delaney, Lupton, & Toth, 1988, p. 107)

Whatever rites of passage may currently exist to guide girls through the liminal period of pubescence and the developmental event of menarche, or have historically existed in other cultures (Delaney, Lupton, & Toth, 1988), have left behind little formal evidence in current North American culture.[5] Perhaps, as a means of exploring the social and emotional meaning of menarche in a profound way, some contemporary rite of passage is in order—grand or humble (Golub, 1992, p. 49). In their recommendations for ways to prepare girls for menarche, post-menarcheal adolescents identified some form of discrete recognition by the parents (or at least the mother) as a way they would want to mark the event, such as a flower, or a special meal out (Koff & Rierdan, 1995). Given the rich tradition of ritual in the Roman Catholic Church, a formal recognition of menarche could work nicely as a formalized rite of passage and could have positive, long-lasting effects: girls whose families celebrated their menarche and framed it positively as a multi-faceted life transition moved more easily into menstruation than those whose families were less supportive, and were pleased to be knowledgeable, prepared, and supported throughout (Teitelman, 2004).

More common than positive recognition of menarche and female sexuality, however, are paradoxical reflections of maturity and shame (Chang, Hayter, & Wu, 2010; Orringer & Gahagan, 2010).

> Conflicting messages congratulating the girls for becoming a woman at the same time that she is cautioned to become virtually obsessed with keeping "it" a secret from others may simply make the task of balancing the positive and negative aspects of menarche too arduous for the young adolescent. The balance seems to shift at menarche, such that menstruation becomes associated primarily with negative affect. (Koff, Rierdan, & Jacobson, 1981, p. 157)

When social messages regarding menarche and menstruation are mixed, girls' perceptions of that ambiguity tend toward the negative; they have difficulty successfully negotiating developing maturity and negative social messages about bleeding, sexual bodies.

While biological and physical development in adolescence is in itself meaningful in human movement through the lifespan, Western socialization around sex and gender that accompanies this physical development is equally weighty. Adolescent females are particularly vulnerable to powerful critiques and prescriptions of the natural bodily phenomena of puberty and adolescence. For many girls, the social messages are internalized, which results in their self-objectification; and, given its mental health consequences, such a response is a problematic one. Coupling female adolescent pubertal development with Elkind's (2001, 1981) theory of the egocentric adolescent provides further theoretical substantiation of the perceived difficulties girls face regarding body image and self-esteem. In the light of Erikson's identification of the developmental stage of adolescence as an identity forming stage (Muuss, 1996), Elkind posits that adolescent egocentrism (as opposed to other developmental egocentrisms) leads them to construct an *imaginary audience:* a sense that they are the centre of attention in all social situations.

The responses of others to an adolescent (as those responses are self-interpreted) tend to confirm her/her positive or negative self-evaluation. Elkind also posits the *personal fable* as a means for adolescents to verify their belief in their own uniqueness (2001). If adolescent females do perceive themselves to be under constant scrutiny as the stars of their own shows, and if they do create a fable to undergird their belief in their own uniqueness, it would be understandable that they would seek both acceptance within a broader social group (and, therefore, go to great lengths to dress similarly to their peers) and recognition as unique (and, therefore, colour their hair blue). In a sense, the dilemma reinforces the double bind for adolescent females—the need to be accepted as the same, and the need to be understood as different.

The biological, sexual development of adolescent females is clearly a complex phenomenon. Despite its universal manifestation in females, its individual location within particular social structures colours girls' perceptions of their bodily, sexual selves in their worlds. Adolescent females' personal experiences of sexuality, including the visible, physical manifestation of a bleeding body, are shaped extensively by social interpretations of menarche and menstruation. Girls meet their sexuality encouraged by social secrecy, and are invited to respond ambivalently to their own embodied selves. In Christian theological terms, we as a church invite adolescent females into an ambivalent relationship with their incarnate selves—their creation in the image of God. From their initial transition into womanhood through to their movement into adult female sexuality, they must hide their own experience of the Incarnation. While Christian ambivalence toward the female bleeding body renders it invisibly incarnate, social ambivalence with the bleeding bodies of females detracts from any positive interpretation of adolescent girls' biological development.

Biological development is just one contributor to the myriad challenges of and potential for flourishing during adolescence. While adolescents are developing their selves and characters throughout this pivotal, hormonal, physiological time, that development is occuring in concert with neural development. Identity formation and adolescent development (including menarche and its social interpretations) are embodied within hormonal surges and social constructs, all while the adolescent brain undergoes its own nuanced shift from childhood to adulthood. This aspect of biological adolescent development requires its own exploration.

Neural Development in Adolescence

While neural development clearly is an aspect of biological and physical development, burgeoning research is yielding a nascent understanding of its particular impact on female and male adolescent development.[6] Historically, the focus of research regarding development through puberty and adolescence was on hormones as the primary factor in the developmental process (Altman, 2004). In recent years, however, the concomitant influence of neural functions on all developmental factors has become more widely recognized (e.g., Romeo, Richardson, & Sisk, 2002; Steinberg, 2010). There is, currently, great promise in our growing understanding of how adolescence is linked to neural development, coupled with recognition of the complexity of developmental factors beyond the brain (Forbes & Dahl, 2010). In this light, neural development is one facet of biological development that works in concert with other aspects of adolescent development toward the creation of human flourishing.

Recognition that the adolescent brain is differently developed from those of children or adults is also rather recent. In the 1960s and 1970s, researchers began to observe and compare post-mortem brains of human children, adolescents, and adults. Only then did they identify the differences among the developing brains and begin investigating the cognitive, affective, and behavioural implications of these differences (Blakemore & Frith, 2005).

This area of biological research has come to complement the prior strategy of focusing on hormonal changes that, over the years, has made modest inroads into understanding adolescent development (Spear, 2000). What has emerged is an appreciation for the complex interaction between neural and hormonal realities in adolescent physical development (Altman, 2004; Dahl, 2004; Romeo, 2003). Researchers in the field of neuroendocrinology have made initial progress in disentangling the intricate process of hormonal and neural triggering around pubertal maturation and adolescent neural development (Romeo, 2003; Sisk & Foster, 2004). Given the nascent nature of these studies, however, much remains underexplored, such as the role of socio-economic status (Noble, Houston, Kan, & Sowell, 2012) or environment in adolescent neural and hormonal development (Blakemore & Choudhury, 2006). It remains premature (and imprudent) to extrapolate causal relationships between adolescent neural development and behaviour from existing data without adequate attention to other developmental research (see DeLisi, Wright, Vaughn, & Beaver, 2010; Sercombe, 2010).

Early studies of the adolescent brain reveal two primary changes from prepubescence to adolescence (Blakemore & Choudhury, 2006). First is the apparent loss of grey matter throughout early adolescence (Giedd et al., 1999; Luna et al., 2001; Spear, 2000). Our current understanding of neural development points to substantial synaptic pruning of grey matter, which housed neural structures from early childhood, and to pubertal synaptogenesis (also known as synaptic proliferation, and meaning the expansion of the brain's capacities). Synaptic pruning, the second primary change in the adolescent brain, allows for synapses that are not well used to make way for more efficient use of functioning synapses, and follows a marked surge in early pubertal synaptic growth.

Concomitant with synaptic pruning is increased myelination (the replacement of grey matter with white matter), whereby the synapses become more efficient in neural processing. White matter is made up of myelinated nerve cells, in which myelin insulates the neural axon and increases the speed and efficiency of transmission of electrical impulses from neuron to neuron (Blakemore & Choudhury, 2006, p. 296). Different areas of the brain undergo synaptic pruning at different points in neural development. Current research indicates that the process of myelination continues to facilitate the development of executive control over behaviour well beyond puberty and does so differently between females and males, suggesting possible implications for dimorphic mental health outcomes (Asato, Terwilliger, Woo, & Luna, 2010). Consequently, although grey matter is decreasing in the adolescent brain, the volume of brain tissue seems to remain stable through the process of myelination (Andersen, 2003; Blakemore & Choudhury, 2006).

Neural functions associated with different areas of the brain yield cognitive, affective, and behavioural changes at different times over the course of adolescence (Blakemore & Frith, 2005; Dahl, 2004; Luna et al., 2001; Paus, 2005; Spear, 2000). It appears that, in the process of development, different parts of the brain undertake similar tasks, depending upon the stage of neural development; as neural development proceeds through adolescence, the brain becomes more proficient and adept at addressing challenges of affect, cognition, and behaviour (Yurgelun-Todd, 2007). In short, using the brain for progressively more challenging tasks is a developmental undertaking that neural development itself facilitates. Under typical circumstances, the brain becomes more functionally streamlined with time and experience. This conclusion appears supported by the generally simultaneous growth in functional capacity of adolescents with the development of the prefrontal cortex.

Study of the still-developing adolescent brain has been greatly facilitated by the introduction of *Magnetic Resonance Imaging (MRI)*, a non-intrusive means of examining and producing high-quality images of the living human brain.[7] Along with structural MRI are *functional MRI (fMRI)* and *Diffusion Tensor Imaging (DTI)*. Functional MRI facilitates observance of the brain, and allows researchers to identify neural activity while persons perform particular cognitive, sensory, and motor functions (Paus, 2005; Yurgelun-Todd, 2007). Diffusion Tensor Imaging (DTI), which "measures water diffusion within brain tissue" (Wang et al., 2012, p. 2) provides an indirect opportunity to "study the microstructural components of white matter, including myelination and axonal organization, in a quantitative manner that complements existing structural MRI studies of white matter volume" (Asato, Terwilliger, Woo, & Luna, 2010, p. 2123). Giedd et al.'s (1999) groundbreaking longitudinal MRI study notes that while the post-pubescent decrease in grey matter follows a surge in pubertal synaptic growth, the changes are "non-linear and regionally specific" (p. 861).

This study also found that white matter changes (i.e., growth) are, in contrast to the grey matter, more linear in accord with age. Asato, Terwilliger, Woo, and Luna's (2010) later study found that myelination correlated with pubertal development, rather than age, and more rapidly in females than in males. In effect, studies suggest that neural development is a process that moves variably through the brain, which might account in part for the functional development of adolescents into adult-required capacities (Asato, Terwilliger, Woo, & Luna, 2010; Blakemore & Choudhury, 2006; Geidd et al., 1999; Luna et al., 2001).

There is a general consensus among developmental researchers that adolescents are in a transitional stage of neural development (Spear, 2000). Contrary to previous suggestions that the brain and its functions experience "critical" phases of development (primarily in childhood), after which various neural capacities cease to be accessible, the human brain appears to develop into and well past adolescence (Blakemore & Choudhury, 2006). Accordingly, these phases of development are now referred to as "sensitive" phases and "natural window[s] of plasticity" (Dahl, 2004, p. 6), in recognition of the brain's capacity to compensate for developmental deficiencies and to continue to develop well past childhood (Andersen, 2003; Dahl, 2004; Romeo & McEwan, 2006).

While adolescents have attained the capacity for some cognitive higher functioning (certainly more than children), they remain less cognitively integrated than adults (Spear, 2000). The implications of this maturational process suggest that, at least to some extent, behavioural (e.g., risk-taking, impulse control, social interaction), cognitive (e.g., integration, abstract reasoning), and affective (e.g., lability, adaptive responses to stress, intensity) changes are correlated with neural development (Casey, Jones, & Hare, 2008; Dahl, 2004; Somerville, Jones, & Casey, 2010; Spear, 2000). Many of these implications seem tied to the relatively late development of the prefrontal cortex of the brain, which "mediates the highest cognitive capacities, including reasoning, planning and behavioral control" (Yurgelun-Todd, 2007, p. 253). The frontal lobes mediate the *executive function* of the brain, "the capacity that allows us to control and coordinate our thoughts and behavior" (Blakemore & Choudhury, 2006, p. 301). Some of the skills attached to executive function include: selective attention (that is, focus); decision-making; voluntary response inhibition, such as suppressing instinctual active responses when indicated to do so; working memory; prospective memory, as when holding intentions for future actions and multi-tasking; and problem solving. Executive function skills typically improve over the course of adolescence (Blakemore & Choudhury, 2006; Yurgelun-Todd, 2007). Couple developing executive function with the relatively immature capacity to regulate impulse control—and the adolescent propensity to heightened response to incentives in particular— and the influence of social and emotional contexts, and it seems teens are more prone to act in ways that seem imprudent to others: primarily adults (Casey, Jones, & Hare, 2008; Luna, Padmanabhan, & O'Hearn, 2010).

In effect, the complexity of intra-personal functions is quite clear in adolescent neural functioning:

> Being a responsible adult requires developing self-control over behavior and emotions to appropriately inhibit and modify behaviors—despite strong feelings—to avoid terrible consequences. It requires that individuals be capable of initiating and carrying out a specific sequence of steps toward a long-term goal even though it may be difficult (or boring) to persist in these efforts. Adolescents need to learn to navigate complex social situations despite strong competing feelings. Skills in self-regulation of emotion and complex behavior aligned to long-term goals must be developed. These self-regulatory processes are complex and mastering behavioral skills involves neurobehavioral systems served by several parts of the brain. The ability to integrate these multiple components of behavior—cognitive *and* affective—in the service of long-term goals involves neurobehavioral systems that are among the last regions of the brain to fully mature. (Dahl, 2004, p. 18)

There also appears to be adolescent development with regard to social cognition (e.g., self-awareness and the ability to attribute distinct mental processes to others), decision-making, and the social brain (i.e., brain regions collectively involved in social cognition; see Blakemore, 2012 & 2008; Burnett & Blakemore, 2009). In keeping with the pubertal synaptic growth and subsequent adolescent synaptic pruning, development of the capacity for social perspective taking undergoes a brief *perturbation* (Blakemore & Choudhury, 2006). This perturbation seems to affect the capacity of adolescents to undertake reasoning and decision-making:

> Early adolescence in humans is associated with a major transformation of cognitive thought leading to abstract reasoning.... This cognitive acquisition is not absolute. The developmental emergence of formal reasoning emerges earlier when addressing problems associated with the physical world than with interpersonal issues, and even in adulthood some individuals do not consistently function at the formal reasoning stage. (Spear, 2000, p. 423)

When reasoning and making decisions, adolescents encounter difficulties not faced by other aged or developed persons; and, when faced with decisions in stressful or perceived stressful situations, such as everyday stress or time-limited situations, adolescents function more poorly than in "optimal test conditions" (Spear, 2000, p. 423).

This cognitive deficit points to the role of emotions and stress in adolescence. Emotion recognition develops over the course of adolescence, following an initial decline at puberty, particularly with regard to strong emotions like fear and disgust (Blakemore & Choudhury, 2006, p. 303). Because social relationships and the growth of independence take on new importance in adolescence, the ability to read and respond appropriately to personal and social cues is a key aspect of development. To function well socially among peers and others, adolescents must develop skills in marshalling incoming information and making decisions about how best to act under the circumstances. This ability appears to be associated with the prefrontal cortex, which facilitates integration and executive functioning in the brain: "As children mature, they show an increased ability to attend to incoming information and control their behavior in a goal-directed manner. . . . This development seems to emerge in conjunction with a progressive frontalization of functional activity associated with inhibitory processing" (Yurgelun-Todd, 2007, p. 255).

Because adolescence is a transitional time on many fronts, stressors and perceived stressors factor heavily into all facets of adolescents' lives. Most adolescents successfully negotiate the transition, with only an estimated 20 percent incidence of psychopathology—a rate similar to that exhibited in adults (Spear, 2000, p. 428). However, elevated reports of depressed mood, emotional lability, disturbed sleep, anxiety, and self-consciousness are common among adolescents (Spear, 2000). While these manifestations and reports of negative affect among adolescents are disproportionately higher than among other persons, the developing performance of the prefrontal cortex mitigates affective volatility over time.

There also seems to be support for the role of neural development in adolescent risk taking (Konrad, Firk, & Uhlhaas, 2013; Steinberg, 2008).[8] Adolescents tend to be disproportionately higher risk takers than both children and adults (Alberts, Elkind, & Ginsberg, 2006; Blakemore & Choudhury, 2006; Dahl, 2004; Spear, 2000; Steinberg, 2008); the synaptic pruning that takes place during adolescence requires substantial amounts of energy, which appears to result in "a major decline in the amount of excitatory stimulation reaching the cortex" (Spear, 2000, p. 439). It is possible, therefore, that adolescent risk-taking and stimuli-seeking behaviours have a neural explanation. One such explanation is that, given the low motivational stimulation of the adolescent brain, "adolescents are driven to seek more extreme incentives to compensate" (Blakemore & Choudhury, 2006, p. 305). As a result of the generally low positive impact that adolescents attain from motivational stimuli, they "may pursue new appetitive reinforcers through increases in risk-taking/novelty-seeking and via engaging in deviant behaviors such as drug-taking" (Spear, 2000, p. 446).

Another explanation for risk-taking is that the adolescent brain does not function as efficiently as the adult brain, and follows a different route to decision-making. "When confronted with a risky scenario, adults' relatively efficient responses were driven by mental images of possible outcomes and the visceral response to those images…however, adolescents relied more on reasoning capacities…hence the relatively effortful responses compared to adults" (Blakemore & Choudhury, 2006, p. 305). The comparatively underdeveloped prefrontal cortex of the adolescent brain works less efficiently than the adult brain in estimating risk (Blakemore & Frith, 2005; Luna, Padmanabhan, & O'Hearn, 2010). It is therefore likely that life experience in decision-making contributes to the neural realities of adult and adolescent decision-making and perceptions of risk-taking.

> A final possible neural explanation for adolescent risk taking, accounts for both the relatively immature executive function of the prefrontal cortex and the non-linear development of the brain. Because of the developmental imbalance within adolescent neural maturity, different processes facilitated by the various areas of the brain will be more or less functional throughout development (Somerville, Jones, & Casey, 2010). While the adolescent prefrontal cortex (and executive function) is still developing, the more maturely developed incentive-seeking areas of the brain overrule executive function (Steinberg, 2008). This could be why adolescents are able to respond appropriately to a given hypothetical situation but are less able to execute proportionate behaviours in practical situations, particularly when emotions run high. The vulnerability of the variously matured brain regions and functions is further exacerbated by perceived peer pressure to gain more rewards by undertaking more risk. While adults seem less susceptible to peer influence, by virtue of a more mature executive function and more extensive practical experience, teens seem to need only the potential of peer pressure to excite sensitive brain regions into risk-taking. (Chein et al., 2010)

Current research suggests that our social expectations of adolescent behaviour ought to be mindful of important factors in adolescent development. Pubertal development and neural restructuring seem, simultaneously, to affect the cognition, affect, and behaviours of adolescents, to varying degrees (e.g., Dahl, 2004). Because social and cultural deliberations over public policy and moral boundaries that affect adolescents are generally informed by empirical data (e.g., age to drive, age of majority, age to enlist in the military, curfews), adult expectations for adolescents ought to reflect a growing awareness of influential factors in human development. It is unwarranted, unhelpful, and imprudent, however, to adopt a reductionist neurobiological stance explaining adolescent development. Rather, most neuro-researchers advocate a more integrated consideration of neural development along with other factors, such as hormonal shifts, socio-economic circumstances, or educational experience, in understanding adolescence (e.g., Altman, 2004; Andersen, 2003; Blakemore & Choudhury, 2006; Blakemore & Frith, 2005; Chein et al., 2010; Dahl, 2004; Romeo, 2003; Spear, 2000; Steinberg, 2008).

A focus on integration of varied studies of adolescent development fits well with a theory of developmental contextualism, such as Lerner's (Muuss, 1996), and a normative sexual ethic based upon human flourishing. Unlike influential theorists preceding him, like Erikson, Piaget, and Kohlberg, Lerner suggests that consideration of contextual factors of development, such as gender development and sexual objectification, ought to weigh more heavily in discussions of adolescence than strict application of generalized patterns and rules of development. Such contextualization opens the door to a diversity of experiences and social circumstances in the formulation of policies and programs aiming to facilitate adolescents' well-being (Muuss, 1996). Adolescent development is clearly constituted by a confluence of individual, social, and physical factors interacting uniquely within each individual person. Within the nascent study of the adolescent brain there exist some key clues for our understanding of adolescence in general, and adolescent sexuality in particular. Working harmoniously with hormonal triggers, neural triggers initiate and sustain the movement of the child toward adolescence. This complex and, at times, tumultuous process gets played out in the social and cultural lives of individual adolescents. Together, the plethora of developmental elements provides the context in which an individual teen girl or boy moves into her or his own sexuality; the various contributors to the life experiences of individuals foster their development as increasingly responsible and integrated persons.

When further applied to adolescent female sexual flourishing, any theory of development that does not consider all aspects of the person—the physical, emotional, psychological, spiritual, intellectual, and social—will clearly fail to account for the embodied experiences of individual females, and of females collectively. When there is room in an ethic to account for adolescents as integrated beings, and as both individuals and a group, the contextual intricacies of their development allow for the elegant unfolding of sexual flourishing in the complexity of actual lives.

SUMMARY

Some aspects of adolescent development that are particularly salient for adolescent female sexuality and flourishing are: gender development; heteronormativity; moral development and voice; self-identity; hormonal, pubertal transitions and the pivotal moment of menarche; neural developments; and social interaction with and interpretation of biological phenomena. Extensive attention to menarche and menstruation highlights the social (and theological) significance of female bleeding in the construction of sexuality and gender.

Insofar as the theoretical structure of feminist natural law calls for a method and procedure open to females' lives and experiences in articulating a sexual ethic, the developmental experiences of prepubescent, pubescent, and post-pubescent adolescent females are essential data in the theological enterprise. Necessary to account for adolescent females in the evolution of sexual theology, this data also begins to fill a void in the Christian tradition. Development, however, is not the only facet of adolescent females' lives relevant to Christian theology. The experiences of adolescents within the context of development add flesh to the bones of their human sexuality. These experiences inform an understanding of adolescent female sexual flourishing, which in turn informs a sexual theology that might be adequate to account for adolescent females' realities.

CHAPTER SEVEN

THIS ONE'S FOR THE GIRLS: ADOLESCENT FEMALES AND FLOURISHING

INTRODUCTION

The transition from empirical evidence and developmental theory pertaining to adolescent females into a discussion of factors that positively affect sexual flourishing recognizes the complexity of experiences of sexuality. My intention is to facilitate a meaningful conversation between the discrete discourses of sexual theology and developmental psychology, and to explore the ways in which this conversation might foster a sexual theology that accounts for, and is meaningful and relevant to, adolescent females. The experiences and interpretations of adolescent female sexuality provide ample evidence that neither a strictly universal nor strictly particular approach to sexual theology is tenable for adolescents. Such a sexual theology requires a framework solid and flexible enough to allow for both aspects of the human experience and the ambiguity of sexuality itself to form its content. With the framework in place, I turn to experiences.

EAGLE WHEN SHE FLIES: ADOLESCENT FEMALES AND FLOURISHING

Based upon the accounts of adolescent females' developmental lives, I address flourishing as the measurement of adequacy for a feminist natural law formulation of sexual theology. To flourish in one's environment means to grow, develop, and thrive beyond the mere parameters of surviving; it is contextual, specific, communal, and individual. What might this mean for adolescent females? What are their concrete and tangible sexual realities? What are their shared experiences in similar contexts? What factors positively facilitate adolescent females' sexual flourishing? And how does empirical data and developmental theory interact with theological constructions within official Roman Catholic sexual theology and teaching?

Not a Girl, Not Yet a Woman: Acknowledging Developmental Realities and Female Bodies

The primary reference for adolescent females' development is their bodies in context. Theoretical and practical understandings of the bodies of adolescent females and the culture(s) in which they develop are the substance upon which I offer here three topics for consideration. First, I consider the ways in which gender constructions and the concept of complementarity might interact in the lives of adolescent females. Second, I address contemporary insights into adolescent female bodies in concert with theological discourse on females and bodies. Finally, I outline factors that facilitate positive female sexual development and long-term sexual health. Woven throughout my consideration of these topics is attention to the sexual flourishing of adolescent females.

Jack and Diane: Gender and complementarity

The first topic is gender and the concept of complementarity. Gender development theory provides a helpful account of how genders (feminine and masculine, primarily) develop in accord with biological sex (or not). Bussey and Bandura's (1999) socio-cognitive theory of the development of gender that meets or defies gender-role norms over the course of development suggests that gender and sex are differentiated by culture and body, respectively. And, even though sex and gender are mutually interactive, sex is not solely responsible for gender identification. Rather, the multi-faceted interaction of factors such as biology, nurturing, social experience, and cultural milieu generally creates movement through a more dynamic than static gender identity. For adolescent females, in particular, the negotiation of gender can be difficult. Although adolescent males also find it difficult, they do not appear to suffer the same negative mental health consequences as females for being gender atypical (Egan & Perry, 2001). Evidence regarding gender points to the personal and social nature of gender development and the potentially hurtful consequences of maintaining prescribed social categories regarding gender and gender-role expression. Broadening gender perceptions might create a social context in which persons "can truly flourish and achieve their maximal psychological health" (Basow, 2006, p. 250).

Gender development is an element of human flourishing; when socially prescribed gender roles do not match a person's self-perception of gender, flourishing can be impeded. In theological discourse on sex and sexuality, this issue is widely debated. On one side are thinkers who would conflate sex and gender and, thereby, reinforce traditional historical gender roles, salted with hints of dualism and patriarchy. In theoretical terms, the conflation of male/female and masculine/feminine support a form of benevolent sexism within which sex and gender are understood as complementary.[1]

Contemporary theory and empirical data addressing sexism toward women identify the complex nature of sexist ideologies and their enactment in daily living. Glick and Fiske (1996, 2001) theorize that, alongside overt and hostile antipathy toward women, more insidious and benevolent expressions of sexism are prevalent internationally and cross-culturally (2001). Their Ambivalent Sexism Theory, and subsequent Ambivalent Sexism Inventory (ASI), identify two types of sexism: hostile sexism (HS), which is a sexist antipathy toward women; and benevolent sexism (BS), which is a relatively positive subjective orientation toward women. Benevolent sexism is "a traditional ideology that idealizes women in traditional female roles. BS is sexist in that it presumes traditional role divisions and gender stereotypes but consists of subjectively positive (for the sexist man) attitudes toward women (e.g., women complete men, women should be cherished and protected by men)."[2] The attitude of males toward females here is not necessarily one of antipathy, but rather one of affection for and protection of women, and for women embodying traditional feminine gender roles in particular (Glick, Diebold, Bailey-Werner, & Zhu, 1997; Glick & Fiske, 1996; and Glick, Lameiras, & Castro 2002).

The theory invokes ambivalence insofar as the benevolently sexist person can be provoked to hostility toward a female who is not fulfilling the traditional gender roles that circumscribe females' choices by gender and sex. The nature of sexism is, therefore, potentially bivalent, moving between outright antipathy and benevolent paternalism (Glick & Fiske, 2001); both valences reap detrimental consequences for females. On the one hand, overt hostility toward females who do not inhabit traditional gender roles, and thereby challenge the dominance of males in the social hierarchy, is threatening in its expression and follow-through. On the other hand, paternalistic benevolence implies weakness and incompetence among females, who require protection from threatening forces—like hostile sexist males (Glick, Diebold, Bailey-Werner, & Zhu, 1997). While both are detrimental to females' well-being, hostile sexism is more easily spotted than benevolent sexism.

Under the guise of good manners and chivalry, benevolent sexism pervades and undercuts females' attempts to flourish outside of traditionally sanctioned gender roles (Dardenne, Dumont, & Bollier, 2007; Good &

Rudman, 2010). By idealizing and rewarding those females who fall within traditional stereotypes of female roles and punishing those who do not, benevolent sexism supports static social structures. While maintaining positive, patronizing stereotypes of females as nurturing, caring, pure, and weak, for example, benevolent sexism secures the relative dominance of males in positions of social, economic, political, and religious power. Sexist ambivalence is elucidated by a categorization of females into favourable (e.g., traditional, chaste, saintly) and unfavourable (e.g., modern, sexually enticing, slutty) sub-types that either support or disturb traditional gender expectations (Sibley & Wilson, 2004). In this way, hostile sexists can justify their affection for the traditional, sexually less experienced female and their disdain for the non-traditional, sexually experienced female, even if the males see themselves as sexual beings and "have greater sexual experience" (Sibley & Wilson, 2004, p. 693). Because HS is concerned with maintaining power relations, gender differentiation, and heterosexuality, any threat to a conventional balance of male power over females in these areas (e.g., females advocating for gender and sex equality and equity, females successfully working in traditionally male jobs, females spurning males' sexual advances) incites hostility toward those females in particular, and toward negative female stereotypes in general (Glick & Fiske, 2001).

Benevolent sexism tends to take a subtler and more patronizing approach to females. Its primary indicators (or sub-factors) are: protective paternalism (males need to protect females from harm; females are weak); complementary gender differentiation (females have positive traits that complete males; each ought to undertake tasks suited to their spheres of competence); and heterosexual intimacy (males require female intimacy; females ought to be available to males for procreation and sexual pleasure; see Glick & Fiske, 1996, 2001). So long as females embody the positive stereotypical traits that ensure the beneficent disparity of power between themselves and males, they receive the benefits of male protection, completion, and intimacy. When females choose not to subscribe to these stereotypes, however, they are disparaged for upsetting the social balance of male/female, masculine/feminine stereotypes.

Given the theoretical construct of ambivalent sexism, Vatican teachings pertaining to sex and gender display signs of benevolent sexism. Based upon a traditional Roman Catholic application of natural law and its procedural inadequacies in regard to females, it is perhaps understandable that benevolent sexism pervades its content and that its commitment to females' flourishing exists outside the realm of practical, concrete circumstances. One Spanish study using the criteria of the Ambivalent Sexism Inventory (Glick & Fiske, 1996), for instance, found that Catholic religiosity predicted for benevolently sexist attitudes in males toward females (Glick, Lameiras, & Castro, 2002).

Drawing on long-standing dualistic gender and sex stereotypes and on the image of Mary, the virgin mother of God in the service of others (as in *Mulieris dignitatem* [John Paul II, 1988, no. 11]), the primary place for women is in the role of mother and nurturer. While chastising social structures that are socio-economically oppressive of women and complimenting women on their wholesale movement into the professional realms of Western cultures, the Roman Catholic Church cautions against the besmirching of women's more noble nature to serve in love (termed the "genius of women" or the "feminine genius") with the adoption of masculine characteristics (CDF, 2004; John Paul II, 1995b). The tripartite subscription to protective paternalism, complementary gender differentiation, and heterosexual intimacy within Roman Catholic teaching of anthropological and sexual theology renders it vulnerable to the charge of benevolent sexism. Clearly, a sexual theology manifesting benevolent sexism is fundamentally problematic and inadequate to support the criterion of female sexual flourishing. That these constructs are further attributed to the will of God for humanity gives them an air of divine authority, as though God herself is benevolently sexist: another untenable proposition.

On the other hand, feminist theologians (and others) maintain that the social creation of gender and the biological reality of sex are significant factors in the oppression of women in the Church and in the world. In contrast to a theological anthropology of complementarity that would confine men and women to Magisterium-sanctioned gender roles and identities, feminist anthropology recognizes the participation of women in the world beyond a feminine genius of reproductivity and service to others. Feminist critique of benevolent sexism, pervasive in official and historical understandings of sex and gender, is precisely aimed at facilitating the flourishing of females. Mindful of the importance of particular realities and manifestations of sex and gender in individual lives, it is hardly helpful to say to a curious lesbian fifteen-year-old that her inherent genius as a female is to complement a male. In fact, empirical evidence regarding gender identity formation and mental health suggests that, particularly for adolescent females, such a suggestion could be detrimental to her flourishing (Holland, Ramazanoglu, Sharpe, & Thompson, 2000; Smiler, Ward, Caruthers, & Merriwether, 2005). The conflation of sex and gender, coupled with an understanding of gender development void of concrete and particular realities of adolescent females, effectively objectifies adolescent females and locates all sexual meaning in their reproductive bodies. Such objectification within a heteronormative assumption requires that females be feminine (in some externally defined way), regardless of their own perceptions and experiences of sex and gender.

Following Traina's (1999) analysis of method and procedure for making tentative claims about the substance of feminist natural law ethics, I question whether a heteronormative notion of sex and gender complementarity is capable of facilitating the full flourishing of females in general, and of developing adolescent females in particular. In a strange twist of theory, the objectification of the female body (and possible resulting self-objectification) within a theology of complementarity does not overtly sexualize females' bodies by casting off all cover and protection (APA, 2007); instead, it seems, covertly, to asexualize them by donning the guise of genius, rather than attending to experiential realities. Menarche, menstruation, and female sexual pleasure are obvious examples of the lack of attention paid to female sexuality; to recognize female bleeding and sexual enjoyment is to recognize, inherently, the practical realities of female sexual experiences. Rather than speaking to female experiences, complementarity defines female sexuality only in relation to males, in vague terms, and with no reference to pleasure: in effect, belittling it and tucking it away from traditional theological discourse.

In this sense, theological method itself is truncated: it is heedless of the garnered wisdom from the actual experiences of adolescent females, and takes away their collective and individual subjective voices. Girls must be (feminine) girls; boys must be (masculine) boys. The convergence here of gender development, benevolent sexism, complementarity, and objectification theories suggests that the theological anthropology informing traditional teachings on males and females diminishes, rather than facilitates, adolescent females' flourishing.

Hips don't lie: Adolescent female bodies

The second topic pertaining to development is the biological/physical realities of adolescent females and their sexual experiences of their bodies. Contemporary Western culture has focused on the biological realities (narrowly perceived) of adolescent development, and paid little attention to concomitant developmental factors. Menarche, the explicit moment of introduction to female sexuality and maturity, and menstruation have become less about the physiological, emotional, and psychological transition into and manifestation of womanhood, and more about an hygienic inconvenience that must be hidden and kept secret, especially from males. Rather than being empowered with an awareness of their own fertility that comes with menstruation, adolescent females are schooled in medical terminology that pathologizes female bleeding and reinforces shame over its very existence (Fingerson, 2006). Female bodies are sexually objectified, beginning in childhood, and are closely monitored for size, beauty, normativity, and attractiveness to the opposite sex. Young girls (and women) are targeted as consumers of products aimed at preserving youthful and socially sanctioned bodies (APA, 2007), while social recognition of a healthy adolescent sexuality eludes them.

Evidence suggests that adolescent females have extensive experience of the negative realities of sexuality. First heterosexual intercourse, for instance, is an ambivalent experience for adolescent females. Factors such as the context of first coitus, sexual messages and values received from parents, gender beliefs, feelings about the body (Smiler, Ward, Caruthers, & Merriwether, 2005), perceived readiness (Hawes, Wellings, & Stephenson, 2010; Skinner, Smith, Fenwick, Fyfe, & Hendriks, 2008), and self-concept (Garriguet, 2005) all contribute to how they perceive their first experience of intercourse. Sharon Thompson's (1990) oft-cited study of teenage girls' accounts of sexual initiation describes a frequent "cognitive gap" between their biological understanding of, and their experiential preparedness for, sexual intercourse. With no foreground conversation about how intercourse actually feels physically, emotionally, or relationally, many girls interpret their experience against a fantasy of romantic and life-altering heterosexual intercourse: they report boredom, pain, coercion, disappointment, and dissociation as primary characteristics of first sex (Thompson, 1990; see also Skinner et al., 2008). In response to their negative first experiences, numerous girls postpone further coitus until they are more comfortable with both the idea and the reality. In fact, data consistently suggests that a later adolescent sexual debut yields a greater likelihood that the person will perceive the experience positively and that her/his ensuing life choices will reflect a positive cognitive, affective, and relational integration of her/his experience (see Armour & Haynie, 2007; Smiler, Ward, Caruthers, & Merriwether, 2005). Data also suggests that when females (more so than males) perceive themselves as ready for intercourse, they enjoy positive experiences of sexual development and activity (e.g., Thompson, 1990; Wight et al., 2008). These findings correspond with those within Michelle Fine's (1988) influential study of alternative discourses of adolescent females' sexual experiences; evidence suggests that at least some girls experience sexual desire, activity, and intercourse in a more positive light.

Adolescent females are capable of attending to and flourishing in their own sexuality when the context is favourable to positive perceptions of that sexuality. Recalling factors that contribute to positive first consensual intercourse (both female and male), context, parental messages, gender ideology, readiness, self-concept, and body satisfaction all play a role. Regarding context, females report that when first sexual intercourse is intentional and planned (rather than coerced and/or impulsive), when a longer period of time has passed in the relationship with their partner, when they are older and more sexually prepared, and when they use contraception, they perceive the experience more positively (Hawes, Wellings, & Stephenson, 2010; Skinner et al., 2008). With regard to the impact of parental messages on experiential perceptions, females who receive more positive messages about sexual freedom that do not endorse a sexual double standard between males and females perceive their experience more positively. For females, ascription to traditional gender roles leads to a more negative experience of first intercourse, while for males, the opposite seems true. And the more comfortable females are with their bodies at the time of first intercourse, the more positively they report the experience (Smiler, Ward, Caruthers, & Merriwether, 2005, pp. 49–52).

Framing adolescent sexuality in a primarily negative light, within a discourse of female victimization (Fine, 1988; Thompson, 1990), is detrimental to adolescent girls' sexual flourishing. From the start, their sexuality is negatively framed by a social introduction to menstruation that emphasizes hiding, secrecy, and uncleanliness. And adolescent females, in particular, regularly encounter a discourse of multi-faceted female risk, danger, and taboo regarding sexual engagement: pregnancy and disease, physical safety, psychological perturbation, and social marginalization. The unfortunate reality of female risk in adolescent sexual behaviours is fuelled by heteronormative assumptions regarding sexuality and their related gender messages. For example, perceptions of sexual virginity and its loss are influenced by gender difference (Carpenter, 2005; Holland, Ramazanoglu, Sharpe, & Thomson, 2000). Males are markedly more positive about their experiences, because their loss of virginity is framed within a masculine construction of sexual meaning: the initiation into manhood (see also Dickson, Paul, Herbison, & Silva, 1998; Guggino & Ponzetti, 1997). It is worth noting, however, that awareness of this particular sexual construction and grappling with it can make the sexual experience more positive for both males and females:

> Where young people have more negotiated relationships, or are influenced by feminism (particularly mothers), then there is a greater awareness of the possibility of differences between male and female experience. Intimacy, friendship, love and an equality of inexperience can create space for resisting the dominance of masculine

meanings and the surveillance of the male peer group. Being able to laugh together at inexperience, rather than her having the power to laugh at him; exploring desires together, rather than her being expected to service his, requires some initial deconstruction of masculinity or outmanoeuvring of heterosexual pressures. (Holland, Ramazanoglu, Sharpe, & Thompson, 2000, p. 227)

A *positive* framework for a discourse of female adolescent sexuality must include some deconstruction of traditional gender roles, heteronormativity, female bleeding, and male sexual privilege (Diamond, 2006; Tolman, 2006).

These are a few of my favourite things: Positive construction of adolescent female sexuality
A positive discourse of adolescent sexuality is necessary to understand why recognition and expression of adolescent female sexuality can be socially and personally dangerous—or, at the least, lacking in pleasure. Initiating such a positive discourse requires a shift in perception and attention: first, to the actual positive sexual experiences of female adolescents; and, second, to the deconstruction of existing barriers to female sexual flourishing (Fine, 1988; Phillips, 1998; Thompson, 1990; Tolman, 2006 & 2002a). A number of factors, outlined below, are pivotal in constructing a positive perception of adolescent female sexual development: parental influences; activities and goals; norms, values, and beliefs; and the pleasure and danger of desire. Each of these factors contributes to an understanding of adolescent female sexual flourishing and also to the content of a feminist natural law ethic that accounts for adolescent sexuality.

Because you loved me: Parental influences on positive adolescent sexuality
The first pivotal factor in positive sexual development among adolescents is parental support and positive messaging about sexuality and sexual behaviour (Miller, Norton, Fan, & Christopherson, 1998; Smiler, Ward, Caruthers, & Merriwether, 2005). Adolescent females' relationships with, and the education levels of, their mothers bear significantly on their sexual attitudes and behaviours (Abma, Driscoll, & Moore, 1998; Houts, 2005). Close monitoring of adolescent activity by parents, a warm and close mother–daughter relationship, and ease of communication between mother and daughter facilitate delayed intercourse and enhance self-esteem and sexual agency among adolescent females (McNeely et al., 2002; Schreck, 1999; Sieving, McNeely, & Blum, 2000). The quality and quantity of the communication and the quality of the existing relationship between adolescents aged 13 to

17 and parents (notably, mothers) mediate the effectiveness of discussions of sexuality between parents and children (Aspy et al., 2007; Lefkowitz & Stoppa, 2006). Data clearly suggests that parental involvement in the sexual education of children and adolescents, an open and loving relationship between parent and child, and accurate and caring information about sexuality as a multi-faceted human experience are beneficial to adolescent sexual development and flourishing (Aspy et al., 2007; Blake et al., 2001; Maguen & Armistead, 2006).

Such a relationship includes the parental capacity to facilitate positive influences in sexual development and to influence an adolescent's understanding and experience of sexuality within a complex social environment. Actual time spent among family can be enough to protect young adolescents from engaging in sexual activity and, to a certain extent, mediate the extensive time that adolescents spend with peers (Barnes et al., 2007). This parental time and influence provide a context for a meaningful critique of persuasive social messages about body image, sexual behaviour, and self-esteem: all critical factors in healthy adolescent female sexual development. Parents are also uniquely positioned to address external influences on sexual development, such as television messages (Schooler, Kim, & Sorsoli, 2006; Sorsoli, Porche, & Tolman, 2005).

The mass media is a prominent example of external influence on adolescent sexuality (J.D. Brown, 2000; Brown, Halpern, & L'Engle, 2005; Ward, 2003). Studies are beginning to establish not only a link between (Gruber & Grube, 2000; Kaestle, Halpern, & Brown, 2007; Ward & Friedman, 2006) but a causal effect of the sexual content within mass media on the sexual attitudes and behaviours of adolescents (Brown et al., 2006; Collins et al., 2004). This data indicates that media depictions of sexual activity, consequences, abstinence, birth control, emotions, gender relationships, and healthy sexual choices will influence adolescents both to refrain from and to engage in sexual activities. Depictions of negative consequences of sexual behaviours, for example, discourage sexual activity, while depictions of no consequences of sexual behaviours encourage sexual activity (Collins et al., 2004; Ward, Day, & Epstein, 2006). The content of media messages about sexuality are as influential as their mere presence. Unfortunately, portrayals of healthy adolescent sexuality are sparse in the mass media (Kunkel et al., 2005; Strasburger, 2005). Parental participation in moderating the sexual media diets of adolescents through their choice and ingestion of, interaction with, and application of sexual media content, combined with critical media literacy, can positively affect the choices their adolescents make for a healthy sexuality (J.D. Brown, 2000; Collins et al., 2004).[3]

Anything you can do: Activities and goals

A second pivotal factor in the development of healthy sexuality among adolescent females is their participation in extracurricular activities and academic goals. Athletic involvement, for example, is a particular focus of research regarding the relationship between adolescent girls' extracurricular activities and their sexual attitudes and behaviours. The factors that mediate the relationship between adolescent female athletes and their sexual attitudes and behaviours are undeniably complex (e.g., age, parental relationships, socio-economic status, race, sexual orientation, and self-esteem). While the links among these factors are apparent, the direction of their interaction seems yet to be firmly identified. Although one study suggests that athletic adolescent girls engage in sexual behaviours, or abstain from them, as a matter of choice rather than as a matter of non-desirable default (Miller et al., 2005), it is not clear if athletic heterosexual adolescent females are choosing behaviours that are protective of sexual health (i.e., they are considered desirable among their male peers, but choose to be sexually active at lower rates than their non-athletic peers) or if their athletic involvement itself contributes to a lack of opportunity to explore sexuality (i.e., they are stigmatized as undesirable to their male peers precisely because of their athletic involvement, and therefore their lower rates of sexual behaviour are by default rather than by choice). However, the generally positive relationship between adolescent girls' involvement in athletics and avoiding risky sexual behaviour, seeking healthy sexual behaviour, and sexual/reproductive health seems well established. One obvious measurable outcome of the relationship between girls and sports is that there are fewer adolescent pregnancies among athletic females than their non-athletic peers (Eitle & Eitle, 2002; Lehman & Koerner, 2004; Sabo et al., 1999; Savage & Holcomb, 1999).

Athletic involvement is only one of numerous activities that seem to protect for healthy general development. Adolescent involvement in any type of extracurricular activity is linked to pro-social development and long-term personal and professional success. Taking part in constructive, non-academic activities, whether school or community structured, facilitates greater school engagement and academic achievement, and provides "opportunities to engage in challenging tasks that promote learning of valued skills," "form strong social bonds with non-familial adults and prosocial peers," and "develop and confirm positive identities" (Eccles, Barber, Stone, & Hunt, 2003, p. 885). Although the direction of effect is unclear, studies suggest a bidirectional relationship between school-related goals and achievements and pro-social behaviours in, for instance, the relationship between age at first sexual intercourse (a potential risk behaviour) and academic goals and achievements (e.g., Uecker, Angotti, & Regnerus, 2008). One longitudinal study suggests that low educational achievement and goals (including parents' educational expectations) predict for earlier sexual initiation, particularly among early adolescent black females. Also, an earlier age of first intercourse in itself predicts for lower longer-term academic achievement and goals (Schvaneveldt, Miller, Berry, & Lee, 2001). Extracurricular activities and long-term academic goals and expectations contribute to adolescent females' sexual self-perceptions, which in turn allow them to envision goals that might be impeded by any negative consequences of early heterosexual intercourse. If the activities and goals themselves both contribute to girls' self-esteem and agency and reduce available discretionary peer-time, which is known to predict for risk behaviours among peers (Barnes et al., 2007), then they are positive factors in adolescent females' flourishing.

Like a virgin: Norms, values, and beliefs

A third pivotal factor in adolescent females' healthy sexual development, which is strongly related to the previous two factors (parental influence, and extracurricular activities and academic goals), is the structure of sexual meaning in girls' lives: how norms, values, and religious beliefs contribute to the healthy sexual development of adolescent females (Paradise et al., 2001). Social norms inform adolescents' perceptions of themselves as sexual, particularly in relation to their peers (Lyons, Giordano, Manning, & Longmore, 2011). When adolescents subjectively perceive themselves to be older than their chronological age, for instance, they tend to adopt behaviours they associate with those who are older—usually late adolescents and young adults (Arbeau, Galambos, & Jansson, 2007). When they understand sexual intercourse to be normative for older persons, adolescents are drawn by the incentive of pseudo-maturity to initiate their own sexual activity in early adolescence. Another reason adolescents might initiate sexual activity is that they perceive that their peers are also sexually active, regardless of whether or not that is the case (Kinsman, Romer, Furstenberg, & Schwarz, 1998; Rosenthal, Smith, & de Visser, 1999). Because earlier sexual initiation is a predictor for sexually related health issues like STIs, unplanned pregnancy, violence and abuse, delay of sexual intercourse is an outcome favourable to adolescent female flourishing.

The inverse of this phenomenon is also somewhat true: when delayed sexual intercourse is understood as normative among adolescents, it also predicts delayed sexual initiation. When the psychosocial factor of delayed sexual initiation is normatively reinforced among adolescents, it also predicts for delay (Carvajal et al., 1999; Santelli et al., 2004). In conjunction with other psychosocial factors, such as parental engagement, media influences, and extracurricular engagement, social reinforcement of delayed sexual initiation as normative among adolescents is a protective factor in the flourishing of adolescent females.

Social norms do not develop in a vacuum. Much of what we consider to be sexually normative in North American culture has been influenced by Judeo-Christian religious values and beliefs. Religious beliefs, while only one aspect among many having an impact on adolescents' sexual decision-making, still hold influential sway in their lives: more than participation in worship and affiliation to a particular tradition, professed religious belief about sexual activity predicts negatively for participation in risk activities, including sex (Sinha, Cnaan, & Gelles, 2007; see also Meier, 2003). A more broadly perceived religiosity that includes identity, behaviours, attitudes, perceptions, and practices regarding religion, also has an impact upon adolescent engagement in health risk behaviours in general, like substance use (Abbott-Chapman & Denholm, 2001; Nonnemaker, McNeely, & Blum, 2003), and upon sexual health risk behaviours in particular, like unprotected intercourse (Hardy & Raffaelli, 2003; Holder et al., 2000; Lefkowitz, Gillen, Shearer, & Boone, 2004; Rostosky, Wilcox, Wright, & Randall, 2004; Uecker, Angotti, & Regnerus, 2008). The most consistent finding regarding religiosity and sexual behaviour is the delay of sexual initiation among adolescent females, which itself predicts for more positive female sexual development from adolescence into adulthood, because it protects for long-term sexual and psychological health, academic and social achievement, and general health and flourishing (Hawes, Wellings, & Stephenson, 2010). Understanding physiological and neural development in adolescents, it seems congruent that the delay of sexual intercourse into late adolescence or early adulthood would provide adolescents with more skill in dealing with its multi-faceted implications.

The phenomenon of public virginity pledges is closely linked to religiosity as an influence on sexual decision-making: "[adolescents] promise to abstain from sex until marriage" (Bearman & Bruckner, 2001, pp. 851–52).[4] A conflation of belief and normativity, the virginity pledge hopes to instill not only sexual continence among its pledgers but also to encourage their abstinence from all *impure* activities. Public pledging activity, however, appears less a factor in maintaining sexual abstinence than a private pledge that more accurately reflects adolescents' personal attitudes, beliefs, and intentions regarding sexual intercourse (Bersamin et al., 2005). When comparing the sexual behaviours of pledgers to non-pledgers with similar beliefs regarding religion, sex, and birth control, there seems to be no protective factor in the pledging itself (Rosenbaum, 2009). Personal beliefs are more predictive of delayed sexual activity, itself a factor in sexual flourishing, than is the act of public pledging.

In a longitudinal follow-up study of the attitudes and behaviours of abstinence pledging adolescents that incorporates the phenomenon of identity movements, pledgers did delay intercourse, particularly among younger adolescents (the average delay ranged from 27 to 38 months, depending on the demographic group; Bearman & Bruckner, 2001). However, interesting social predictors colour the profiles of pledgers, their identification with the movement, and the environmental factors affecting the success of the pledge movement. First, the more pubertally developed, cognitively able, and experienced at dating an adolescent is, the less likely that he/she will pledge: "pledgers tend to be more religious, from more normative backgrounds, and less physically developed than their non-pledging peers" (Bearman & Bruckner, 2001, p. 909). Second, the more effectively the pledging movement creates a community of identity through, for example, the use of various pledging paraphernalia (e.g., pledge rings, bracelets, books), the more successful the pledgers will be at maintaining abstinence. Individual public pledgers living outside of a visible pledging community are less successful at maintaining abstinence by virtue of the pledge alone. Finally, the pledging effect has a threshold of about 40 percent; once a community of pledgers reaches approximately 40 percent of the entire population (e.g., students in a particular school), then the identity effect collapses and the protective factor of the pledge begins to decline. The pledge identity requires an element of non-normativity for its success: "the community is effective only if it has self-conscious recognition, which presumes minority status" (Bearman & Bruckner, 2001, p. 901).

The success of delayed intercourse for adolescent females is clearly a benefit of the pledging phenomenon, yet this benefit seems to be lost when it comes to the transmission of sexually transmitted infections (STIs). In a third-wave follow-up to their previous study, Bruckner and Bearman (2005) undertook a comparison examination of rates of STIs among pledgers and non-pledgers. Although pledgers delayed their sexual debuts about two to three years longer than their non-pledging peers and married younger than their non-pledging peers, most did eventually engage in premarital vaginal intercourse. Whether married or not, however, pledgers contracted STIs at about the same rate as non-pledgers. Despite having fewer sexual partners and fewer opportunities for sexual intercourse, pledgers test positive for STIs as consistently as non-pledgers. Although abstinence as an ideal for premarital sexual activity seems to work to reduce sexual risk among early adolescent pledgers, it cannot alone be considered an effective strategy for promoting lifelong flourishing and sexual health.

Norms, values, and religious beliefs do affect sexual decision-making among adolescents, yet the social context in which the values and beliefs exist also contributes to their efficacy in promoting sexual health. The realities of community, nonconformity, identity, and relational development influence the ways in which adolescents identify and integrate social and parental values and norms into their own structures of meaning. Knowing that adolescents are strongly committed to exploring their identities in relation to their parents, community, and peers means that adult attempts to inculcate the norms, values, and beliefs of existing social groups into young people can be tricky. Although, as adults, we might have insight and wisdom into the benefits of sexual abstinence among early adolescents, for instance, articulating that insight and wisdom to them in a meaningful way requires interrelational respect, attention to social factors, and a long-term commitment to human sexual flourishing. A promulgation of rules and expectations for sexual behaviour is no guarantee of respect for and a capacity to maintain those rules and expectations.

What a girl wants: The pleasure and danger of desire

One final factor pivotal in the healthy sexual development of adolescent females is sexual desire; a seemingly internal emotional experience of sexuality, desire is actually shaped by the socio-political context in which it is experienced. The importance of the phenomenon of desire in adolescent females' sexual perceptions and experiences warrants its consideration at length, here in its own section. The politically charged discussion of desire in adolescent females is reminiscent of the ways in which females' sexualities have been rendered taboo and dangerous in the evolution of Western culture, and in theological sexual ethics. Its extensive consideration here introduces the parallel dearth of engagement with female sexuality in the evolution of theological discourse. The need for a sexual theology that is more attentive to female sexualities is evidence of the importance of this lack of representation: correcting this lack forms the substance of my final discussion.

In 1988, Michelle Fine critiqued the typical American sexual education experience as perpetuating an anti-sex and victimizing account of adolescent female sexuality. Countering the discourse of victimization in sexual education, Fine identified what she termed the "missing discourse of desire" with regard to girls' sexuality. By focusing sex education solely on the negative outcomes of (hetero)sexual activity, the curricula were, by default, excluding discourse about the inherently positive character of sexuality in general. In so glossing over the possibility that adolescent sexuality might be more ambiguous in its experience than merely negative, many protective factors for adolescent females' healthy sexual development were lost. Fine then proposed that a discourse of desire become central to sexual education and, in particular, to sexual education among adolescent females.

In 2006, almost twenty years after her initial proposal, Fine returned to sexual education programs in the United States. She and Sara McClelland (2006) investigated the impact of abstinence-only, nationally funded sexual education programs on adolescent sexual development and health. Having found little progress with regard to the implementation of a discourse of desire, and having found evidence to suggest that the people most negatively affected by abstinence-only education and subsequent policies are those young people already socially marginalized (e.g., lesbian, gay, bisexual, queer, immigrant, undocumented, and women with disabilities), Fine and McClelland proposed a more refined take on desire as a "friendly amendment" to Fine's 1988 essay (2006, p. 300). They suggest a "framework of *thick desire*"—a recognition of the multiplex factors that shape adolescent females' experiences of desire—to address the missing discourse of desire in its own environment: that is, to understand the broader context in which females' sexual desire is situated.

Sexual desire is one of a number of desires that capture the attention of young people, including the desire to be socially, politically, and intellectually engaged in ways that invite meaning and value into their lives. Young people desire to contribute to and receive from social and economic systems respectful of their personhood and dignity. And they desire to envision a place for themselves that encompasses their past, facilitates their present, and nurtures their future well-being (Fine & McClelland, 2006). Most notably, Fine and McClelland are committed to exploring *thick desire* in the "embodied intersections" where young women and girls live: in their racial, gendered, economic, social, and political situations, which yield sexual experiences that are at once pleasurable and dangerous. Like Traina's (1999) thesis that any adequate ethical consideration of women's experiences must start within a *thick telic anthropology* that provides a preferential option for females in the broader circumstances of their actual lives, Fine and McClelland's thesis posits that any adequate sexual education for adolescent females must address their thick desire within a contextual analysis of their embodied sexual realities. Recognizing the politics that undergird sexuality education in the United States, Fine and McClelland (2007) suggest that abstinence-only sexuality education (or any other model that limits females' sexual realities) does, in fact, more harm to females than good.

Although Fine and McClelland's return to the discourse of desire found American sexuality education wanting, numerous researchers (particularly feminist and female scholars) have taken up the task of investigating the reality of adolescent females' sexual desires in the wake of Fine's 1988 identification of the missing discourse of desire. Deborah Tolman's (2005, 2002a, 2000, 1994) extensive attempts to capture the voices of adolescent females in their expression of sexual desire have nudged our discussions of female adolescent sexuality into a more positive framework. Responding to an historical construction of adolescent female sexuality as problematic and corresponding research focusing on behaviours and outcomes, Tolman (2002b, 1999) and other researchers (Harris, 2005; Impett, Schooler, & Tolman, 2006; Smiler, Ward, Caruthers, & Merriwether, 2005) are attending to a broader, more contextual construction of adolescent girls' sexualities. In exploring female adolescent sexual desires, recent research attests to the ambiguity of sexuality, sexual experience, and adolescent sexual development.

First, sexual desire among adolescent girls is complex in and of itself. For females in general, sexual desire has historically been constructed as their sexual desirability to males. The gendered social construction of femininity "encourages girls and women to be desirable but not desiring" (Tolman, 2002a, p. 115). In such an historical context, girls who have internalized their own objectification as desirable to males tend to associate their own desire with their desire to please males, because prominent social gender constructs consider female sexual desire anathema. In its most blatant expression, the objectification of the desirable sexual adolescent female is located in the commodification of female sexuality in an economy of market profit. Taken one step further, when a discourse of adolescent female sexual desire *is* articulated, it is also vulnerable to being co-opted into the market economy:

> Images and discourses of young women's sexual desire are commodified and sold back to them through fashion, beauty and lifestyle products, music and accessories. In this way, the articulation of the missing discourse of desire has enabled the constitution of young women as consumer citizens, and at the same time it produces them as new kinds of desiring subjects of, and desirable objects for, (hetero)-sexual consumption. (Harris, 2005, p. 40)

The discourse of sexual desire among adolescent females is as potentially confounding as its silence. When eliciting a discourse of desire, it is important to ensure a safe space for its elucidation and a welcoming social context for its expression (Harris, 2005).

Second, the complexity of articulating adolescent female sexual desire highlights its social construction. Examining the role of gender in the construction of sexual desire finds "femininity" itself can be a barrier to the sexual health of adolescent females (Tolman, 2002a, 2002b, 1999; see also Averett, Benson, & Vaillancourt, 2008). Placing gender assumptions that diminish females' capacity and agency in all realms of health at the forefront of her interpretive framework, Tolman recognizes that social heteronormativity, in turn, places females at a disadvantage regarding sexual desire: sexual females are perceived dichotomously as either virgins (non-desiring) or whores (desiring). This dichotomy places females who have internalized gender femininity in a double bind. If they do not acknowledge their own sexual desire, they are by default assumed to be the object of male sexual desire. If they do acknowledge their own sexual desire, they are negatively stigmatized outside of dominant social roles. Because adherence to prescribed gender roles can be harmful to adolescent females' sexual development, their automatic identification with "femininity" may, in fact, hinder and harm their healthy sexuality (Impett, Schooler, & Tolman, 2006; Tolman, 2002a & 2000).

The gap between "want" and "get" in sexual satisfaction is one manifestation of the social construction of gender and females' inability to articulate their sexual desires, a disparity most prominent in heterosexual sexual encounters (Tolman, 2002a). Although popular social discourse might suggest that females' sexual agency has progressed significantly into the twenty-first century, the gendered realities of female sexual desires still prevail in Western cultures. In her exploration of the "gap between desired and lived heterosexual relationships in the twenty-first century," Sieg (2007) finds that females are still willing to accept the deferral of their own desires for the fulfillment of their male partners' desires. And, females accept this situation based on a common assumption of male–female relationship and socially constructed gender roles: that males cannot control their sexual desires and thus must have their needs and wants met, regardless of females' needs and wants. This assumption, the "male sexual drive discourse" (Phillips, 2000, pp. 57–61), "tells us that men possess a natural sexual drive that is inherently compelling and aggressive in its quest for fulfillment" (p. 58). This discourse privileges male sexual desire to the detriment both of women's sexual fulfillment and their safety, insofar as it suggests that the male sexual drive must be satisfied, regardless of females' satisfaction, even to the point of abuse or violence. By suppressing a discourse of female sexual desire at the behest of social constructions of gender, females stand a diminished chance of experiencing their own sexual pleasure as normative and, indeed, even natural.

Finally, adolescent females' experienced ambivalence regarding the expression of sexual desire is notable. In a social context that, historically, has declared female sexual desire suspect and unpalatable (Phillips, 2000; Tolman, 2002a), females have grown to struggle with both the danger and pleasure of their own sexuality. In close examination of the narrative accounts of young females' experiences of sexuality and sexual expression, while an emerging female discourse of desire does exist, there exists no corresponding discourse of male accountability regarding actual sexual expression (Phillips, 2000, pp. 76–78). In the gendered reality of female sexuality, the expression of desire is precariously perched on the construct of male sexual privilege: females know that the expression of their desire is concomitant with danger to self and social risk.

Such risk and danger are made manifest in the ambivalence around wanting and not wanting sex, and consent and coercion to sex. The ambivalence that accompanies heterosexual interaction, and the motives for both wanting and not wanting sex, yields complex feelings in young people: arousal, attraction, guilt, fear, harm to image, enhancement of image, and fear of pregnancy, to name a few (Muehlenhard & Peterson, 2005, p. 17). Sex can be unwanted and consensual, or wanted but not consensual; the olio of feelings that young people experience and report regarding sexual desire indicates that a discourse of desire cannot be removed from a discourse of vulnerability. Qualitative and quantitative studies find that, for adolescent females, ambiguity colours their accounts of sexual desire and expression. In particular, sexual violation predicts for more disembodied accounts of sexual activity, and notably lower accounts of ensuing sexual pleasure (Tolman & Szalacha, 1999).

For females with same-sex desires, however, the ambiguity differs. Studies of girls' narrative accounts of same-sex sexual experiences suggest the pleasure and danger of sexual desire directly conflict with the heteronormative social reality in which they are experienced (Thompson, 1995; Tolman, 2002a). Unlike girls' accounts of heterosexual encounters, lesbian experiences focused more on the pleasure of the encounters themselves (as sexually satisfying, orgasmic, and mutual) and the danger of the social context (as non-normative and cause for alarm): "Orgasms—as rare as hen's teeth in the heterosexual narratives—were reported in every lesbian account. Only girls who had been with men initially saw orgasm as a feat" (Thompson, 1995, p. 184). For these lesbian girls, the expectation for sexual activity was, ultimately, pleasure.

The danger that lesbian girls experience in their sexual encounters is more commonly associated with social expectations of heterosexuality.

While it might seem as if girls who feel desire for girls or both girls and boys are somehow exempt from the institution of heterosexuality, in fact they stand in a very different and threatening relationship to it, by violating its most core principle: that we are, by nature, attracted to the opposite gender only. Like other women who do not enter into the socially sanctioned heterosexual relationship—women who are single, divorced, or widowed, or nuns—these girls have an "uncontained" sexuality that heightens social anxiety and thus instigates violent reactions.... While true in some sense for all adolescent girls, girls who desire girls instigate intense alarm. They commit a double violation: they feel sexual desire, and it is for girls. (Tolman, 2002a, pp. 184–85)

Unlike girls who desire heterosexually, the danger that lesbian girls experience is less likely to come from within the intimacy of the relationship than from external social norms and their own need, in expressing their desires, to contravene heteronormativity. For adolescent females, regardless of the objects of their desires, there exists a tension between what they wish to experience and what they actually do experience. The pleasure and danger of sexual desire are bound up in a social understanding of adolescent female sexuality.

Adolescent females' experiences of sexual desire plot a course of both danger and pleasure—careful ambivalence. Any reduction of sexual desire to either pleasure or danger is a misrepresentation of females' own experiences, and potentially more confounding to the girls themselves. Their struggles with "the constructed concepts of adulthood, agency, danger, and desire" exist fully immersed in a society that is, itself, wary of female sexuality (Phillips, 2000, p. 83). Coupled with social ambivalence of female sexuality in general, adolescent girls are also in the midst of the broader developmental realities of adolescence. Remembering the interactive components of adolescent development (i.e., biological, neurological, personal, and social), adolescents experience burgeoning sexuality in concert with their holistic movement toward adulthood. And because that development is ongoing, they are both drawing from their own experiences to grow as individuals and attending to the social realities that would have them flourish and be relationally capable. The confounding factors of growth spurts, neural inefficiencies, relational challenges, and their transitional status as no-longer-children but not-yet-adults, combine with sexual desire to create a whirlwind of adolescent ambiguity; danger and pleasure are intertwined.

Phillips's (2000) study presents the voices of young, socio-politically astute, feminist women as they articulate their experiences of female sexual desire. Most striking about their accounts is their constant negotiation between seemingly dichotomous experiences that are conflated realities of their sexual desires. As Phillips understands them, these negotiations represent strategies of both recognizing and acting on their own sexual desires, and actuating safety in potentially threatening circumstances. In this manner, females maintain heteronormative male sexual privilege (and are mindful of the social ambiguity of their part in that) while attending to their own desires. Phillips recounts narratives wherein females manipulate their experiences of vulnerability as a means of "damage control" when circumstances are beyond their control. Some of these narratives include: "stroking egos" (ensuring males' sexual egos are not bruised and do not trigger a "ballistic" response), "mastering the male body" (ensuring one's control over the outcome of a sexual encounter), "trying to like it" (attempting mentally to reconstruct a violent, out-of-control sexual encounter), or "hoping he'll notice" (feigning exhaustion to exit a "boring" or overdrawn sexual encounter) (Phillips, 2000, pp. 136–48). In each of these circumstances, the females' own sexual desires are deferred to accommodate the males' sexual experience. Also, many females are loathe to identify their own experiences as abuse, battering, rape, or assault, even though they are quick to recognize them in the experiences of other females. Not wanting to self-identify in the role of sexual victim, these women often go to great lengths to resist the naming of abuse, to take some responsibility for males' behaviours, and to construct strategies for coping with the reality of danger and pleasure in the expression of their sexual desires.

Stories accounting for female sexual desire are not framed exclusively by the multi-faceted forms of danger. The ambiguity of sexual desire also indicates concomitant experiences of pleasure and fulfillment. For example, accounts by both Thompson (1995) and Tolman (2002a) of lesbians' and sexually self-aware females' sexual experiences recall pleasure and desire. Investigation into adolescent females' desires points to a heartening expression of sexual pleasure among some of them. While recognizing the danger of the social context of their desire, there are still girls who chose purposefully to act upon and find safety in the expression of their sexual desire. Noting the dilemmas of desire they experienced in negotiating social expectations of female sexuality and their own subjective desire for sexual pleasure, both lesbian and straight girls who were adamant about their expectations of desire and fulfillment generally expressed a healthy sense of themselves and the parameters for their sexual flourishing (Tolman, 2002a, pp. 118–65). The girls who have refused to succumb to a heteronormative construction of male sexual privilege, in particular, have figured out that they have the power to refuse to care, and have chosen not to care, *because* they understand and reject the inequity of a system that gives desire and entitlement to boys and keeps it from girls. They make what is a risky choice to stand apart from the institution of heterosexuality. They use their knowledge and affirmation of their own bodies to defy categories that are meant to keep them out of relationship with themselves and with other girls. They will not enact this form of social control by regulating themselves or policing other girls. (Tolman, 2002a, pp. 164–65)

These girls are aware of their bodies, and incredulous that sexual pleasure within sexual interactions would not be an expectation for all females. In voicing their personal commitment to equity of both desire and fulfillment in sexual encounters (most pointedly, with males), these females are cognizant of the social barriers to their sexual agency and capable of defining their own parameters of pleasure.

A compelling factor for these females is the reality that most of them had little or no capacity to locate their own dilemmas of desire within the broader social construction of sexual relationships (Tolman, 2002a). This dearth of capacity seems mired in the lack of appropriate and meaningful conversations about their embodied sexualities with one another, and/or with mature adult women. The unshared wisdom of preceding generations of females about their sexual desire leaves an efficacy gap in our attempts at sexually educating young females. On many levels, the norms set out for moral behaviour of adolescent females have been inattentive to their real, embodied experiences of an ambivalent, thick, sexual desire. And, while it is likely that these girls are not the first to have experienced ambivalence about their burgeoning adolescent sexualities, we have chosen in Western culture to persist in a curious lack of meaningful engagement.

Yet, it seems clear that a dialogue about adolescent female sexual desire could work positively to provide girls with a sense of sexual agency, and the capacity to choose or refuse sexual activity based on their own embodied experiences. When females construct their sexual expressions around their own hopes for pleasure, intimacy, and satisfaction, they are differentiating between their own experiences of desire and the experience of being desirable to others. In so differentiating, they have the power to direct their own sexuality toward long-term sexual health, as evident in sexual autonomy, positive and intimate relationships, sexual pleasure, and physical health, among other indicators. Further, to affirm adolescent female sexual desire as socially normative, and personally and relationally acceptable, is to

diminish the heteronormative assumption of male privilege in sexual relationships. At a practical level, this shift in understanding provides a safer
social environment for female same-sex desire and expression, and a safer
interpersonal environment for female opposite-sex desire and expression.
The recognition of adolescent female sexual desire, therefore, contributes
to the sexual flourishing of adolescent females in both practice and theory.

And so, a positive framing of adolescent female sexuality is needed in
order to actuate the potential benefits of acknowledging and accepting
female sexual desire. In the context of a heteronormative social environment that has silenced discussion of female sexuality in general, and adolescent female sexuality in particular, the existing dialogue deficit among
females of all ages has limited our capacity to teach, mentor, and accompany adolescent females in their sexual development (Tolman, 2006).
Openness to the realities of adolescent sexuality, as a matter of course, has
the potential to create a positively focused understanding of adolescent
female (and male) sexual development.

> If one considers the end point of adolescent sexuality development
> to include the incorporation of the pleasures of sexuality—physical,
> emotional, relational—along with awareness of the vulnerabilities of
> sexuality into one's sexual self-concept—then we include pleasure,
> passion, mutuality, safety, embodiment, agency, experiencing emo-
> tions, and vulnerability as developmentally expected for both girls
> and boys, expanding in tandem (perhaps with deepening intimacy)
> through adolescence. (Tolman, 2006, p. 86)

SUMMARY

Researchers, scholars, and educators advocating on behalf of adolescent
females in the positive and pleasurable development of their sexualities are
currently navigating the ambiguities of female sexuality. The integrated
consideration of what factors contribute to positive adolescent female sexual
development stands to benefit adolescent girls in their sexual desires and
sexual experiences, and in their long-term sexual flourishing. By addressing
the dynamic interaction and evolution of physiological (including neurological), psychological, and social factors contributing to sexual development, I
am positioned to provide a theological account of sexual flourishing among
adolescent girls. To frame female sexuality positively, such a theological
account must be rooted in an account of female sexual pleasure. To assume
a preferential option for female sexuality and sexual pleasure in Christian

sexual theology is to disrupt the historical silence of the female bodies of evidence in the Church. The following chapter will integrate the preceding data within a feminist natural law framework, aiming to construct a robust sexual theology appropriate to adolescent females. The criterion of adequacy for a normative sexual theology will be adolescent female sexual flourishing.

CHAPTER EIGHT

GIRLS AND GOD: ADOLESCENT FEMALES AND A SEXUAL THEOLOGY OF FLOURISHING

OH. MY. GOD. THEOLOGY, SEX, AND ADOLESCENT FEMALES

Seeing the terms "theology," "sex," and "adolescent females" together in one phrase is unusual in theological discourse. The gist of this project, however, is precisely to explore the possibilities that arise from introducing discrete discourses pertaining to each of these concepts. So far, the various realms of theological anthropology, natural law, feminist natural law, feminist theory, sexual theology, adolescent female development, sexuality, experience, and context have all come to bear upon this articulation of a sexual theology accounting for adolescent females.

In this chapter, I address female sexual realities in general, and adolescent female realities in particular. Recounting some characteristics of female sexual flourishing within a feminist natural law framework situates the content of an appropriate sexual ethic that accounts for adolescent females. Ultimately, I outline both prerequisites for female sexual flourishing and some normative content for a theological sexual ethic. These last two endeavours are the culmination of the interdisciplinary dialogue undertaken throughout this project.

AN ACCEPTABLE LEVEL OF ECSTASY: FEMALE SEXUAL PLEASURE

Christian theology has, historically, focused disproportionately on the negative aspects of female sexuality and expression; recalling the dualistic accounts of human anthropology that have coloured the evolution of the Christian tradition, it is not surprising that positive accounts of female sexuality did not explicitly make their way into sexual theologies until the twentieth century. When women began, as a matter of course, to enter the academy and the discipline of theology, they consistently observed that sexual theology bore the biases of patriarchy and misogyny (Andolsen, 1996). Feminist theologians began to counter an almost two-thousand-year dearth of women's recorded experience in Christian theology with a systematic preferential option for the stories of women, recovering accounts of women in scripture and in the Judeo-Christian intellectual tradition. With a hermeneutic of suspicion, these recovered accounts led to the realization that, like Fine's (1988) missing discourse of desire in sexuality education, there was a missing discourse of sexual pleasure and fulfillment for/of females in theological discourse. Feminist theologians, instead, uncovered a long history of ambivalence toward, and often vilification of, female sexuality, and a general ignorance about female sexual experience (Andolsen, 1996; Jung, 2000).

Feminist attempts to fill the lacunae have emerged slowly. Encountering, by turns, hostile and benevolent sexisms within Christian Churches, women have been addressing the methodology, procedure, and content of Christian sexual ethics with a preferential option for females' sexual experiences (e.g., Blodgett, 2002; Cahill, 1996 & 1985; Farley, 2006; Gudorf, 1994; Heyward, 1989). These emerging theologies provide a glimpse into an adequate theological ethic that is attuned to adolescent female sexuality. They also highlight a lack of exploration of the goodness of sexual pleasure within traditional, historical sexual theologies. This lack obtains most profoundly to female realities, simply by dint of the exclusion of female experiences in the development of sexual theology.

Speaking generally of the Christian theological tradition, William Stayton points out numerous Western cultural barriers to the "development of a creative theology for sexual pleasure" (1996):

1. the "sexual traumatization" of Western [perhaps North American?] culture by the contrasting exploitative and commercial social presentation of sexuality and the "anti-sex" Church presentation of sexuality;
2. the valuation of sexual ignorance—for example, abstinence-only sexual education;
3. the secrecy of sexual desire and pleasure by their relegation to the realm of mystery; and
4. the devaluation of sexual pleasure by the Church. (pp. 342–44)

Stayton responds to these barriers by returning to a biblical value structure that is focused on the integral nature of human persons in relationships. Rather than limiting sexual pleasure to the procreative and, at times, projecting anti-sex attitudes in response to the commercialization of sexuality, he suggests that theology locate sexual pleasure within the context of the human capacity to reflect divine love in relationship. That we are capable of experiencing beautiful, humbling, and whole moments of sexual ecstasy with another is a blessing of God's grace in the union of spirit and flesh. In his effort to deconstruct barriers to a Christian sexual theology that is attentive to, and welcoming and nurturing of, sexual pleasure, Stayton proposes renewed attention to the gift of relationship to self, others, and God that may be nourished in pleasurable sexual experience. This proposal invites the privileging of female sexual experience in a feminist sexual theology; it welcomes sexual experiences of pleasure that have traditionally been absent from the development of theology.

The Roman Catholic Tradition once found redemption for sexual activity only in its link to procreation, and it continues currently to link procreation and unity inextricably in sexual expression. Each act of marital sexual intercourse must be physically open to both the possibility of procreation—meaning no artificial contraception, for example—and the union of the couple—meaning, for instance, no artificial reproductive technologies (Paul VI, 1968). The theology supporting this teaching and its subsequent development is situated within the patriarchal and hierarchal structures of the Church that exclude females and female sexual experiences (Andolsen, 1996; Gudorf, 1994; Jung, 2000). These teachings ostensibly reflect a male-oriented coital experience linking orgasm (pleasure/unity) to ejaculation (procreation). Because female sexual pleasure (regardless of whether or not orgasm is achieved) is by no means linked to male ejaculation or, for that matter, to penile–vaginal intercourse, females' experiences of sexual pleasure are absent from the ethical construction of morally acceptable intercourse.

Although, in typical situations, the procreative aspect of sexual intercourse is available to females, pleasure may not be. The unitive aspect of sexual intercourse for females is reduced to physical participation, irrespective of any concomitant manifestations of unity, like pleasure, intimacy, mutuality, or trust (Jung, 2000, p. 28). Ironically, while procreativity (which is located in the female capacity for pregnancy) has been very much privileged in the history of Christian sexual theology, females' menstruating and reproducing sexual bodies, and any pleasure deriving therefrom, have been considered suspicious, when considered at all (Andolsen, 1996). As noted above, such suspicion of menstruation is witnessed in the Western social construction of the adolescent female experiences of menarche and menstruation, whereby the Church and society maintain menstruation to be a hidden hygienic crisis.

Contemporary feminist theologians are now recreating sexual theology mindful of the complexity and ambiguity of female sexuality and female sexual experiences, and are explicitly exploring the moral significance of female orgasm (Gudorf, 1994; Jung, 2000; Pellauer, 1994). The corrective for a lack of female experience in theological accounts of human sexuality lies not only in its identification, but also in more adequate accounts of female sexual experiences. Female pleasure and orgasm in sexual theology is only adequately represented with females' own accounts of pleasure (physical, emotional, spiritual, sexual) and orgasm. Themes related to the experience of orgasm, such as presence, sensations, ecstasy, vulnerability, power, and uncertainty (Pellauer, 1994, pp. 154–58), suggest ways in which theologians can consider what female sexual pleasure means within a foundational or experiential theological sexual ethic. Gudorf (1994) and Jung (2000) suggest that mutual sexual pleasure ought to be *normative* in theological sexual ethics; although sexual pleasure cannot be the only norm of ethical sexual expression, its introduction is certainly a fresh element in Christian theological thought. Such proposals stem from a conviction of the goodness of the female sexual body, regardless of its participation in procreation.

Toward the goal of explicitly incorporating female sexual pleasure into the content of sexual theology, feminist theology counters the official Roman Catholic opposition to masturbation by advocating its promotion of sexual pleasure and delight for females. Although official teaching allows for developmental factors in its moral judgment of masturbation, a narrowly understood male-centred sexuality still defines its moral character; in effect, masturbation is an "intrinsically and gravely disordered action" (except when culpability is mitigated in cases of affective immaturity, anxious obsession, addiction, or social pressure), because sexual pleasure is dissociated from procreative capacity (*Catechism*, 1995, no. 2352). What seems to inform this teaching is an assumption that sexual pleasure will, by default, be achieved within heterosexual marital sexual intercourse, open to procreation. While this is generally true for heterosexual males who marry, it is not necessarily so for females. Further, this assumes that masturbation is an action that exists solely for individual sexual pleasure, removed from the context of mutually satisfying sexual expression within a couple: it is selfish because disconnected from the possibility of procreation. However, if sexual pleasure were to be considered a good to be pursued toward sexual flourishing, and were female sexual pleasure considered seriously within a theological sexual ethic, then masturbation could be considered more self-interested (i.e., toward one's own best interest in light of one's communal and faith context) than selfish (i.e., inwardly focused to the exclusion of others' well-being). Shifting sexual ethics away from a practical emphasis on reproduction as the primary good pertaining to sexual expression toward its inclusion in a number of goods, such as pleasure, comfort, intimacy, or solace, could nurture the self-knowledge that facilitates sexual pleasure (self-pleasure or pleasure with a partner) that seems requisite for sexual flourishing. The female sexual self-knowledge that comes with masturbation and the exploration of personal sexual response patterns enhances both individual flourishing and relational intimacy (Gudorf, 1994, pp. 91–95; see also Jung, 2000).

Because sexual self-knowledge lends to sexual pleasure (both personally and relationally), masturbation is intimately linked to female sexual flourishing. Thus, a moral norm against masturbation detracts decidedly from the female capacity for sexual pleasure. Females who do not experience sexual pleasure from coitus are left with no sanctioned space to explore their own sexual pleasures, and no reason to believe that this is anything but their own problem. In the historical theological understanding of heterosexual intercourse, female pleasure (or lack thereof) is merely "an accident" of the action; it is not necessary for the function of male orgasm and ejaculation, and for the ensuing procreative possibilities (Jung, 2000). Theologically speaking, sexual pleasure is gender-biased toward males.

> It is peculiar that so few ethical discussions of sexuality take up female orgasm, let alone its problematic character or its importance to flourishing. Much more emphasis and lingering philosophical care has been spent on desire. This may be one of the distinguishing marks of patriarchy in sexual ethics: Men are able to take pleasure for granted in sex. Or perhaps they translate pleasure into desire.... The progress from desire to pleasure to ecstasy is precisely what women cannot take for granted in our society.... We do not have a language fully empowered and inflected with women's sexual experiences. (Pellauer, 1994, p. 161)

Orgasm plays an important role in female sexual flourishing (Pellauer, 1994), and human sexual pleasure and mutual delight are integral to human well-being and the human relationship with the Divine (Andolsen, 1996; Farley, 2006; Jung, 2000; Stayton, 1996). The gift of human sexuality is the expression of intimate relationship in which we have the capacity to experience the ecstasy of covenant with God via mutual interpersonal vulnerability. To move toward God is to encounter, in human experience, the possibility of flourishing in relational sexual grace. The Christian theological tradition has largely overlooked this capacity for sexual flourishing in favour of a procreative ethic and diminishment of sexual pleasure, particularly among females.

By extension, the traditional inattention to females' actual experiences of sexuality has also left the Christian community parched for a meaningful sexual theology for adolescent females. The complex negotiation of sexuality facing adolescent females (e.g., biological and neural development, menarche and menstruation, gender identity construction, socialization, objectification, sexualization, danger and pleasure, personal health, safety) requires that theologians cultivate a more robust sexual theology. More general comfort with meaningful conversation about sexuality and its context would also facilitate, certainly among females in the Church, a more authoritative mentorship role in their development. In this light, I address the substantive construction of a theological sexual ethic that is attentive to adolescent females' sexual realities in Western culture and useful for their healthy and meaningful sexual development.

Smells Like Teen Spirit: Adolescent Female Flourishing

The call to frame adolescent female sexuality positively in developmental psychological discourses is echoed in feminist theological accounts of female sexuality in general; meaningful dialogue between these two schools of thought can be based in human flourishing. Not to romanticize the human experience overly, it is noteworthy that human flourishing is a complicated enterprise. It requires attention to the concrete particular circumstances of each individual, the broader context in which he or she lives, and the complex interaction of each one with the other. While we can propose, speculate, and imagine what such flourishing might entail in theory, in practice it is a messy business.

People's real, concrete lives do not submit easily to the neatness of theory. The interaction of theory and practice must, therefore, progress lightly and with humility to allow for error in the elusive attainment of human goods. Such complexity is especially true when dealing with human sexuality. A loving and just ethic of sexuality accounting for adolescent females must tolerate ambiguity and the flux of the human spirit. When human flourishing is the crux of discourse on ethics, sexuality, and the developing person, it is necessary to allow for its thickness to emerge.

Is There Something I Should Know? The Thickness of Flourishing

Adopting flourishing as the central criterion for an adequate sexual theology, and allowing for its thickness, is effective in both feminist theology and adolescent sexual development. Traina (1999) proposes flourishing as the primary criterion for morality; to effect flourishing, the human agent is characterized by a thick, vague anthropology that assumes the embrace of God as its telos. Such an anthropology, necessary for theological regeneration, admits ambiguity and ambivalence in human relationships and understanding. Indeed, female flourishing relies on such ambiguity and ambivalence; departing from merely theoretical notions of equality or freedom and moving into the complexities of women's actual lives are prerequisites for truly free choices. Traina challenges the assumption that these prerequisites are already in place for females by listing their practical manifestations: "healthy bodies, healthy relationships, and a degree of economic and political security. Sexual and reproductive self-possession, as well as a social position secure enough to enable women truly to choose intercourse, childbirth, or parenting, are thus among the prerequisites for women's flourishing" (1999, p. 147). Thick human flourishing is complicated for women by persistent barriers to its basic prerequisites.

The call to recognize the thickness of human flourishing is echoed by Michelle Fine and Sara McLelland's 2006 revisitation of Fine's (1988) "missing discourse of desire" essay, in which they acknowledge adolescent female sexual desire as inherently shaped by the socio-political context in which it is experienced. Heteronormativity, male sexual privilege, and adolescent female sexual desire as anathema, all contribute to the tension of pleasure and danger that comes with experiencing and acting upon desire. Given that sexual desire is shaped by social realities, to flourish sexually requires not just attention to sexual desire itself, but to the ways in which sexual desire is monitored, regulated, and disparaged in both theological and social contexts. Recognition of the complexities of these contexts requires attention not just to the negative outcomes of adolescent female sexual expression, like unplanned pregnancy, STIs, or violence, but also to social privileging of male sexual pleasure, ignorance of female sexual pleasure, adolescent developmental realities, and assumptions of heterosexuality. To flourish sexually is, both theologically and developmentally, a complex and intriguing enterprise: it is thick.

Adolescent females experience the desire to engage sexually parallel to a host of desires for other engagement: intellectual, political, economic, and social (Fine & McClelland, 2006), which require publicly recognized and funded *enabling conditions* similar to *prerequisites* for flourishing:

[O]pportunities to: (a) develop intellectually, emotionally, economically, and culturally; (b) imagine themselves as sexual beings capable of pleasure and cautious about danger without carrying the undue burden of social, medical, and reproductive consequences; (c) have access to information and health-care resources; (d) be protected from structural and intimate violence and abuse; and (e) rely on a public safety net of resources to support youth, families, and community.

A framework of thick desire situates sexual well being within structural contexts that enable economic, educational, social, and psychological health. (Fine & McClelland, 2006, pp. 300–301)

The thickness of adolescent female desire is layered with the prerequisites for whole human flourishing. For a female to flourish sexually requires a renewed dialogue about social and religious perceptions of desire, pleasure, and the context within which each female lives. With respect for the complexity and thickness of sexuality, a feminist natural law framework invites interaction with adolescent female experiences in the renaissance of a theology of human sexual flourishing.

CALLING ALL ANGELS: SEXUAL THEOLOGY AND ADOLESCENT FEMALES

The explicit integration of adolescent female sexualities and experiences into sexual theology is both possible and desirable within a feminist natural law framework. Preceding chapters have addressed the theological and empirical data that is helpful in achieving such integration. Mindful of this data, I articulate prerequisites for adolescent female sexual flourishing and the norms by which sexual flourishing might occur. First, however, the ambiguous spiritual character of the Christian life warrants recollection, for this ambiguity is abundantly apparent in the Christian endeavour to live sexuality well.

A Hazy Shade of God: Ambiguity

The Christian theological enterprise is characterized by tension between what is already now (the immanent God, made manifest in the person Jesus Christ) and what is not yet (the transcendent God, to be known in beatitude). This tension characterizes not only the discipline of theology but the reality of human experience: we are complete when we rest in the heart of the Divine. The unfolding knowledge of sexual goods in the long history of human sexual experience indicates growth in the human capacity to recognize the patterns of God's grace in the gift of sexuality. If our telos is union with God, then we are simultaneously already now there and not yet arrived at both the individual and the social levels. Growth in understanding sexuality within the human community continues more adequately to reveal the subtleties of intimacy, power, pleasure, refuge, vulnerability, delight, and fruitfulness concomitant with sexual experience.

In our striving toward beatitude, our vehicle is human embodiment; perpetual growth toward the Divine takes place only in the reality of our bodies. And, although we would like our experiences of both our bodies and the Divine always to be pleasurable, in reality, they are not. Sexual intimacy is prone to be muddled and messy; bodily incapacity, emotional uncertainty, relational distance, confused intentions, or even cruel abuses indicate clearly that, whatever sexual relationships could be, they are not always so. Growing in wisdom and capacity to discern God's presence in the midst of such a muddle, we are vulnerable to the ambiguity both of sexual experience and intimacy with God: our limitations of faith, doubt, and despair, for instance. Yet, only through the ambiguous experience of authentic human interaction with self, others, and creation, is God's grace apparent. When human love, compassion, sorrow, or joy is reflected in the face of another, we meet God. When we experience our own bodily delight, we meet God. This is not, however, the whole of the human story. Too frequently, we experience the physical violence of another's anger, the embarrassment of bodily decay or disease, or natural destruction in a punishing environment, which may cause us to question the presence and love of the Divine. Embodied human experience is already now in the embrace of God, but not yet fully so.

The theological ambiguity of the Christian experience is writ large in human sexuality, its complexity known in the ambiguity of our experiences and its bodily manifestations. For instance, its positive manifestation of trust and intimacy witnesses to the inherent goodness of sexuality and the contextual goodness of sexual expression. Yet, its negative manifestation in the abuse of power and in violence is also witness to the ways in which sexuality and sexual expression can be used as means of oppression and diminishment. Neither is human sexuality definitively expressed in each body: individual attraction, sexed and gendered bodies, the interaction of these with one another, and interpretations of these phenomena are not uniform; there is uncertainty, confusion, or ambivalence toward social norms and first-hand experience of human sexuality. The tension between pleasure and danger in human sexual desire and the complexity of human sexual flourishing attest, in theological terms, to the Christian understanding of the slow, painstaking, yet ultimately hopeful revelation of God. Sexual expression can facilitate and deter human flourishing; the moral task at hand is to discern, among the expressions, which will do which.

Natural law discussions within the Roman Catholic theological tradition have attempted, in various ways, to clarify the morality of sexual expression, and have done so with varied success. Recalling Thomas Aquinas's natural law, there is a degree of tolerance in it for ambiguity that has not always been mirrored in successive discussions. Thomas iterates little content for natural law: he recognizes that human persons have varying capacities for practical wisdom and prudence (which one might never develop), and that situations and details will obscure or colour our moral reasoning. In this way, although we can speculate on universal moral truths, the more detailed the particulars in reality, the more difficult it is to discern those truths. Ethics and morality can be difficult.

Thomas's vague account of natural law is attentive to both the universal and the particular. Although human persons all have a capacity for practical moral reasoning in typical situations, we would be foolish to expect the degree of that capacity to be uniform for all human persons, regardless of circumstance. Further, what ought to be done in any particular circumstance is by no means a de facto conclusion. To reason and act well in practical moral situations takes time, experience, practice, attention, understanding, good judgment, and responsibility, all of which are substantial to moral development through actions; they are habits. Human understanding and wisdom are multi-faceted: they ebb and flow with continual movement. We reach our destinations, and yet the wise realize that the destination is not the goal. We might already be there, but we are still not yet. Habits can be both positive and negative, so that our virtues and vices can bring us closer to or farther away from God.

In traditional theological terms, this ambiguity is summed up in the tension between virtue and sin. Because our telos is the Divine, virtue and virtuous actions are necessarily those that are directed toward relationship with God. We can be wise, loving, just, and free only insofar as we ideally direct our lives toward communion with God. But we also have the capacity to sin. Virtue does not manifest itself fully at birth; rather, it requires growth in character, and skill in human moral reasoning and action. In so developing, we are humbled by our own inadequacies and growth in wisdom and integrity. We negotiate our freedom to act with our ultimate freedom in relationship with the Divine. We attend to our own sinfulness in the hope of ongoing growth in virtue and love (see Farley, 2006, pp. 240–44).

Such ambiguity in sexual moral decision-making can be acute in the burgeoning self of adolescence. This time of transition between childhood and adulthood signals the onset of the between times: the already-now sexual and the not-yet sexually mature. Adolescents are already and still developing the capacities that will facilitate their moral decision-making: physiological, neural, hormonal, spiritual, social, cognitive, and affective developments are colliding in the magical melee that is teen spirit. Depending on age, circumstance, and personal characteristics, adolescents will be variously thoughtful and stupid, adventurous and lazy, happy and sad, energetic and tired, polite and rude, chatty and brooding. They will also run the continuum of realities between each extreme. In short, they will surprise and delight, and disappoint and anger us. If looking in from the outside at adolescent realities is confusing and ambiguous, so too it must be from within. They are no longer children, but are still not adults: they are not yet wise to the ambiguity of human sexuality.

This ambiguity lies squarely in adolescents' negotiation of the transition time into adulthood. They must engage the complexity of what is already within their capacity in order to develop toward what is not yet firmly in place. For adolescents to mature and develop sexually, they must try, practise, and experience their sexual bodies. They must learn the skills of attention to desire, care of self and another, self and mutual pleasure, and responsible expression of sexuality, to edge ever closer to full flourishing in their sexualities and their lives.

Moral theological discourses have struggled with the general tensions of sexual ambiguity in the history and development of moral theology, variously vilifying, glorifying, and ignoring the human sexual body. This is where we encounter the wisdom of ambiguity. Attention to the tensions present in practical moral reasoning and prudence provides a cornerstone for understanding and accounting for diverse adolescent female sexualities in Christian theology. Attending to both the individual particular realities of each female, and the broader universal patterns for females in general, is proving a struggle. Sexual ethics often is lacking in usefulness for adolescent females, precisely because those same females are excluded methodologically, procedurally, and substantively from our discourses. Unyielding norms for sexual behaviour that are inattentive to the realities of adolescence and females are often both irrelevant and potentially harmful.

Given the thickness of female adolescent sexual desire and flourishing, and the historical exclusion of their experiences in Christian sexual theologies, feminist theoretical discourse is a helpful corrective to oppressive theologies imbued with patriarchy and misogyny. Addressing the particular lives of adolescent females in sexual theology requires first acknowledging and unravelling the patriarchal constructs within which theology has developed. Feminist theorists and feminist theologians have systematically deconstructed the heteronormative, and at times misogynist, characteristics of preceding generations' male-dominated scholarship. Attention to the particular, a hallmark of feminist theory, enables accounting for difference in sexual ethical theory and practice.

While attention to the particular has been a necessary development in theoretical and theological discourse, it has led to some consternation with regard to universally recognized rights and ethical standards against which we can declare some actions clearly wrong. One prominent example of moral hand-wringing as regards universal and particular norms, globally speaking, is over the practice of female genital cutting (female genital mutilation or female circumcision). The way in which one names this practice is likely to identify whether one views it as a culturally sanctioned activity over which external cultures have no moral sway, or as a universally maleficent practice that ought always to be denounced. Such an example highlights the need for feminist discourse to have some critical leverage for identifying and denouncing what might clearly be wrong. Traina's feminist natural law takes seriously the moral ambiguity that arises when considering the particular and the universal in females' lives (1999). Although willing to admit of normative sexual behaviour, her revisable universals are fluid enough to incorporate the particular lived realities of individual persons. With regard to adolescent female sexuality, a sexual theology constructed within such a framework would provide a tenuous recognition of both the dangers and pleasures inherent in sexual desire and expression.

WHAT A GIRL NEEDS: PREREQUISITES FOR ADOLESCENT FEMALE SEXUAL FLOURISHING

Prerequisites for sexual flourishing facilitate useful integration of the norms, and assume the previously mentioned prerequisites for thick female flourishing and sexual desire. This assumption situates adolescent females' sexual flourishing within the broader social, political, economic, educational, religious, and environmental contexts in which they live. There cannot be promotion of sexual flourishing that is inattentive to the concomitant existential realities of individual persons.

The first prerequisite for adolescent female sexual flourishing is an open social awareness and acceptance of the functioning female sexual body. It is insufficient to maintain menarche and menstruation as a covert reality that virtually all females experience but none are known to experience at any given time. And it is insufficient not to educate females about the fertility intrinsic to their sexual bodies. The current disconnection of the female reproducing body from the female sexual body diminishes the meaning of menstruation in the lives of girls and women, and reinforces an individualistic perception of menstruation as hidden and private. Although menarche and menstruation are private, they are also public in their social reception and interpretation, which are, to date, sorely stigmatizing. Current Western perceptions of female monthly bleeding, as distinct from female sexual attraction and expression, has led to the bifurcation of individual and social female sexual bodies. This bifurcation further leads to dissociation of the sexual female body from actual embodied females. Thus, Western culture perpetuates the objectification of female sexual bodies, the disconnection of fertile and sexual bodies, the premature sexualization of girls, and the commodification of female sexual desire.

At a theological level, acceptance of the integrated female sexual body can only be accomplished when theological discourse systematically reconciles the quizzical construction of the sexual female as virgin (non-desiring but procreative) and whore (desiring but non-procreative). Morally upstanding girls do not talk about or demonstrate their sexuality, so their virginal silence of desire meets the patriarchal requirement of silence in discourse about the female sexual body. Morally bereft girls might speak about and demonstrate their sexuality but are not fit to be mothers, so their whorish voices sit outside of the patriarchal discourse of sexuality in general. Their explicitly sexual, menstruating bodies are inappropriate for theological discussion. Within such a construction female bodies are denied the dignity of equal access to the Divine in sacramental life.[1]

The second prerequisite for sexual flourishing is explicit recognition not only that sexuality is inherently good and sexual expression is good, but also that sexual pleasure itself is good, that female sexuality itself is good, and that female sexual pleasure itself is good. In particular, these goods must be recognized even if they are physically separated from the possibility of procreation. The long-standing Roman Catholic theological tradition that offers tenuous acceptance to females has led to official sexual teachings that exclude female sexual pleasure. The privileging of male sexual pleasure in discourse around moral sexual activity has especially diminished adolescent females' sexual agency in heterosexual relationships. Further, such male privilege virtually denies the possibility of pleasurable sexual experience outside of penile–vaginal penetration. Female sexuality and sexual pleasure are not a modified male sexuality and sexual pleasure, which must be made explicit if sexual flourishing is to be nurtured in normative sexual expression.

The third prerequisite for sexual flourishing is the broad recognition that sexual development occurs within a communal context. Much of what facilitates and complicates our self-evolution into and within our sexuality is its interaction with the social context in which we sit. If adolescent females are to flourish in their sexual development, then there must be a broad consensus of community support for relational development, female sexual well-being and safety, sexual knowledge, and the beneficent possibilities of sexual interaction. When all sexual expression among adolescent females is viewed with suspicion, negatively framed, or silenced, girls learn early that their sexuality is dangerous and that they will be ostracized for non-normative sexual expression; that silence serves not to protect them sexually, but to isolate them. For any society to be supportive of healthy adolescent female sexual development, it must be indicated by adult comfort with addressing the topic. If parents, teachers, coaches, mentors, or leaders in the community refuse openly to address adolescent sexuality with candour and security, adolescents will follow suit. A prerequisite, therefore, of adolescent females' sexual flourishing is a social commitment to their healthy development.

The final prerequisite for adolescent females' sexual flourishing pertains most obviously to the sexed and gendered anthropological constructions persistent in official Roman Catholic teachings. For adolescent (and adult) females to flourish in their sexualities, particularly within the Roman Catholic context, the hierarchical Church must divest itself of anthropological formulations that diminish the fullness of females' humanity. In particular, the narrow anthropological assumption of gender complementarity that riddles contemporary Catholic teachings embodies gendered assumptions that conflate sex and gender. In so doing, the teachings promulgate a benevolent sexism that patronizes females and reduces their genius to reproduction and child rearing.

Insofar as magisterially articulated gender complementarity reinforces stereotypical gender roles, the Church continues to diminish female sexual agency with a deferral to feminine receptivity (in contrast to male initiation) and a negation of female sexual desire (in contrast to uncontrollable male sexual desire). Females' participation in the Divine image is predicated on their completion of males, since female bodies do not biologically reflect the body of Christ (see John Paul II, 1994). The construction of complementarity advanced within official Roman Catholic anthropology is, therefore, one that limits the capacities of both females and males, based on its adoption of sexual dualisms and gender.

If to flourish sexually includes having a sense of one's sexual agency and capacity for control over one's body, then to be slotted into a stereotypically feminine construction of virginal sexual procreativity would be the exact opposite of flourishing. Eradication of the sin of sexism, which is manifest in the oppressive relegation of females to stereotypical gender roles, is overdue. For females to have a sense of the gift from God that is their sexuality, they must be able to voice their perceptions and experiences that depart from the construction of complementarity; they must have the divinity of their actual sexual bodies affirmed. This divinity must also be recognized to exist not only in biologically complementary opposite-sex relationships but also in the varied sexualities within females' experiences. Enough empirical evidence exists to confirm that human sexual flourishing occurs outside imposed compulsory heterosexuality. Only when theological, anthropological discourse welcomes sex and gender roles that are more amenable to females' diverse experiences will adolescent females flourish sexually.

In meeting these prerequisites for a theological sexual ethic that accounts for the realities of adolescent females, we would, as a community, indicate social willingness and support for the creation of an environment of flourishing. In so doing, we would also indicate our willingness to entertain and instill a sexual ethic that permits ambiguity and tentativeness. Thus, the norms that would embody that ethic would be, simultaneously, essential and accidental, universal and particular, static and dynamic. This premise is a difficult rock upon which to build an ethic. Feminist natural law's tolerance for uncertainty and ambiguity, to negotiate the already-now and not-yet of human sexual understanding and morality, however, provides the ideal starting point for moral normativity.

WHAT'S A GIRL TO DO? A THEOLOGICAL SEXUAL ETHIC ACCOUNTING FOR ADOLESCENT FEMALES

One of the primary tasks of feminist theologians is to rethink sexual theology and ethics for a contemporary, post-modern culture. The underlying currents of patriarchy and misogyny within the Roman Catholic sexual theological tradition require systematic defusing in order for theology to be more relevant and helpful for adolescent females. Renewal of the tradition is buoyed with a spirit of love and fidelity to the revelation of God throughout human history. Accompanying women's contribution to contemporary theological discourse are accounts of the wisdom of the female body. These accounts, which voice females' sexualities, sexual desires, and sexual experiences, are revelation of the Divine hope for sexual flourishing. In these voices are the incarnation of females' sexual lives, and theologians are called to a normative account of what nurtures their sexual flourishing. This account, the content of a feminist natural law sexual ethic, is the articulation of a sexual theology accounting for adolescent females. Assuming the prerequisites for sexual flourishing outlined above, the following are six basic norms (or revisable universals) for an adequate sexual ethic.[2]

First is a normative understanding that personal sexual knowledge of one's body is a good. As evidence shows, when adolescent females (and others) know their own bodies as sexual, pleasing, and fruitful, they are better equipped to make sexual choices that will both protect and facilitate their own well-being. In this light, masturbation, as a means of sexual self-exploration, promotes female sexual flourishing. Thus, to declare masturbation inherently sinful ought itself to be considered sinful. Because this prohibition places females' (and males') sexual development and ensuing sexual health at risk, a reconsideration of its place in sexual theology is in order. To take adolescent females' sexual flourishing seriously in the Christian community, we must condone the factors that nurture their development. Masturbation is one such factor.

Masturbation among females further serves to diminish male sexual privilege in deliberations on morally acceptable sexual interaction. Evidence suggests that females who have masturbated and have an intimate understanding of their sexual bodies are more likely to experience sexual pleasure both alone and with a partner. More specifically, females are less likely to reach orgasm by penile–vaginal intercourse than they are by other means of stimulation. Promoting that aspect of sexual pleasure ought to be as normative as the promotion of male orgasm and ejaculation. Masturbation as normative recognizes the equal necessity of sexual pleasure for females and males. If the acceptance and promotion of sexual pleasure is prerequisite for flourishing, then knowing how to attain sexual pleasure will facilitate flourishing.

Mindful of adolescent females' sexual experiences, a second norm for sexual activity is the delay of heterosexual sexual intercourse. The later persons (especially females) debut sexually, and the more sexually mature they are when they do, the better are their chances for long-term sexual and personal well-being. Because heterosexual intercourse is imbued with the social realities of gender differentiation, objectification of the female body, male sexual privilege, and heteronormativity, this particular sexual activity is best delayed until there is a commensurate level of maturity to carry its ensuing implications. This reality has long been recognized by the Christian community in its normative understanding of sexual abstinence outside of marriage. To deal well with the implications of sexual activity, the partners must first have reached a level of respect both for their own selves, and for the other. Further, they must have a sense of personal pleasure that will inform their sexual experiences. Knowing the long course of neural, hormonal, affective, and social development through adolescence, it seems clear that persons are best able to integrate sexuality in later adolescence/early adulthood. This second norm is tied intimately to the first norm; self-knowledge of the sexual body promotes healthy delay of intercourse among adolescents.

A third normative aspect of ethical sexual expression is equity of power and appropriate vulnerability.[3] I refer to *equity* rather than *equality* because of basic differences that might occur between partners (e.g., disparity of physical strength); equality is not sufficient to describe the notions of mutuality and interdependence that ought to exist within an equitable relationship. Although chronological age, typically, will contribute to power differences that might occur in intimate relationships (a prominent factor accounting for abuse),[4] this is not necessarily the case. The sexual norm calling for equity of power and appropriate vulnerability insists that persons engaging in coupled sexual activity share relational power between them that is just and respectful. Consequently, appropriate vulnerability addresses the disparity of power, in any of its manifestations (i.e., physical, emotional, social, financial, etc.), that leads to oppressive or abusive relational inequity. Any sexual expression makes its participants vulnerable. At the level of ethical loving sexual expression, such vulnerability would be appropriate only insofar as equity of power and personal maturity yield a level of trust that facilitates flourishing and safety. This would clearly rule out of court directly violent or coercive acts such as rape, sexual assault, or sexual abuse.

Appropriate vulnerability and equity of power also exclude sexual activity between any persons whose relationship is clearly structured around the control, manipulation, or abuse of one partner over the other. Also, when a person in a position of power over another (e.g., a teacher, supervisor, or employer) initiates and/or undertakes a sexual (or otherwise intimate) relationship with that person (e.g., a student, subordinate, or employee), this cannot be ethically acceptable. The power differential between these two parties is such that one person will always be inappropriately vulnerable to the influence or control of the other. A norm that attends to the appropriateness of sexual vulnerability in the context of power in relationships is protective of the developmental maturation process that contributes to human sexual flourishing.

The fourth norm for sexual ethics follows from the previous norm dealing with power and vulnerability; partnered sexual expression must embody a mutual relationship. Such a mutual relationship will include a sense of reciprocal respect and dignity between partners. Sexual expression in such a mutual relationship will thus adhere to the minimum requirements that there is consent between partners[5] and that no intentional harm is done. Given that the current Western heteronormative social structure supports a tacit relational bias toward male sexual privilege, the attainment of mutuality in sexual expression is particularly difficult for adolescent females. Assuming the prerequisites for personal and sexual flourishing (the assumption of the goodness of both female sexual knowledge and female sexual pleasure) and the norm of personal sexual awareness, it is possible to envision a social conversion toward relational mutuality. Truly

to commit to female flourishing, we must also commit to sexual and relational mutuality as normative.

*A fifth norm for sexual ethics implies an intentional openness to fruitful-
ness in sexual expression, although this openness need not be physical.* Heterosexual sexual expression clearly has creation as one of its purposes.
However, that procreative possibility need not be normatively present in
every sexual expression. Rather, intentional openness to creative possibilities arising from sexual intimacy supports a broader understanding
of human sexual persons and acknowledges that not every act of sexual
intercourse will be potentially procreative. Christian wisdom has long
acknowledged that couples physically unable to have children, for a variety
of reasons, still behave morally when sexually active. Sexual intimacy in
such situations has value, regardless of its lack of procreative possibility.
The creative possibilities of physical expression here surpass mere physical
procreativity and heteronormativity. While mindful of the reproductive
possibilities and pitfalls that arise with heterosexual sexual intercourse,
they need not override the broader relational aspects of sexual intimacy.

Committing to being intentionally open to the creative possibilities of
sexual expression further recognizes the potential for same-sex partners to
engage in fruitful sexual sharing. Following the prerequisite divestiture of
a theological anthropology of complementarity, openness to sexual fruitfulness need not require that procreation be inherent in every sexual act.
When same-sex partners express the depth of a loving and mutual relationship sexually, such intimacy is capable of extending creatively, beyond
itself. Intentional openness to fruitful creativity in such cases reflects the
same intentional openness of heterosexual partners unable to procreate.

*Finally, sexual expression must entail commitment to self, to other, and to
God.* At its simplest, relational commitment serves to delay sexual intercourse, and such a delay promotes immediate and long-term sexual flourishing. Beyond the practical, however, is the spiritual: the divinity of the
sexual gift and the ways in which we see God in relationship with others and self. Such human relationship must envision some promise of the
future, some entrusting of a share of one's personal well-being to another.
Relational commitment provides a sense not just of momentary pleasure,
but also of continued development in flourishing. The security that commitment provides positively supports the psychological, physical, and
emotional outcomes of sexual activity, especially for females. Given the
disparity of interpretation of sexual experience between males and females
in general, but especially so among adolescents, commitment as normative
is particularly important in heterosexual relationships. Further, in recognizing a future orientation as normative for ethical sexual expression, we

attest in human relationships to the tension between what is already now, but not yet. Flourishing is not facilitated by individual experiences void of context. Rather, flourishing implies a past and a future into which this experience is woven: a context of meaning. To flourish, we require a sense of our place in the world that provides a modicum of security. Such relational commitment serves to insulate our sexual vulnerability through its promotion of trust and mutual respect.

These six norms for ethical sexual activity, which take into account the realities and experiences of adolescent females, hardly constitute the end of the discussion. Much investigation remains to be done regarding adolescent females, sexuality, theology, and flourishing. The layered reality of individual girls' experiences as both sexual and spiritual persons sits hidden beneath the weight of centuries of social construction. The discussion of adolescent females' sexual flourishing is in its nascence and normative proposals are, therefore, made with humility and dynamic openness. In God's renewed and ongoing revelation of herself in the world, we understand human sexuality more clearly as graced.

BRAVE NEW GIRL: SUMMARY

Within a feminist natural law framework, the sexual realities of adolescent females are methodologically and procedurally included in this proposed Christian sexual theology. While its normative content departs from official Roman Catholic teaching, this sexual theology still sits squarely within the Roman Catholic theological tradition. Its personalist approach to human sexual development, maturity, and relationships (mindful of Pope John Paul II), incorporates a secondary analysis of data, which makes it more relevant to adolescent females' experiences. That is, the morality of sexual expression is based upon individuals acting within their contexts and relationships with God and others, rather than upon the location of sexual expression in a person's particular state in life. While the proposal of such content in the form of prerequisites for the flourishing of adolescent females and the norms that accompany them are universally accessible, their application will still be concrete and particular in the lives of adolescent females. I submit this proposal, yet recognize that its very substance is tentative and revisable.

The Christian faith recognizes the human capacity for sin by way of inattention, stupidity, unreasonableness, imprudence, and indifference, amongst other means. The between-times experience of the Christian story acknowledges that, although we may see now what we ought to do, still we might not see it clearly. In beatitude, we will see all truth face-to-face, yet in our current circumstance, truth can seem vague (1 Cor. 13:12).

The tension of sin and grace colours moral reflection in Christian sexual ethics. This tension is particularly palpable in the lives of adolescents, who are experiencing the moral and developmental ambiguity between child-hood and adulthood. Given the realities proposed by current develop-mental studies, sexual theology must be mindful of the disparity of moral capacity between adolescents and adults. A social commitment (including the Church community) to mentor adolescents and nurture healthy sexu-alities is paramount in the formation of sexually mature Christian persons and integration of the elusive wisdom of the body.

The sexual theology that I propose is focused on the sexual (both individ-ual and social) realities of girls and women. This theology gives hermeneuti-cal preference to females' experiences of sexuality as a means of highlighting their particular questions in sexual morality. This hermeneutical privilege provides unique insight into the dearth of such engagement in the historical and traditional development of sexual theology. That acknowledgement or consideration of female sexual pleasure, for instance, is virtually absent from theological discourse, indicates that female perspectives have been largely irrelevant in the Christian tradition of sexual theology.

A theology that privileges female experiences, and those of adolescent females in particular, forwards an inclusive sexual theological discourse within the Roman Catholic tradition. Such inclusive discourse takes for granted the communal nature of faith development and learning. Recog-nition of the developmental realities of adolescence requires an ongoing discussion about adult mentorship in adolescents' sexual understandings. Their evolving capacity to integrate the various aspects of sexuality and sexual experience (i.e., cognitive, affective, spiritual, physical, relational) means that patience is required in the articulation and habitual enactment of sexual ethical norms.

Such articulation and enactment continues to require attention to and reaffirmation of the wisdom of the Roman Catholic theological tradition. Sexual theology cannot abandon the values ensconced in the tradition that have served and continue to serve us well: commitment, chastity, pru-dence, mutuality, maturity, gift, responsibility, dignity, relationship, and respect among them. In teaching and modelling these values, the Christian community invites children, adolescents, and adults to reflect prayerfully on the meaning and place of sexuality in their lives. To enhance the impact of these values on the lives of the faithful requires continual attention to and reiteration of their meaning in contextual, historically relevant reali-ties. Such work could include ongoing engagement in the lives of the faith-ful through reciprocal discourse, attention to empirical data, and prayerful reflection on the role of the Christian/Catholic Church in contemporary societies. In so doing, perhaps official and unofficial theological discourse could avoid the experiential gap that currently plagues Roman Catholic teachings with regard to sex, sexuality, and the lives of the faithful.

Finally, I do not consider this proposal definitive or complete. The explicit inclusion of adolescent females' sexual realities in sexual theological ethics merely marks one moment among many of awakening to this and other missing discourses that plague the history and tradition of Roman Catholic/Christian sexual theology and practice. All thought unfolds in the course of history, as witnessed by changing perceptions of justice, love, and human dignity over time. The evolution of sexual theology is located in human realities and contexts that shift and groan, all while remaining constant before God. As sexual theology unfolds, new questions for consideration will surface among future generations of faithful Christians. I look forward with hope to ongoing revelation of the Divine in sexual theologies, the questions that arise therefrom, and the flourishing that accompanies the answers.

NOTES

Chapter One

1 In response to Pope John Paul II's call for a new feminism—in contrast, one supposes, to the old, unsuitable feminism—numerous scholars have articulated a new feminist theology that serves primarily to bolster the anthropological and moral claims of John Paul II's theology of the body (e.g., Allen, 2006; for contrast, see Beattie, 2006).

2 The discussion of authority (particularly moral authority) and Roman Catholic teachings regarding sexuality has been inflamed in recent decades by the revelation of a global epidemic of child sexual abuse committed by members of the clergy. All levels of the hierarchical Church have been implicated not only in the perpetration of abuse, but also in the inept and scandalous handling of priests, victims, survivors, families, and the laity in general. Clearly, this reality has created a credibility gap for the Magisterium in promulgating authoritative sexual teachings to the laity. Further, it remains to be seen how the laity of the global Church perceive its authoritative teachings on the family and related matters (e.g., sacraments and divorced/remarried Catholics, birth control, same-sex marriage), which was the focus of an October 2014 Extraordinary Synod of Bishops, called by Pope Francis and its subsequent Ordinary Synod in October 2015.

3 The discussion of flourishing extends well beyond moral and ethical theory; it is prominent, for instance, in global development initiatives and political philosophy (Nussbaum, 2000, 1988). A brief survey of recent scholarly literature also finds discussion of flourishing within the areas of nursing and health care (Bunkers, 2010; Low, 2011; Taylor & Dell'Oro, 2006), technology (Poore, 2011), organizational strategy (Ghaye, 2010), psychology (Barber, Bagsby, & Munz, 2010), suffering (Hall, Langer, & McMartin, 2010), and education (Howell, 2009; Low, 2011).

4 A thorough history and development of the Aristotelian understanding of *eudaimonia* in Western philosophical thought is beyond the scope of this

work. There is by no means scholarly consensus on either moral theory in general or Aristotle's understanding of *eudaimonia*. The contemporary discussions of human flourishing that I address here provide a snapshot of current scholarship.

Chapter Two

1 Thomas (variously referred to as *Thomas* or *Aquinas*) wrote the *Summa theologica* (my primary source for his thought) during the years between 1267 and 1273. He applied the scholastic method of dialectic reasoning, and posing and responding to disputed questions, to explore issues of faith and reason. Throughout this work I refer to the translation undertaken by the Fathers of the English Dominican Friars (1947).

2 Regarding Thomas's understanding of historicity, Traina states: "Although Thomas clearly allows in theory for variation and change in practical moral conclusions, he just as clearly does not expect that the amplitude of their oscillations will be very large. Although his own culture was hardly ossified or ignorant of other societies—and his own theology was initially intellectually disruptive rather than pacific—his ideal was relative homogeneity. Making peace with the panoply of functioning sets of norms coexisting in the contemporary dynamic, plural global culture was a task he certainly did not envision. Nor did he anticipate the historicism that makes casuistry continuously necessary." And: "The bounds and conclusions of Thomas's own use of prudence...are thus very narrow. But because they leave small openings for innovation, they do not permanently mark the limits of prudence's range. And the wider the variation one admits in time and circumstances, the 'more the great commandments of love of God and of neighbor, the great principles of justice and charity'—rather than any specific set of concrete precepts—appear as the primary criteria of natural law's conclusions" (both citations: Traina, 1999, p. 69).

3 See, for example, Finnis, 1980; Grisez, 1965; Grisez, Boyle, & Finnis, 1987; and May, 2003, 1998.

4 In contrast, see Finnis's (1992) critique of historical consciousness in theology.

5 For a sustained critique of the confessional nature of the New Natural Law and, in particular, John Finnis's development of NNL in secular legal theory, see Bamforth and Richards (2008), who are most concerned with the conservative conclusions the NNL theorists reach regarding social issues pertaining to sexuality and gender.

Chapter Three

1 To this end, Margaret Farley proposes "norms for just sex" in her 2006 work, *Just Love: A Framework for Sexual Ethics* (pp. 216–32). Although the nuance of her discussion is diminished in this brief note, the articulation of her norms is still quite helpful. She proposes two norms based specifically on

autonomy, from within a principle-based ethic; four norms based upon a relational ethic; and one norm based upon a social ethic. The norms are:

1. Do No Unjust Harm (autonomy-based)
2. Free Consent (autonomy-based)
3. Mutuality (relationally-based)
4. Equality (relationally-based)
5. Commitment (relationally-based)
6. Fruitfulness (relationally-based)
7. Social Justice (socially-based)

Although Farley recognizes the precariousness of outlining norms for sexual relationships and expression, and the delicacy required in their application, still she proceeds. For "if sexuality is to be creative and not destructive in personal and social relationships, then there is no substitute for discerning ever more carefully the norms whereby it will be just" (Farley, 2006, p. 232).

Chapter Four

1 To avoid confusion between the collection of Pope John Paul II's Wednesday sermons entitled *The theology of the body* and the unified school of thought known as "theology of the body," the text will be capitalized and italicized when referring to John Paul's work. When referring to the school of thought, the text will be in a lower-case, regular font.

2 Excellent scholarly discussions on the body in the Christian tradition include *The body and society: Men, women, and sexual renunciation in early Christianity* (P. Brown, 1988), *Fragmentation and redemption: Essays on gender and the human body in medieval religion* (Bynum, 1991), and "Why all the fuss about the body? A medievalist's perspective" (Bynum, 1995).

3 The creation accounts in Genesis present a pre-lapsarian understanding of humanity (i.e., humanity in its created ideal, prior to the fall into sin [Gen. 3]). The text is as much an account of the human capacity for sin as it is an account of God's work of creation. Its explanatory nature provides insight into both human frailty and God's will for human goodness. See Clifford and Murphy (1990) and Trible (1978).

4 The dual aspects of marital sexual intercourse—the unitive and procreative—were first affirmed in the encyclical *Casti connubii* (Pius XI, 1930) and became ensconced as inseparable aspects, willed by God, in *Humanae vitae* (Paul VI, 1968). These documents mark the first magisterial teachings to recognize the unitive reality of marital sexual intercourse. The ensuing theological discussion of these inseparable aspects within *Humanae vitae* reflects a watershed moment in Roman Catholic sexual theology.

5 Christopher West is largely recognized as the most popular Western interpreter of John Paul II's theology of the body. Because John Paul's own work

is dense, many persons interested in the theology of the body turn to West's (2004) basic introduction as a means of accessing the Pope's work.

6 Salzman and Lawler (2008) have undertaken a sustained and cogent critique of John Paul's biologically focused understanding of complementarity and suggested a *holistic* complementarity accounting for sexual orientation, reproductivity, and personal, affective communion within the sexual person. Although theirs is not a specifically feminist account of theological anthropology, its more robust account of complementarity lends itself to a broad understanding of human sexual flourishing.

7 In response to Johnson's critique, Christopher West suggests that Johnson's dissatisfaction with John Paul's theology of the body arises from the fact that he "simply hasn't penetrated the Pope's project"; "in layman's terms, he just doesn't 'get it'" (West, 2005).

8 Lebacqz's concerns are borne out by Canadian statistics regarding physical and sexual violence against females, starting early in the home. In 2009, while boys and girls (up to and including 17 years of age) experienced similar rates of physical assault in the home, girls experienced sexual offences in the home at four times more than the rate for boys (Canadian Centre for Justice Statistics: Statistics Canada [CCJS-SC], 2011, p. 5). The domestic sphere tends to be more dangerous for women than for men. In 2009, 15 males and 49 females were victims of spousal homicide in Canada: "While males were more likely to be the victims of homicide, females were more likely to be the victims of family-related homicide, particularly spousal homicide. Over the past 30 years, the rate of spousal homicides against females has consistently been about three to four times higher than that for males" (CCJS-SC, 2011, p. 33). Even when homicide is not the final result, women still experience violence more frequently and with greater severity than males: "In 2009, females who reported spousal violence were about three times more likely than males (34% versus 10%) to report that they had been sexually assaulted, beaten, choked or threatened with a gun or a knife by their partner or ex-partner in the previous five years" (CCJS-SC, 2011, p. 10).

9 *Gender trouble* was originally published in 1990 and was re-released in a tenth-anniversary edition in 1999. I cite the 1999 publication.

Chapter Five

1 Some of that barrage comes from print magazines aimed at adolescent females, along with their online equivalents: *GL/Girls' Life* (www.girlslife .com), *Glitter* (www.glittermagrocks.com), *J-14* (www.j-14.com), *justine* (www.justinemagazine.com), *Nylon* (www.nylonmag.com), *Seventeen* (www.seventeen.com), *Teen Vogue* (www.teenvogue.com), and *Twist* (www.twistmagazine.com). These magazines tend to be derivatives of adult fashion magazines, reformatted with information deemed appropriate for

adolescents. Teen-focused magazines, however, generally feature advertising, content, and product endorsement similar to adult magazines. They also tend to focus on fashion, dating (boys), body size, and sex. In contrast to fashion magazines, there are some adolescent-focused magazines that attempt to counter the cultural focus on appearance and boys with attention to contemporary issues, broader life questions, and strong female role models: *Discovery Girls* (www.discoverygirls.com), *Shameless* (www.shamelessmag.com), *Teen Graffiti* (www.teengraffiti.com), *Teen Ink* (www.teenink.com), and *Teen Voices* (www.teenvoices.com).

2 For a helpful history of gender development research, see Zosuls, Miller, Ruble, Martin, and Fabes (2011). For an overview and critique of various trends in the field, see Perry and Pauletti (2011). And for a review of current trends, including both gender normative and gender variant development, see Steensma, Kreukels, de Vries, and Cohen-Kettenis (2013).

3 Following the 1999 publication of their social cognitive theory (SCT), Bandura and Bussey (2004) have participated in a lively dialogue with Martin, Ruble, and Szkrybalo (2002, 2004). Although Martin, Ruble, and Szkrybalo disagree with them on some points, such as the directionality of influences on and sequence of gender development, and the comprehensiveness of SCT, Martin, Ruble, and Szkrybalo note, "there is widespread agreement in the field that a complete understanding of gender development requires an integration of many different perspectives" (2002, p. 928). See the primary sources for a more detailed account of their differences.

4 That is, a multi-dimensional theoretical framework including feminist theory and its critique of compulsory heterosexuality and social injustices regarding gender; social construction theory and phenomenology; relational theory regarding adolescent development; and ecological development theory (Tolman, Striepe, & Harmon, 2003, pp. 7–9).

5 It seems unlikely that Tolman, Striepe, and Harmon (2003) are in accord with the official Roman Catholic understanding of gender complementarity in theological anthropology and concomitant sex and gender discussions, as developed in Pope John Paul II's theology of the body.

6 See DeRosa et al. (2010); Lindberg, Jones, and Santelli (2008).

7 See Brewster and Tillman (2008); Cornell and Halpern-Felsher (2006); DeRosa et al. (2010); Halpern-Felsher, Cornell, Kropp, and Tshann (2005); Lindberg, Jones, and Santelli (2008).

8 See Lindberg, Jones, and Santelli (2008); Markham et al. (2009); Song and Halpern-Felsher, (2011).

9 See Bersamin, Walker, Fisher, and Grube (2006); Dake, Price, Ward, and Welch (2011).

10 See Council of Ministers of Education, Canada (2003); Dake, Price, Ward, and Welch (2011); DeRosa et al. (2010).

11 See Roberts, Kippax, Spongberg, and Crawford (1996).

12 Cornell and Halpern-Felsher (2006); Dake, Price, Ward, and Welch (2011); and DeRosa et al. (2010).

13 Based on the 2006–2008 National Survey of Family Growth (NSFG), a representative national study.

14 Seyla Benhabib (1987) offers a succinct account of Kohlberg's response to Gilligan's critique of his work, and an interesting theoretical exploration of the place of feminist theory in the development of moral philosophy in Western thought.

15 She also notes the possible liabilities associated with exceedingly high self-esteem for some individuals. When combined with narcissistic tendencies, low empathy for others, and high sensitivity to negative evaluation, these individuals are prone to react violently to threats to their own egos (Harter, 2003, pp. 633–34).

Chapter Six

1 Although there are likely myriad global experiences of pubertal females, I limit my discussion here primarily to scholarly discussions of such experiences in Western/North American cultures, for the purposes of focus and brevity. I further recognize the wide diversity of cultural realities within Western/North American society, and indicate significant distinctions when possible.

2 Each cultural group recounted ambivalence regarding first menstruation, but in different ways. A more cross-cultural examination of menstrual experience goes beyond this project, but would make an interesting study in its own right.

3 Websites directed at adolescent females are the newest form of menstrual education/advertising offered by producers of "feminine hygiene" products. The Procter and Gamble–administered website *BeingGirl* offers information on menstruation and its management. Conveniently, their products (i.e., Tampax tampons and Always pads) will work for you. In the "My Period" column, advertisements for Procter & Gamble products feature heavily in anticipation of the reader's first menstruation (see www.beinggirl.com). Kimberley-Clark offers the Kotex line of products, including the "UByKotex" campaign for tampons and liners, encouraging females to take charge of their periods and "decide what works for yourself" (see www.ubykotex.com).

4 Martin (1996) also notes that menarche and menstruation are laden with associations to dirt, shame, taboo, and danger in their link to excrement and excretion. Martin suggests that "girls learn these cultural meanings from peers, parents, siblings, advertising, and boys' joking" (1996, p. 29).

5 A possible exception to the dearth of meaningful ritual in adolescent females' lives is the Latin American ritual celebration of Quinceanera, a girl's fifteenth birthday. Although it is not tied explicitly to menarche or menstruation, the celebration certainly has overtones of transition

into womanhood. This is not, however, a ritual universally celebrated in Latin American cultures and contexts, nor is it universally understood in its meaning and purpose. For useful and diverse explorations of the Quinceanera, see Cantu, 1999; Davalos, 1996; Gomez, 1997; Horowitz, 1993; and Stavans, 2010.

6 The differences and similarities between adolescent female and male neural development are not yet well understood; current data suggests more similarities than differences (Giedd, Raznahan, Mills, & Lenroot, 2012). Although in their large-scale, longitudinal neuro-imaging study Lenroot et al. (2007) found size differences between males' and females' brains (males' brain size is "consistently reported to be ~8–10% larger" than females' [p. 1]), they noted that the developmental differences were not linear across the brain. Further, their study did not explore the functional differences between male and female adolescent brains. As they point out, there remains "a particular paucity of data on sexual dimorphism of human brain anatomy between 4 and 22 years of age, a time of emerging sex differences in behavior and cognition" (Giedd, Raznahan, Mills, & Lenroot, 2012, p. 1). To date, tentative conclusions regarding neural sexual dimorphism include differences in size, timing differences in growth and development, continuing divergence of brain volumes throughout development toward adulthood, and differences of incidence, timing, and manifestation of mental illnesses and disorders. For example, although some recent research suggests that sexual maturity/pubertal status is more closely associated with neural development than chronological age, and progresses differently between males and females (Hu, Pruessner, Coupe, & Collins, 2013), data is mixed and inconclusive (Blakemore, 2012; Lenroot & Giedd, 2010; Luna, Padmanabhan, & O'Hearn, 2010). Also inconclusive is the data regarding the neural mechanisms of the non-linear developmental process (Lenroot & Giedd, 2010).

7 "Magnetic Resonance Imaging (MRI) uses a very large magnetic field to produce high-quality three-dimensional images of brain structures without injecting radioactive tracers. A large cylindrical magnet creates a magnetic field around the person's head, and a magnetic pulse is sent through the magnetic field. Different structures in the brain (so-called white matter and grey matter, blood vessels, fluid, and bone, for example) have different magnetic properties and therefore they appear different in the MRI image. Sensors inside the scanner record the signals from the different brain structures and a computer uses the information to construct an image. Using MRI, it is possible to image both surface and deep brain structure in great anatomical detail" (Blakemore & Choudhury, 2006, p. 298).

8 Adolescent risk-taking is a debated topic in the study of adolescent development (Arnett, 2010). See the exchange between Males (2009, 2010), who charges that neuroscience has perpetuated a false, biodeterminist understanding of the dangers of adolescence, and a bevy of neuroscientists (Chein

et al., 2010; DeLisi et al., 2010; Johnson, Sudhinaraset, & Blum, 2010; Sercombe, 2010; Steinberg, 2008), who dispute Males' biodeterminist accusations with an appeal for interdisciplinary studies of adolescent development.

Chapter Seven

1 An interesting contemporary manifestation of this attitude is found in the "Purity Ball" movement within some evangelical Christian churches. The premise of the Ball is to promote sexual abstinence until marriage: the father takes a pledge to "cover" his pubertal daughter "as her authority and protection in the area of purity," and the daughter (as young as 10 years of age), princess for the day, pledges her purity until marriage. They often exchange purity rings or a locket with a key the father protects until the daughter's marriage. There is no equivalent phenomenon for adolescent males, although young males are invited to witness how fathers treat their daughters (see www.generationsoflight.com).

2 See Glick, Diebold, Baily-Werner, and Zhu, 1997, p. 1323.

3 There are a number of websites, the goals of which are to foster media literacy among females regarding pervasive sexual messages, and to instill a healthy critical stance toward those messages. See, for example: About-Face (www.about-face.org), The Action Coalition for Media Education (www.smartmediaeducation.net), Geena Davis Institute on Gender in the Media (www.seejane.org), Girls Inc. (www.girlsinc.org), Media Awareness Project (www.mediaawareness.org), The Media Education Foundation (www.mediaed.org), and Media Watch (www.mediawatch.com).

4 Along with the aforementioned Purity Ball are the less extravagant expressions of the virginity pledge. See, for example, the True Love Waits approach, which incorporates purity pledging with various symbols (e.g., jewellery, apparel, certificates), ceremonies, and programs, and offers support resources for Christian communities, such as the True Love Project:

> **Reintroducing True Love Waits:** Twenty years ago a small group of students in the Nashville area committed themselves to Christ in the pursuit of purity. Little did they know that shortly thereafter there were going to be thousands of additional students join them in what came to be known as the movement of True Love Waits. Over the years True Love Waits has witnessed hundreds of thousands of young people commit their sexual purity to God, while at the same time offering the promise of hope and restoration in Christ for all who have sinned sexually. It has been a tremendous movement, orchestrated by God, to further spread the biblical message of sex and purity to a younger generation. (LifeWay, n.d.)

Chapter Eight

1 Tina Beattie (2003) provides an astute critique of the sacred and secular constructions of female sexual bodies: "On the one hand, femininity is a transcendent ideal of perfection—a manufactured and commodified body that bears little resemblance to the living realities of the female flesh. On the other hand, real women have no voice with which to offer a different, more authentic account of women's embodied personhood as a source of dignity, meaning and worth. If the men of God invested the female body with all their sexual anxieties and robbed her of her capacity to image God, the men of Mammon have exploited that culture of denigration by using it to position women in a constant state of inadequacy and shame, perpetuated now not by spiritual fantasies of idealized femininity but by consumerist fantasies of the female body as a marketable commodity" (p. 128).

2 I am indebted to Margaret Farley's articulation of norms for an ethic of "just sex" (2006, pp. 216–32); my digression from her articulation reflects my endeavour to address adolescent female concerns specifically. As Farley notes, it is not clear that her account is appropriate for adolescents in general, given their developmental realities (2006, pp. 232–35).

3 I first encountered the articulation of *appropriate vulnerability* in Lebacqz (1987).

4 Hence, the so-called *Romeo and Juliet* clauses adopted within some legal jurisdictions, which provide for legal sexual activity among minors who are close in age.

5 "Consent" is an ambiguous requirement for sexual expression (e.g., in the simultaneous occurrence of consent, coercion, desire, and acquiescence); in the context of a mutual relationship, the negotiation of ambivalence between partners contributes to its very character as mutual.

REFERENCES

Abbott-Chapman, J., & Denholm, C. (2001). Adolescents' risk activities, risk hierarchies and the influence of religiosity. *Journal of Youth Studies 4* (3), 279–97. doi: 10.1080/13676260120075428

Abma, J., Driscoll, A., & Moore, K. (1998). Young women's degree of control over first intercourse: An exploratory analysis. *Family Planning Perspectives 30* (1), 12–18.

Abraham, S., Boyd, C., Lal, M., Luscombe, G., & Taylor, A. (2009). Time since menarche, weight gain and body image awareness among adolescent girls: Onset of eating disorders? *Journal of Psychosomatic Obstetrics and Gynecology 30* (2), 89–94. doi: 10.1080/01674820902950553

Alberts, A., Elkind, D., & Ginsberg, S. (2006). The personal fable and risk-taking in early adolescence. *Journal of Youth and Adolescence 36,* 71–76. doi: 10.1007/s10964-006-9144-4

Alkire, S. (2000). The basic dimensions of human flourishing: A comparison of accounts. In N. Biggar & R. Black (Eds.), *The revival of natural law: Philosophical, theological and ethical responses to the Finnis-Grisez school* (pp. 73–110). Aldershot, England: Ashgate Publishing House.

Allen, P. (2006). Man–woman complementarity: The Catholic inspiration. *Logos 9* (3), 87–108.

Alterman, E. (1999). Blowjobs and snowjobs. *The Nation,* December 20. Retrieved from http://www.thenation.com/article/blowjobs-and-snow-jobs#

Altman, J. (2004). Gonadal hormones humour the brain. *Neuroendocrinology 79* (6), 287–95. doi: 10.1159/000080045

American Academy of Pediatrics & American College of Obstetricians and Gynecologists. (2006). Menstruation in girls and adolescents: Using the menstrual cycle as a vital sign. *Pediatrics 118* (5), 2245–50. doi: 10.1542/peds.2006-2481

American Psychological Association (2002). *Developing adolescents: A reference for professionals.* Washington, DC: American Psychological Association.

American Psychological Association, Task Force on the Sexualization of Girls (2007). *Report of the APA Task Force on the Sexualization of Girls.* Washington, DC: American Psychological Association.

Andersen, S. (2003). Trajectories of brain development: Point of vulnerability or window of opportunity? *Neuroscience and Biobehavioral Reviews 27,* 3–18. doi: 10.1016/S0149-7634(03)00005-8

Andolsen, B.H. (1996). Whose sexuality? Whose tradition? Women, experience, and Roman Catholic sexual ethics. In C.E. Curran, M.A. Farley, & R.A. McCormick (Eds.), *Readings in moral theology: No. 9. Feminist ethics and the Catholic moral tradition* (pp. 207–39). Mahwah, NJ: Paulist Press.

Annas, J. (1993). *The morality of happiness.* New York: Oxford University Press.

Aquinas, T. (1947). *Summa theologica.* Benziger Bros. Edition. Fathers of the English Dominican Province (Trans.). Retrieved from http://www.ccel.org/ccel/aquinas/summa.toc.html

Aquinas, T. (1986). *Division and methods of the sciences: Questions V and VI of his Commentary on the De Trinitate of Boethius* (Armand Mauer, Trans.; 4th Rev. ed.). Toronto, ON: Pontifical Institute of Medieval Studies, 1986.

Arbeau, K.J., Galambos, N.L., & Jansson, S.M. (2007). Dating, sex, and substance use as correlates of adolescents' subjective experience of age. *Journal of Adolescence 30,* 435–47. doi:10.1016/j.adolescence.2006.04.006

Aristotle. (1985). The moral virtues (J.A.K. Thomson, Trans.). In C.H. Sommers (Ed.), *Vice and virtue in everyday life* (pp. 148–58). San Diego, CA: Harcourt Brace Jovanovich.

Armour, S., & Haynie, D.L. (2007). Adolescent sexual debut and later delinquency. *Journal of Youth and Adolescence 36,* 141–52. doi: 10.1007/s10964-006-9128-4

Arnett, J.J. (1999). Adolescent storm and stress, reconsidered. *American Psychologist 54* (5), 317–26.

Arnett, J.J. (2010). Editor's note: Section on the adolescent brain and risk taking. *Journal of Adolescent Research 25* (1), 3. doi: 10.1177/0743558409357231

Asato, M.R., Terwilliger, R., Woo, J., & Luna, B. (2010). White matter development in adolescence: A DTI study. *Cerebral Cortex 20,* 2122–31. doi: 10.1093-cercor/bhp282

Aspy, C.B., Vesely, S.K., Oman, R.F., Rodine, S., Marshall, L., & McLeroy, K. (2007). Parental communication and youth sexual behaviour. *Journal of Adolescence 30,* 449–46. doi: http://dx.doi.org.login.ezproxy.library.ualberta.ca/10.1016/j.adolescence.2006.04.007

Augustine, Saint (1952). *Continence.* M.F. McDonald (Trans.). Boston, MA: Daughters of St. Paul.

Augustine, Saint (1955). *The good of marriage.* C.T. Wilcox (Trans.). Boston: Daughters of St. Paul.

Averett, P., Benson, M., & Vaillancourt, K. (2008). Young women's struggle for sexual agency: The role of parental messages. *Journal of Gender Studies 17* (4), 331–44. doi: 10.1080/09589203802420003

Backstrom, L., Armstrong, E.A., & Puentes, J. (2012). Women's negotiation of cunnilingus in college hookups and relationships. *Journal of Sex Research 49* (1), 1–12. doi: 10.1080/00224499.2011.585523

Bamforth, N., & Richards, D.A.J. (2008). *Patriarchal religion, sexuality, and gender: A critique of new natural law.* New York: Cambridge University Press.

Bandura, A., & Bussey, K. (2004). On broadening the cognitive, motivational, and sociostructural scope of theorizing about gender development and functioning: Comment on Martin, Ruble, and Szkrybalo (2002). *Psychological Bulletin 130* (5), 691–701. doi: 10.1037/0033-2909.130.5.691

Barber, L.K., Bagsby, P.G., & Munz, D.C. (2010). Affect regulation strategies for promoting (or preventing) flourishing emotional health. *Personality & Individual Differences 49* (6), 663–66. doi: 10.1016/j.paid.2010.06.002

Barnes, G.M., Hoffman, J.H., Welte, J.W., Farrell, M.P., & Dintcheff, B.A. (2007). Adolescents' time use: Effects on substance use, delinquency and sexual activity. *Journal of Youth and Adolescence 36,* 697–710. doi: 10.1007/s10964-006-9075-0

Basow, S.A. (2006). Gender role and gender identity development. In J. Worrell & C.D. Goodheart (Eds.), *Handbook of girls' and women's psychological health* (pp. 242–251). Oxford: Oxford University Press.

Bay-Cheng, L.Y. (2003). The trouble of teen sex: The construction of adolescent sexuality through school-based sexuality education. *Sex Education 3* (1), 61–74. doi: 10.1080/1468181032000052162

Bay-Cheng, L.Y., & Fava, N.M. (2011). Young women's experiences and perceptions of cunnilingus during adolescence. *Journal of Sex Research 48* (6), 531–42. doi: 10.1080/00224499.2010.535221

Bearman, P.S., & Bruckner, H. (2001). Promising the future: Virginity pledges and first intercourse. *American Journal of Sociology 106* (4), 859–912. doi: 10.1086/320295

Beattie, T. (2003). *Woman: New century theology.* London, UK: Continuum.

Beattie, T. (2006). *New Catholic feminism: Theology and theory.* New York: Routledge.

Benedict XVI, Pope (2006a). *Homily, mass in Pilsudzki Square, May 26, 2006.* Retrieved from http://www.vatican.va/holy_father/benedict_xvi/homilies/2006/documents/hf_ben-xvi_hom_20060526_varsavia_en.html

Benedict XVI, Pope (2006b). *Homily, Eucharistic concelebration with the members of the International Theological Commission, October 6, 2006.* Retrieved from http://www.vatican.va/holy_father/benedict_xvi/homilies/2006/documents/hf_ben-xvi_hom_20061006_commissione-teologica_en.html

Benedict XVI, Pope (2007). *Address to the participants in the General Assembly of the Pontifical Academy for Life, February 24,2007.* Retrieved from http://www.vatican.va/holy_father/benedict_xvi/speeches/2007/february/documents/hf_ben-xvi_spe_20070224_academy-life_en.html

Benhabib, S. (1987). The generalized and the concrete other: The Kohlberg–Gilligan controversy and feminist theory. In S. Benhabib & D. Cornell

(Eds.), *Feminism as critique* (pp. 77–95, 174–81). Minneapolis: University of Minnesota Press.

Bersamin, M.M., Walker, S., Fisher, D.A., & Grube, J.W. (2006). Correlates of oral sex and vaginal intercourse in early and middle adolescence. *Journal of Research on Adolescence 16* (1), 59–68. doi: 10.1111/j.1532-7795.2006.00120.x

Bersamin, M.M., Walker, S., Waiters, E.D., Fisher, D.A., & Grube, J.W. (2005). Promising to wait: Virginity pledges and adolescent sexual behavior. *Journal of Adolescent Health 36,* 428–36. doi: 10.1016/j.jadohealth.2004.09.016

Biddlecom, A.E. (2004). Trends in sexual behaviours and infections among young people in the United States. *Sexually Transmitted Infections 80* (Suppl II), ii74–ii79. Retrieved from http://sti.bmjjournals.com

Blake, S.M., Simkin, L., Ledsky, R., Perkins, C., & Calabrese, J.M. (2001). Effects of a parent–child communications intervention on young adolescents' risk for early onset of sexual intercourse. *Family Planning Perspectives 33* (2), 52–61.

Blakemore, S.J. (2008). The social brain in adolescence. *Nature Reviews: Neuroscience 9,* 267–77. doi: 10.1038/nrn2353

Blakemore, S.J. (2012). Imaging brain development: The adolescent brain. *NeuroImage 61,* 397–406. doi:10.1016/j.neuroimage.2011.11.080

Blakemore, S.J., & Choudhury, S. (2006). Development of the adolescent brain: Implications for executive function and social cognition. *Journal of Child Psychology and Psychiatry 47* (3/4), 296–312. doi: http://dx.doi.org/10.1111/j.1469-7610.2006.01611.x

Blakemore, S.J., & Frith, U. (2005). *The learning brain: Lessons for education.* Malden, MA: Blackwell Publishing.

Blodgett, B.J. (2002). *Constructing the erotic: Sexual ethics and adolescent girls.* Cleveland: Pilgrim Press.

Blume, J. (1970). *Are you there God? It's me, Margaret.* New York: Dell Publishing.

Bordini, B., & Rosenfield, R.L. (2011). Normal pubertal development: Part II: Clinical aspects of puberty. *Pediatrics in Review 32* (7), 281–92. doi: 10.1542/pir.32-7-281

Brewster, K.L., & Tillman, K.H. (2008). Who's doing it? Patterns and predictors of youths' oral sexual experiences. *Journal of Adolescent Health 42,* 73–80. doi: 10.1016/j/jadohealth.2007.08.010

Brooks-Gunn, J. (1992). The impact of puberty and sexual activity upon the health and education of adolescent girls and boys. In S.S. Klein (Ed.), *Sex equity and sexuality in education* (pp. 97–126). New York: State University of New York Press.

Brooks-Gunn, J., & Ruble, D.N. (1983). The experience of menarche from a developmental perspective. In J. Brooks-Gunn & A.C. Petersen (Eds.), *Girls at puberty: Biological and psychosocial perspectives* (pp. 155–77). New York: Plenum Press.

Brown, J.D. (2000). Adolescents' sexual media diets. *Journal of Adolescent Health 27S,* 35–40.

Brown, J.D., Halpern, C.T., & L'Engle, K.L. (2005). Mass media as a sexual super peer for early maturing girls. *Journal of Adolescent Health 36,* 420–27. doi:10.1016/j.jadohealth.2004.06.003

Brown, J.D., L'Engle, K.L., Pardun, C.J., Guo, G., Kenneavy, K., & Jackson, C. (2006). Sexy media matter: Exposure to sexual content in music, movies, television, and magazines predicts black and white adolescents' sexual behavior. *Pediatrics 117,* 1018–27. doi: 10.1542/peds.2005-1406

Brown, L.M., & Gilligan, C. (1992). *Meeting at the crossroads: Women's psychology and girls' development.* New York: Ballantine Books.

Brown, P. (1988). *The body and society: Men, women, and sexual renunciation in early Christianity.* New York: Columbia University Press.

Bruckner, H., & Bearman, P. (2005). After the promise: The STD consequences of adolescent virginity pledges. *Journal of Adolescent Health 36,* 217–78. doi: 10.1016/j.jadohealth.2005.01.005

Brumberg, J.J. (1997). *The body project: An intimate history of American girls.* New York: Random House.

Bunkers, S.S. (2010). A focus on human flourishing. *Nursing Science Quarterly 23* (4), 290–95. doi: http://dx.doi.org/10.1177/0894318410380258

Burnett, S., & Blakemore, S.J. (2009). The development of adolescent social cognition. *Values, Empathy, and Fairness across Social Barriers: Annals of the New York Academy of Sciences 1167,* 51–56. doi: 10.1111/j.1749-6632 .2009.04509.x

Bussey, K., & Bandura, A. (1999). Social cognitive theory of gender development and differentiation. *Psychological Review 106* (4), 676–713.

Butler, J. (1993). *Bodies that matter: On the discursive limits of "sex."* New York: Routledge.

Butler, J. (1997). *Excitable speech: A politics of the performative.* New York: Routledge.

Butler, J. (1999). *Gender trouble: Feminism and the subversion of identity.* New York: Routledge. (Original work published 1990).

Butler, J. (2004a). *Undoing gender.* New York: Routledge.

Butler, J. (2004b). Imitation and gender insubordination. In S. Salih with J. Butler (Eds.), *The Judith Butler reader* (pp. 119–37). Malden, MA: Blackwell Publishing. (Original work published in 1991).

Butler, J. (2004c). The end of sexual difference? In *Undoing gender* (pp. 174–203). New York: Routledge.

Bynum, C.W. (1991). *Fragmentation and redemption: Essays on gender and the human body in medieval religion.* New York: Zone Books.

Bynum, C.W. (1995). Why all the fuss about the body? A medievalist's perspective. *Critical Inquiry 22* (Autumn), 1–33.

Cahill, L.S. (1985). *Between the sexes: Foundations for a Christian ethics of sexuality.* Philadelphia: PA: Fortress Press.

Cahill, L.S. (1995). "Embodiment" and moral critique: A Christian social perspective. In L.S. Cahill and M.A. Farley (Eds.), *Embodiment, morality, and medicine* (pp. 199–215). Netherlands: Kluwer Academic Publishers.

Cahill, L.S. (1996). *Sex, gender, and Christian ethics.* New studies in Christian ethics series. Cambridge, UK: Cambridge University Press.

Cahill, L.S. (1997). Natural law: A feminist reassessment. In L.S. Rouner (Ed.), *Is there a human nature?* (pp. 78–91). Notre Dame, IN: University of Notre Dame Press.

Canadian Centre for Justice Statistics: Statistics Canada (2011). *Family violence in Canada: A statistical profile.* Catalogue no. 85-224-X. Ottawa, ON: Minister of Industry.

Cantu, N.E. (1999). La quinceanera: Towards an ethnographic analysis of a life-cycle ritual. *Southern Folklore 56* (1), 73–101.

Carpenter, L.M. (2005). *Virginity lost: An intimate portrait of first sexual experiences.* New York: New York University Press.

Carvajal, S.C., Parcel, G.S., Basen-Engquist, K., Banspach, S.W., Coyle, K.K., Kirby, D., & Chan, W. (1999). Psychosocial predictors of delay of first sexual intercourse by adolescents. *Health Psychology 18* (5), 443–52.

Casey, B.J., Jones, R.M., & Hare, T.A. (2008). The adolescent brain. *Annals of the New York Academy of Sciences 1124,* 111–26. doi: 10.1196/annals.1440.010

Catechism of the Catholic Church. (1995). New York: Doubleday.

Cauffman, E., & Steinberg, L. (1996). Interactive effects of menarcheal status and dating on dieting and disordered eating among adolescent girls. *Developmental Psychology 32* (4), 631–35.

Chambers, W.C. (2007). Oral sex: Varied behaviors and perceptions in a college population. *Journal of Sex Research 44* (1), 28–42.

Chandra, A., Mosher, W.D., Copen, C., & Sionean, C. (2011). Sexual behavior, sexual attraction, and sexual identity in the United States: Data from the 2006–2008 National Survey of Family Growth. *National Health Statistics Reports,* 36. Hyattsville, MD: National Center for Health Statistics.

Chang, Y-T., Hayter, M., & Wu, S-C. (2010). A systematic review and meta-ethnography of the qualitative literature: Experiences of menarche. *Journal of Clinical Research 19,* 447–60. doi: 10.1111/j.1365-2702.2009.03019.x

Chein, J., Albert, D., O'Brien, L., Uckert, K., & Steinberg, L. (2011). Peers increase adolescent risk taking by enhancing activity in the brain's reward circuitry. *Developmental Science, 14* (2) F1–F10. doi: 10.1111/j.1467-7687 .2010.01035.x

Chopp, R. (1991). *The power to speak: Feminism, language, God.* New York: Crossroad.

Chrisler, J.C., & Zittel, C.B. (1998). Menarche stories: Reminiscences of college students from Lithuania, Malaysia, Sudan, and the United States. *Health Care for Women International 19,* 303–12.

Chrysostom, Saint John (1986). *On marriage and family life.* Trans. C.P. Roth & D. Anderson. Crestwood, NY: St. Vladimir's Seminary Press.

Clark, E.A. (1983). *Women in the early Church*. Wilmington, DE: Michael Glazier Inc.

Clifford, R.J., & Murphy, R.E. (1990). Genesis. In R.E. Brown, J.A. Fitzmyer & R.E. Murphy (Eds.), *The new Jerome biblical commentary* (pp. 8–43). Englewood Cliffs, NJ: Prentice Hall.

Cloutier, D. (2006). Heaven is a place on earth? Analyzing the popularity of Pope John Paul II's theology of the body. In L.S. Cahill, J. Garvey, & T.F. Kennedy (Eds.), *Sexuality and the U.S. Catholic Church: Crisis and renewal* (pp. 18–31, 200–203). New York: Crossroad Publishing Company.

Coakley, S. (2002). *Powers and submissions: Spirituality, philosophy and gender*. Malden, MA: Blackwell Publishing.

Coleman, E. (2002). Masturbation as a means of achieving sexual health. *Journal of Psychology and Human Sexuality 14* (2/3), 5–16. doi: 10.1300/J056v14n02_02

Coll, R. (1994). *Christianity and feminism in conversation*. Mystic, CN: Twenty-third Publications.

Collins, R.L., Elliott, M.N., Berry, S.H., Kanouse, D.E., Kunkel, D., Hunter, S.B., & Miu, A. (2004). Watching sex on television predicts adolescent initiation of sexual behavior. *Pediatrics 114*, e280–e289. doi: 10.1542/peds.2003-1065-L

Congregation for the Doctrine of the Faith (1986). *Letter to the bishops of the Catholic Church on the pastoral care of homosexual persons*. Retrieved from http://www.vatican.va/roman_curia/congregations/cfaith/documents/rc_con_cfaith_doc_19861001_homosexual-persons_en.html

Congregation for the Doctrine of the Faith (1987). *Donum vitae (Instruction on respect for human life in its origin and on the dignity of procreation)*. Retrieved from http://www.vatican.va/roman_curia/congregations/cfaith/documents/rc_con_cfaith_doc_19870222_respect-for-human-life_en.html

Congregation for the Doctrine of the Faith (2004). *Letter to the bishops of the Catholic Church on the collaboration of men and women in the Church and in the world*. Retrieved from http://www.vatican.va/roman_curia/congregations/cfaith/documents/rc_con_cfaith_doc_20040731_collaboration_en.html

Conly, S. (1988). Flourishing and the failure of the ethics of virtue. *Midwest Studies in Philosophy 13* (1), 83–95.

Cook, D.T., & Kaiser, S.B. (2004). Betwixt and be tween: Age ambiguity and the sexualization of the female consuming subject. *Journal of Consumer Culture 4* (2), 203–27. doi: 10.1177/1469540504043682

Cornell, J.L., & Halpern-Felsher, B.L. (2006). Adolescents tell us why teens have oral sex. *Journal of Adolescent Health 38*, 299–301. doi: 10.1016/j.jadohealth.2005.04.015

Council of Ministers of Education, Canada (2003). *Canadian youth, sexual health and HIV/AIDS study: Factors influencing knowledge, attitudes and behaviours*. Toronto, ON: Author.

Crysdale, C. (1995). Revisioning natural law: From the classicist paradigm to emergent probability. *Theological Studies 56*, 464–84.

Cuffee, J.J., Hallfors, D.D., & Waller, M.W. (2007). Racial and gender differences in adolescent sexual attitudes and longitudinal associations with coital debut. *Journal of Adolescent Health 41*, 19–26. doi: 10.1016/j.jadohealth.2007.02.012

Curran, C.E. (1991). Natural law in moral theology. In C.E. Curran & R. McCormick (Eds.), *Readings in moral theology, No. 7. Natural law and theology* (pp. 247–95). New York: Paulist Press.

Curran, C.E. (1999). *The Catholic moral tradition today: A synthesis.* Washington, DC: Georgetown University Press.

Dahl, R.E. (2004). Adolescent brain development: A period of vulnerabilities and opportunities (Keynote Address). *Annals of the New York Academy of Science 1021*, 1–22. doi: 10.1196/annals.1308.001

Dake, J.A., Price, J.H., Ward, B.L., & Welch, P.J. (2011). Midwestern rural adolescents' oral sex experience. *Journal of School Health 81* (3), 159–165. doi: http://dx.doi.org/10.1111/j.1746-1561.2010.00575.x

Daly, M. (1968). *The Church and the second sex.* New York: Harper & Row.

Daly, M. (1973). *Beyond God the father: Toward a philosophy of liberation.* Boston, MA: Beacon Press.

Dardenne, B., Dumont, M., & Bollier, T. (2007). Insidious dangers of benevolent sexism: Consequences for women's performance. *Journal of Personality and Social Psychology 93* (5), 764–79. doi: 10.1037/0022-3514.93.5.764

Davalos, K.M. (1996). La quinceanera: Making gender and ethnic identities. *Frontiers: A Journal of Women's Studies 16* (2/3), 101–27.

Delaney, J., Lupton, M.J., & Toth, E. (1988). *The curse: A cultural history of menstruation* (Rev. ed.). Chicago, IL: University of Illinois Press.

DeLisi, M., Wright, J.P., Vaughn, M.G., & Beaver, K.M. (2010). Nature and nurture by definition means both: A response to Males. *Journal of Adolescent Research 25* (1), 24–30. doi: 10.1177/0743558409353063

Dell, M.L. (2000). She grows in wisdom, stature, and favor with God: Female development from infancy through menarche. In J. Stevenson-Moessner (Ed.), *In her own time: Women and developmental issues in pastoral care* (pp. 117–43). Minneapolis, MN: Fortress Press.

DeRosa, C.J., Ethier, K.A., Kim, D.H., Cumberland, W.G., Afifi, A.A., Kotlerman, J., Loya, R.V., & Kerndt, P.R. (2010). Sexual intercourse and oral sex among public middle school students: Prevalence and correlates. *Perspectives on Sexual and Reproductive Health 42* (3), 197–205. doi: 10.1363/4219710

Diamond, L.M. (2006). Introduction: In search of good sexual-developmental pathways for adolescent girls. In R.W. Larson & L.A. Jensen (Series Eds.) & L. Diamond (Vol. Ed.) *New directions for child and adolescent development: No. 112. Rethinking positive adolescent female sexual development* (pp. 1–7). San Francisco: Jossey-Bass.

Dickson, N., Paul, C., Herbison, P., & Silva, P. (1998). First sexual intercourse: Age, coercion, and later regrets reported by a birth cohort. *British Medical Journal 316*, 29–33. doi: http://dx.doi.org/10.1136/bmj.316.7124.29

Diorio, J.A., & Munro, J.A. (2000). Doing harm in the name of protection: Menstruation as a topic for sex education. *Gender and Education 12*, 347–65.

Eccles, J.S., Barber, B.L., Stone, M., & Hunt, J. (2003). Extracurricular activities and adolescent development. *Journal of Social Issues 59* (4), 865–89.

Egan, S.K., & Perry, D.G. (2001). Gender identity: A multidimensional analysis with implications for psychosocial adjustment. *Developmental Psychology 37* (4), 451–63. doi: 10.1037/0012-1649.37.4.451

Eitle, T.M., & Eitle, D.J. (2002). Just don't do it: High school sports participation and young female adult sexual behavior. *Sociology of Sport Journal 19*, 403–18.

Elkind, D. (1981). Understanding the young adolescent. In L.D. Steinberg (Ed.), *The life cycle* (pp. 167–76). New York: Columbia University Press.

Elkind, D. (2001). Egocentrism in adolescence. In E. Aries (Ed.), *Adolescent behavior: Readings and interpretations* (pp. 107–15). United States: McGraw-Hill/Dushkin.

Erchull, E.J., Chrisler, J.C., Gorman, J.A., & Johnston-Robledo, I. (2002). Education and advertising: A content analysis of commercially produced booklets about menstruation. *Journal of Early Adolescence 22*, 455–74. doi: 10.1177/027243102237192

Ewing Lee, E.A., & Troop-Gordon, W. (2011). Peer processes and gender role development: Changes in gender atypicality related to negative peer treatment and children's friendships. *Sex Roles 64*, 90–102. doi: 10.1007/s11199-010-9883-2

Farley, M. (1993). Feminism and universal morality. In G. Outka & J.P. Reeder, Jr. (Eds.), *Prospects for a common morality* (pp. 170–90). Princeton, NJ: Princeton University Press.

Farley, M. (2006). *Just love: A framework for Christian sexual ethics.* New York: Continuum.

Fine, M. (1988). Sexuality, schooling, and adolescent females: The missing discourse of desire. *Harvard Educational Review 58* (1), 29–53.

Fine, M., & McClelland, S. (2006). Sexuality education and desire: Still missing after all these years. *Harvard Educational Review 76* (3), 297–338.

Fine, M., & McClelland, S. (2007). The politics of teen women's sexuality: Public policy and the adolescent female body. *Emory Law Journal 56* (4), 993–1038.

Fingerson, L. (2006). *Girls in power: Gender, body, and menstruation in adolescence.* Albany, NY: State University of New York Press.

Finnis, J. (1980). *Natural law and natural rights.* Oxford: Oxford University Press.

Finnis, J. (1992). *"Historical consciousness" and theological foundations.* Toronto, ON: Pontifical Institute of Medieval Studies.

Finnis, J. (1994). Law, morality, and "sexual orientation." *Notre Dame Law Review 69* (5), 1049–76.

Forbes, E.E., & Dahl, R.E. (2010). Pubertal development and behavior: Hormonal activation of social and motivational tendencies. *Brain and Cognition 72,* 66–72. doi: 10.1016/j.bandc.2009.10.007

Fredrickson, B.L., & Roberts, T.A. (1997). Objectification theory: Toward understanding women's lived experiences and mental health risks. *Psychology of Women Quarterly 21,* 173–206.

Fulkerson, M.M. (1997). Contesting the gendered subject: A feminist account of the *imago dei.* In R.S. Chopp & S.G. Davaney (Eds.), *Horizons in feminist theology: Identity, tradition, and norms* (pp. 99–115, 244–45). Minneapolis, MN: Fortress Press.

Garriguet, D. (2005). Early sexual intercourse. *Health Reports (Statistics Canada) 16* (3), 9–18.

Gerressu, M., Mercer, C.H., Graham, C.A., Wellings, K., & Johnson, A.M. (2008). Prevalence of masturbation and associated factors in a British national probability survey. *Archives of Sexual Behavior 37,* 266–78. doi: 10.1007/s10508-006-9123-6

Ghaye, T. (2010). In what ways can reflective practices enhance human flourishing? *Reflective Practice 11* (1), 1–7. doi: http://dx.doi.org/10.1080/14623940903525132

Giedd, J.N., Blumenthal, J., Jeffries, N.O., Castellanos, F.X., Liu, H., Zijdenbos, A., & Paus, T. (1999). Brain development during childhood and adolescence: A longitudinal MRI study. *Nature Neuroscience 2* (10), 861–63.

Giedd, J.N., Raznahan, A., Mills, K.L., & Lenroot, R.K. (2012). Review: Magnetic resonance imaging of male/female differences in human adolescent brain anatomy. *Biology of Sex Differences 3* (1), 19-27. doi: 10.1186/2042-6410-3-19

Gilligan, C. (1982/1993). *In a different voice: Psychological theory and women's development.* Cambridge, MA: Harvard University Press.

Glick, D.J. (1986). Recovering morality: Personalism and theology of the body of John Paul II. *Faith & Reason 12,* 1, 7–25.

Glick, P., Diebold, J., Bailey-Werner, B., & Zhu, L. (1997). The two faces of Adam: Ambivalent sexism and polarized attitudes toward women. *Personality and Social Psychology Bulletin 23* (12), 1323–34.

Glick, P., & Fiske, S.T. (1996). The Ambivalent Sexism Inventory: Differentiating between hostile and benevolent sexism. *Journal of Personality and Social Psychology 70* (3), 491–512.

Glick, P., & Fiske, S.T. (2001). An ambivalent alliance: Hostile and benevolent sexism as complementary justifications for gender inequality. *American Psychologist 56* (2), 109–18.

Glick, P., Lameiras, M., & Castro, Y.R. (2002). Education and Catholic religiosity as predictors of hostile and benevolent sexism toward women and men. *Sex Roles 47* (9/10), 433–41.

Golub, S. (1992). *Periods: From menarche to menopause.* Newbury Park, CA: Sage Publications.

Gomez, R. (1997). Celebrating the quinceanera as a symbol of faith and culture. In K.G. Davis (Ed.), *Misa, mesa y musa: Liturgy in the U.S. Hispanic Church* (2nd ed., pp. 104–115). Schiller Park, IL: World Library Publications.

Good, J.J., & Rudman, L.A. (2010). When female applicants meet sexist interviewers: The costs of being a target of benevolent sexism. *Sex Roles 62,* 481–93. doi: 10.1007/s11199-009-9685-6

Grabe, S., Hyde, J.S., & Lindberg, S.M. (2007). Body objectification and depression in adolescents: The role of gender, shame, and rumination. *Psychology of Women Quarterly 31,* 164–75.

Grisez, G. (1965). First principle of practical reason: A commentary on the *Summa Theologiae,* 1–2, Question 94, Article 2. *Natural Law Forum 10,* 168–201.

Grisez, G. (1993). *The way of the Lord Jesus: Volume two, living a Christian life.* Quincy, IL: Franciscan Press.

Grisez, G., Boyle, J., & Finnis, J. (1987). Practical principles, moral truth, and ultimate ends. *American Journal of Jurisprudence 32,* 99–151.

Grisez, G., & Shaw, R. (1991). *Fulfillment in Christ: A summary of Christian moral principles.* Notre Dame: University of Notre Dame Press.

Gruber, E., & Grube, J.W. (2000). Adolescent sexuality and the media: A review of current knowledge and implications. *Western Journal of Medicine 172,* 210–14.

Gudorf, C. (1994). *Body, sex, and pleasure: Reconstructing Christian sexual ethics.* Cleveland, OH: Pilgrim Press.

Guggino, J.M., & Ponzetti, J.J. (1997). Gender differences in affective reactions to first coitus. *Journal of Adolescence 20,* 189–200.

Hall, M.E.L., Langer, R., & McMartin, J. (2010). The role of suffering in human flourishing: Contributions from positive psychology, theology, and philosophy. *Journal of Psychology & Theology 38* (2), 111–21.

Halpern-Felsher, B. (2008). Oral sexual behavior: Harm reduction or gateway behavior? *Journal of Adolescent Health 43,* 207–8. doi: 10.1016/j/jadohealth.2008.07.001

Halpern-Felsher, B.L., Cornell, J.L., Kropp, R.Y., & Tschann, J.M. (2005). Oral versus vaginal sex among adolescents: Perceptions, attitudes, and behavior. *Pediatrics 115,* 845–51. doi: 10.1542/peds.2004-2108

Hardy, S.A., & Raffaelli, M. (2003). Adolescent religiosity and sexuality: An investigation of reciprocal influences. *Journal of Adolescence 26,* 731–39. doi: http://dx.doi.org/10.1016/j.adolescence.2003.09.003

Harris, A. (2005). Discourses of desire as governmentality: Young women, sexuality and the significance of safe spaces. *Feminism & Psychology 15* (1), 39–43. doi: 10.1177/0959353505049702

Harter, S. (1999). *The construction of the self: A developmental perspective.* New York: Guilford Press.

Harter, S. (2003). The development of self-representations during childhood and adolescence. In M. Leary & J. P. Tangney (Eds.), *Handbook of self and identity* (pp. 610–642). New York: Guilford Press.

Harter, S., Waters, P.L., Whitesell, N.R., & Kastelic, D. (1998). Level of voice among female and male high school students: Relational context, support, and gender orientation. *Developmental Psychology 34* (5), 892–901.

Havens, B., & Swenson, I. (1988). Imagery associated with menstruation in advertising targeted to adolescent women. *Adolescence 23* (89), 89–97.

Hawes, S.C., Wellings, K., & Stephenson, J. (2010). First heterosexual intercourse in the United Kingdom: A review of the literature. *Journal of Sex Research 47* (2–3), 137–52. doi: 10.1080/00224490903509399

Hayes, D.L. (1996). *And still we rise: An introduction to black liberation theology.* New York: Paulist Press.

Hayes, D.L. (2011). *Standing in the shoes my mother made: A womanist theology.* Minneapolis, MN: Fortress Press.

Heyward, C. (1989). *Touching our strength: The erotic as power and the love of God.* New York: HarperCollins.

Himes, M.J. (1989). The human person in contemporary theology: From human nature to authentic subjectivity. In R.P. Hamel & K.R. Himes (Eds.), *Introduction to Christian ethics: A reader* (pp. 49–62). New York: Paulist Press.

Hittinger, R. (1997). Natural law and Catholic moral theology. In M. Cromartie (Ed.), *A preserving grace: Protestants, Catholics, and natural law* (pp. 1–30, 175–79). Grand Rapids, MI: Ethics and Policy Center and Wm. B. Eerdmans Publishing Co.

Hogarth, H., & Ingham, R. (2009). Masturbation among young women and associations with sexual health: An exploratory study. *Journal of Sex Research 46* (6), 558–67. doi: 10.1080/00224490902878993

Holder, D.W., Durant, R.H., Harris, T.L., Daniel, J.H., Obeidallah, D., & Goodman, E. (2000). The association between adolescent spirituality and voluntary sexual activity. *Journal of Adolescent Health 26*, 295–302.

Holland, J., Ramazanoglu, C., Sharpe, S., & Thomson, R. (2000). Deconstructing virginity—young people's accounts of first sex. *Sexual and Relationship Therapy 15* (3) 221–32.

Horowitz, R. (1993). The power of ritual in a Chicano community: A young woman's status and expanding family ties. *Marriage and Family Review 19* (3/4), 257–80.

Houts, L.A. (2005). But was it wanted? Young women's first voluntary sexual intercourse. *Journal of Family Issues 26* (8), 1082–102. doi: 10.1177/0192513X04273582

Howell, A.J. (2009). Flourishing: Achievement-related correlates of students' well-being. *Journal of Positive Psychology 4* (1), 1–13. doi: 10.1080/17439760802043459

Hu, S., Pruessner, J.C., Coupe, P., & Collins, D.L. (2013). Volumetric analysis of medial temporal lobe structures in brain development from childhood to adolescence. *NeuroImage 74,* 276–87. doi: 10.1016/j .neuroimage.2013.02.032

Hunt, L.H. (1999). Flourishing egoism. In E.F. Paul, F.D. Miller, & J. Paul (Eds.), *Human flourishing* (pp. 72–95). New York: Cambridge University Press.

Hursthouse, R. (2007). Virtue ethics. *Stanford encyclopedia of philosophy.* Retrieved from http://plato.stanford.edu/entries/ethics-virtue

Hyde, J.S., & Jaffee, S.R. (2000). Becoming a heterosexual adult: The experiences of young women. *Journal of Social Issues 56* (2), 283–96.

Impett, E.A., Schooler, D., & Tolman, D.L. (2006). To be seen and not heard: Femininity ideology and adolescent girls' sexual health. *Archives of Sexual Behavior 35* (2), 131–44. doi: 10.1007/s10508-005-9016-0

Irigaray, L. (1993). *An ethics of sexual difference* (C. Burke & G.C. Gill, Trans.). Ithaca, NY: Cornell University Press.

Isasi-Diaz, A.M. (1993). *En la lucha = in the struggle: A Hispanic women's liberation.* Minneapolis, MN: Fortress Press.

Jaffee, S., & Hyde, J.S. (2000). Gender difference in moral orientation: A metaanalysis. *Psychological Bulletin 126* (5), 703–26. doi: 10.1037/0033-2909.126 .5.703

Jantzen, G.M. (2002). Good sex: Beyond private pleasure. In P.B. Jung, M.E. Hunt, & R. Balakrishnan (Eds.), *Good sex: Feminist perspectives from the world's religions* (pp. 3–14, 177–179). Piscataway, NJ: Rutgers University Press.

John Paul II, Pope (1981). *Familiaris consortio* [Role of the Christian family in the modern world]. Retrieved from http://www.vatican.va/holy_father/ john_paul_ii/apost_exhortations/documents/hf_jp-ii_exh_19811122_ familiaris-consortio_en.html

John Paul II, Pope (1988). *Mulieris dignitatem* [On the dignity and vocation of women]. Retrieved from http://www.vatican.va/holy_father/john_paul_ ii/apost_letters/documents/hf_jp-ii_apl_15081988_mulieris-dignitatem _en.html

John Paul II, Pope (1993). *Veritatis splendor* [On the splendor of truth: Regarding certain fundamental questions of the Church's moral teaching]. Retrieved from http://www.vatican.va/holy_father/john_paul_ii/ encyclicals/documents/hf_jp-ii_enc_06081993_veritatis-splendor_en.html

John Paul II, Pope (1994). *Ordinatio sacerdotalis* [On reserving priestly ordination to men alone]. Retrieved from http://www.vatican.va/holy _father/john_paul_ii/apost_letters/documents/hf_jp-ii_apl_22051994_ ordinatio-sacerdotalis_en.html

John Paul II, Pope (1995a). *Evangelium vitae* [The value and inviolability of human life]. Retrieved from http://www.vatican.va/holy_father/john_paul_ii/encyclicals/documents/hf_jp-ii_enc_25031995_evangelium-vitae_en.html

John Paul II, Pope (1995b). *Letter to women*. Retrieved from http://www.vatican.va/holy_father/john_paul_ii/letters/documents/hf_jp-ii_let_29061995_women_en.html

John Paul II, Pope (1997). *The theology of the body: Human love in the divine plan*. Boston, MA: Daughters of St. Paul.

Johnson, L.T. (2001). A disembodied "theology of the body": John Paul II on love, sex and pleasure. *Commonweal 128*, 2, 11–17.

Johnson, S.B., Sudhinaraset, M., & Blum, R.W. (2010). Neuromaturation and adolescent risk taking: Why development is not determinism. *Journal of Adolescent Research 25* (1), 4–23. doi: 10.1177/0743558409353339

Jones, S. (1997). Women's experience between a rock and a hard place: Feminist, womanist, and *mujerista* theologies in North America. In R.S. Chopp & S.G. Davaney (Eds.), *Horizons in feminist theology: Identity, tradition, and norms* (pp. 33–53, 234–35). Minneapolis, MN: Fortress Press.

Jones, S. (2000). *Feminist theory and Christian theology: Cartographies of grace*. Minneapolis, MN: Fortress Press.

Jonsen, A.R., & Toulmin, S. (1988). *The abuse of casuistry: A history of moral reasoning*. Berkeley and Los Angeles: University of California Press.

Jung, P.B. (2000). Sexual pleasure: A Roman Catholic perspective on women's delight. *Theology & Sexuality 12*, 26–47.

Jung, P.B. (2002). Sanctifying women's pleasure. In P.B. Jung, M.E. Hunt, & R. Balakrishnan (Eds.), *Good sex: Feminist perspectives from the world's religions* (pp. 77–95, 186–91). New Jersey: Rutgers University Press.

Kaestle, C.E., & Allen, K.R. (2011). The role of masturbation in healthy sexual development: Perceptions of young adults. *Archives of Sexual Behavior 40* (5), 983–94. doi: 10.1007/s10508-010-97220

Kaestle, C.E., Halpern, C.T., & Brown, J.D. (2007). Music videos, pro wrestling, and acceptance of date rape among middle school males and females: An exploratory analysis. *Journal of Adolescent Health 40*, 185–87. doi: 10.1016/j.jadohealth.2006.08.010

Kalman, M.B. (2003a). Adolescent girls, single-parent fathers, and menarche. *Holistic Nursing Practice 17* (1), 36–40.

Kalman, M.B. (2003b). Taking a different path: Menstrual preparation for adolescent girls living apart from their mothers. *Health Care for Women International 23*, 868–79. doi: 10.1080/07399330390244275

Kaveny, C. (2003). What women want: 'Buffy', the pope & the new feminists. *Commonweal 130* (19), 18–24.

Keenan, J.F. (1996). The return of casuistry. *Theological Studies 57*, 123–139.

Keenan, J.F. (1999). Applying the seventeenth-century casuistry of accommodation to HIV prevention. *Theological Studies 60*, 492–512.

Kinsman, S.B., Romer, D., Furstenberg, F.F., & Schwarz, D.F. (1998). Early sexual initiation: The role of peer norms. *Pediatrics 102,* 1185–92.

Koff, E., & Rierdan, J. (1995). Preparing girls for menstruation: Recommendations from adolescent girls. *Adolescence 30,* 795–811.

Koff, E., & Rierdan, J. (1996). Premenarcheal expectations and postmenarcheal experiences of positive and negative menstrual related changes. *Journal of Adolescent Health 18,* 286–91.

Koff, E., Rierdan, J., & Jacobson, S. (1981). The personal and interpersonal significance of menarche. *Journal of the American Academy of Child Psychiatry 20,* 148–58.

Kohlberg, L. (1976). Moral stages and moralization. In T. Lickona (Ed.), *Moral development and behavior* (pp. 72–98). New York: Holt, Rinehart & Winston.

Konrad, K., Firk, C., & Uhlhaas, P.J. (2013). Brain development during adolescence: Neuroscientific insights into this development period. *Deutsches Arzteblatt International 110* (25), 425–431. doi: http://dx.doi.org/10.3238/arztebl.2013.0425

Kristeva, J., & Clement, C. (2001). *The feminine and the sacred* (J.M. Todd, Trans.). New York: Columbia University Press.

Kunkel, D., Eyal, K., Finnerty, K., Biely, E., & Donnerstein, E. (2005). *Sex on TV4: A Kaiser Family Foundation Report.* Menlo Park, CA: Henry J. Kaiser Family Foundation. Retrieved from http://kff.org/other/event/sex-on-tv-4/

Kwok, P-l. (1992). *Chinese women and Christianity, 1860–1927.* Atlanta: Scholars Press.

Kwok, P-l. (2005). *Postcolonial imagination & feminist theology.* Louisville, KY: Westminster John Knox Press.

Laqueur, T.W. (2003). *Solitary sex: A cultural history of masturbation.* New York: Zone Books.

Lebacqz, K. (1987). Appropriate vulnerability: A sexual ethic for singles. *Christian Century 104* (15), 435–38.

Lebacqz, K. (1994). Love your enemy: Sex, power, and Christian ethics. In L.K. Daly (Ed.), *Feminist theological ethics: A reader* (pp. 244–61). Louisville, KY: Westminster John Knox Press.

Lee, J. (2008). "A kotex and a smile": Mothers and daughters at menarche. *Journal of Family Issues 29* (10), 1325–47. doi: 10.1177/0192513X08316117

Lefkowitz, E.S., Gillen, M.M., Shearer, C.L., & Boone, T.L. (2004). Religiosity, sexual behaviors, and sexual attitudes during emerging adulthood. *Journal of Sex Research 41* (2), 150–59.

Lefkowitz, E.S., & Stoppa, T.M. (2006). Positive sexual communication and socialization in the parent-adolescent context. In R.W. Larson & L.A. Jensen (Series Eds.) & L. Diamond (Vol. Ed.) *New directions for child and adolescent development: No. 112. Rethinking positive adolescent female sexual development* (pp. 39–55). San Francisco: Jossey-Bass.

Lehman, S.J., & Koerner, S.S. (2004). Adolescent women's sports involvement and sexual behavior/health: A process-level investigation. *Journal of Youth and Adolescence 33* (5), 443–55.

Lemmons, R.M.H. (2002). Equality, gender, and John Paul II. *Logos 5* (3), 111–30.

Lenroot, R.K., & Giedd, J.N. (2010). Sex differences in the adolescent brain. *Brain and Cognition 72,* 46–55. doi: 10.1016/j.bandc.2009.10.008

Lenroot, R.K., Gogtay, N., Greenstein, D.K., Wells, E.M., Wallace, G.L., Clasen, L.S., & Blumenthal, J.D. (2007). Sexual dimorphism of brain developmental trajectories during childhood and adolescence. *NeuroImage 36,* 1065–73. doi: 10.1016/j.neuroimage.2007.03.053.

Levine, J. (2002). *Harmful to minors: The perils of protecting children from sex.* Minneapolis, MN: University of Minnesota Press.

Lewin, T. (1997). Teen-agers alter sexual practices, thinking risks will be avoided. *New York Times,* Women's Health, April 5.

Lindberg, L.D., Jones, R., & Santelli, J.S. (2008). Noncoital sexual activities among adolescents. *Journal of Adolescent Health 43*(3), 231–38. doi: 10.1016/j.jadohealth.2007.12.010

Lonergan, B. (1957). *Insight: A study of human understanding.* New York: Harper & Row.

Lonergan, B. (1972). *Method in theology.* Minneapolis, MN: Winston Press.

Lorde, A. (1994). Uses of the erotic: The erotic as power. In J.B. Nelson & S.P. Longfellow (Eds.), *Sexuality and the sacred: Sources for theological reflection* (pp. 75–79). Louisville, KN: Westminster/John Knox Press.

Low, K.G. (2011). Flourishing, substance use, and engagement in students entering college: A preliminary study. *Journal of American College Health 59* (6), 555–61. doi: http://dx.doi.org/10.1080/07448481.2011.563432

Luna, B., Padmanabhan, A., & O'Hearn, K. (2010). What has fMRI told us about the development of cognitive control through adolescence? *Brain and Cognition 72,* 101–13. doi: 10.1016/j.bandc.2009.08.005

Luna, B., Thulborn, K.L., Munoz, D.P., Merriam, E.P., Garver, K.E., Minshew, N.J., Keshavan, D.S., et al. (2001). Maturation of widely distributed brain function subserves cognitive development. *NeuroImage 13,* 786–93. doi:10.1006/nimg.2000.0743

Lyons, H., Giordano, P.C., Manning, W.D., & Longmore, M.A. (2011). Identity, peer relationships, and adolescent girls' sexual behavior: An exploration of the contemporary double standard. *Journal of Sex Research 48* (5), 437–49. doi: 10.1080/00224499.2010.506679

MacIntyre, A.C. (2007). *After virtue: A study in moral theory* (3rd ed.). Notre Dame, IN: University of Notre Dame Press. (Originally published in 1981)

Maguen, S., & Armistead, L. (2006). Abstinence among female adolescents: Do parents matter above and beyond the influence of peers? *American Journal of Orthopsychiatry 76* (2), 260–64. doi: 10.1037/0002-9432.76.2.260

Males, M. (2009). Does the adolescent brain make risk taking inevitable? A skeptical appraisal. *Journal of Adolescent Research 24* (1), 3–20. doi: 10.1177/0743558408326913

Males, M.A. (2010). Is jumping off the roof *always* a bad idea? A rejoinder on risk taking and the adolescent brain. *Journal of Adolescent Research 25* (1), 48–63. doi: 10.1177/0743558409353780

Markham, C.M., Peskin, M.F., Addy, R.C., Baumler, E.R., & Tortolero, S.R. (2009). Patterns of vaginal, oral, and anal sexual intercourse in an urban seventh-grade population. *Journal of School Health 79* (4), 193. doi: 10.1111/j.1746-1561.2008.00389.x

Martin, C.L., Ruble, D.N., & Szkrybalo, J. (2002). Cognitive theories of early gender development. *Psychological Bulletin 128* (6), 903–33. doi: 10.1037/0033-2909.128.6.903

Martin, C.L., Ruble, D.N., & Szkrybalo, J. (2004). Recognizing the centrality of gender identity and stereotype knowledge in gender development and moving toward theoretical integration: Reply to Bandura and Bussey (2004). *Psychological Bulletin 130* (5), 702–10.

Martin, K.A. (1996). *Puberty, sexuality, and the self: Boys and girls at adolescence.* New York: Routledge.

May, W.E. (1998). Germain Grisez on moral principles and moral norms: Natural and Christian. In R.P. George (Ed.), *Natural law and moral inquiry: Ethics, metaphysics, and politics in the life of Germain Grisez* (pp. 3–35). Washington, DC: Georgetown University Press.

May, W.E. (2003). *An introduction to moral theology.* Huntington, IN: Our Sunday Visitor.

McCormick, R.A. (1978). Ambiguity in moral choice. In R.A. McCormick & P. Ramsey (Eds.), *Doing evil to achieve good: Moral choice in conflict situations* (pp. 7–53). Chicago: Loyola University Press.

McGrory, A. (1990). Menarche: Responses of early adolescent females. *Adolescence 25* (98), 265–70.

McNeely, C., Shew, M.L., Beuhring, T., Sieving, R., Miller, B.C., & Blum, R.W. (2002). Mothers' influence on the timing of first sex among 14- and 15-year-olds. *Journal of Adolescent Health 31,* 256–265. doi: http://dx.doi.org/10.1016/S1054-139X(02)00350-6

Meier, A.M. (2003). Adolescents' transition to first intercourse, religiosity, and attitudes about sex. *Social Forces 81* (3), 1031–52. doi: 10.1353/sof.2003.0039

Merskin, D. (1999). Adolescence, advertising, and the ideology of menstruation. *Sex Roles 40,* 941–57.

Miller, B.C., Norton, M.C., Fan, X., & Christopherson, C.R. (1998). Pubertal development, parental communication, and sexual values in relation to adolescent sexual behaviours. *Journal of Early Adolescence 18,* 27–52.

Miller, K.E., Farrell, M.P., Barnes, G.M., Melnick, M.J., & Sabo, D. (2005). Gender/racial difference in jock identity, dating, and adolescent sexual risk. *Journal of Youth and Adolescence 34* (2), 123–36. doi: 10.1007/s10964-005-3211-0

Modras, R. (1988). Pope John Paul II's theology of the body. In J. Grammick & P. Furey (Eds.), *The Vatican and homosexuality* (pp. 119–25). New York: Crossroads Publishing Company.

Moore, S.M. (1995). Girls' understanding and social constructions of menarche. *Journal of Adolescence 18*, 87–104.

Moreau-Gruet, F., Ferron, C., Jeannin, A., & Dubois-Arber, F. (1996). Adolescent sexuality: The gender gap. *AIDS Care 8* (6), 641–54.

Muehlenhard, C.L., & Peterson, Z.D. (2005). Wanting and not wanting sex: The missing discourse of ambivalence. *Feminism & Psychology 15* (1), 15–20. doi: 10.1177/0959-353505049698

Muuss, R.E. (1996). *Theories of adolescence* (6th ed.). New York: McGraw-Hill.

Nelson, J.B. (1978). *Embodiment: An approach to sexuality and Christian theology.* Minneapolis, MN: Augsburg Publishing House.

Nelson, J.B. (1992). Body theology and human sexuality. In R.M. Green (Ed.), *Religion and sexual health* (pp. 37–54). Netherlands: Kluwer Academic Publishers.

Nelson, J.B., & Longfellow, S.P. (1994). Introduction. In J.B. Nelson & S.P. Longfellow (Eds.), *Sexuality and the sacred: Sources for theological reflection* (pp. xiii–xviii). Louisville, KN: Westminster/John Knox Press.

Newcomer, S.F., & Udry, R. (1985). Oral sex in adolescent population. *Archives of Sexual Behavior 14* (1), 41–46.

Noble, K.G., Houston, S.M., Kan, E., & Sowell, E.R. (2012). Neural correlates of socioeconomic status in the developing human brain. *Developmental Science 15* (4), 516–27. doi: 10.1111/j.1467-7687.2012.01147.x

Nonnemaker, J.M., McNeely, C.A., & Blum, R.W. (2003). Public and private domains of religiosity and adolescent health risk behaviors: Evidence from the National Longitudinal Study of Adolescent Health. *Social Science & Medicine 57*, 2049–54. doi:10.1016/j.socscimed.2005.11.052

Nussbaum, M.C. (1988). Non-relative virtues: An Aristotelian approach. *Midwest Studies in Philosophy 13* (1), 32–53.

Nussbaum, M.C. (2000). *Women and human development: The capabilities approach.* Cambridge, UK: Cambridge University Press.

Orringer, K., & Gahagan, S. (2010). Adolescent girls define menstruation: A multiethnic exploratory study. *Health Care for Women International 31*, 831–47. doi: 10.1080/07399331003653782

Oswalt, S.B., Cameron, K.A., & Koob, J.J. (2005). Sexual regret in college students. *Archives of Sexual Behavior 34* (6), 663–69. doi: 10.1007/s10508-005-7920-y

Paradise, J.E., Cote, J., Minsky, S., Lourenco, A., & Howland, J. (2001). Personal values and sexual decision-making among virginal and sexually experienced urban adolescent girls. *Journal of Adolescent Health 28* (5), 404–9.

Patton, M.S. (1985). Masturbation from Judaism to Victorianism. *Journal of Religion and Health 24* (2), 133–46.

Paul VI, Pope (1968). *Humanae vitae* [On human life]. Retrieved from http://www.vatican.va/holy_father/paul_vi/encyclicals/documents/hf_p-vi_enc_25071968_humanae-vitae_en.html

Paus, T. (2005). Mapping brain maturation and cognitive development during adolescence. *TRENDS in Cognitive Sciences 9* (2), 60–68. doi: 10.1016/j.tics.2004.12.008

Pellauer, M.D. (1994). The moral significance of female orgasm: Toward sexual ethics that celebrates women's sexuality. In J.B. Nelson & S.P. Longfellow (Eds.), *Sexuality and the sacred: Sources for theological reflection* (pp. 149–68). Louisville, KY: Westminster/John Knox Press.

Perry, D.G., & Pauletti, R.E. (2011). Gender and adolescent development. *Journal of Research on Adolescence 21* (1), 61–74. doi: 10.1111/j.1532-7795.2010.00715.x

Petersen, J.L., & Hyde, J.S. (2010). A meta-analytic review of research on gender differences in sexuality, 1993–2007. *Psychological Bulletin 136* (1), 21–38. doi: 10.1037/a0017504

Phillips, L. (1998). *The girls report: What we know and need to know about growing up female.* New York: National Council for Research on Women.

Phillips, L.M. (2000). *Flirting with danger: Young women's reflections on sexuality and domination.* New York: New York University Press.

Pinkerton, S.D., Bogart, L.M., Cecil, H., & Abramson, P.R. (2002). Factors associated with masturbation in a collegiate sample. *Journal of Psychology and Human Sexuality 14* (2/3), 103–21.

Pius XI, Pope (1930). *Casti connubii* [On Christian marriage]. Retrieved from http://www.vatican.va/holy_father/pius_xi/encyclicals/documents/hf_p-xi_enc_31121930_casti-connubii_en.html

Poore, M. (2011). Digital literacy: Human flourishing and collective intelligence in a knowledge society. *Literacy Learning: The Middle Years 19* (2), 20–26.

Porter, J. (1993). Basic goods and the human good in recent Catholic moral theology. *The Thomist 57* (1), 27–49.

Porter, J. (1999). *Natural and divine law: Reclaiming the tradition for Christian ethics.* Ottawa, ON: Novalis, St. Paul University.

Posner, R.B. (2006). Early menarche: A review of research on trends in timing, racial differences, etiology and psychosocial consequences. *Sex Roles 54*, 315–22. doi: 10.1007/s11199-006-9003-5

Prendergast, S. (1995). 'With gender on my mind': Menstruation and embodiment at adolescence. In J. Holland, M. Blair, & S. Sheldon (Eds.), *Debates and issues in feminist research and pedagogy* (pp. 196–213). Bristol, PA: Open University.

Rasmussen, D.B. (1999). Human flourishing and the appeal to human nature. In E.F. Paul, F.D. Miller, & J. Paul (Eds.), *Human flourishing* (pp. 1–43). New York: Cambridge University Press.

Rathus, S.A., Nevid, J.S., Fichner-Rathus, L., McKenzie, S.W., & Bissell, M. (2005). *Essentials of human sexuality* (2nd Cdn. ed.). Toronto, ON: Pearson Education Canada.

Ratzinger, J. (2005). *Homily, mass "Pro Eligendo Romano Pontifice," April 18, 2005.* Retrieved from http://www.vatican.va/gpII/documents/homily-pro-eligendo-pontifice_20050418_en.html

Reirden, D.H., Forke, C.M., Rudy, B., Hodinka, R., & Schwarz, D.F. (2007). Oral sex behavior in urban adolescent women. *Journal of Adolescent Health 40*, S19–S54.

Remez, L. (2000). Oral sex among adolescents: Is it sex or is it abstinence? *Family Planning Perspectives 32* (6), 298–304.

Rickert, V.I., Sanghvi, R., & Wiemann, C.M. (2002). Is lack of sexual assertiveness among adolescent and young adult women a cause for concern? *Perspectives on Sexual and Reproductive Health 34* (4), 178–83.

Roberts, C., Kippax, S., Spongberg, M., & Crawford, J. (1996). 'Going down': Oral sex, imaginary bodies and HIV. *Body & Society 2* (3), 107–24.

Roberts, T.A, Goldenberg, J.L., Power, C., & Pyszczynski, T. (2002). "Feminine protection": The effects of menstruation on attitudes towards women. *Psychology of Women Quarterly 26*, 131–39.

Roberts, T.A., & Waters (2004). Self-objectification and that "not so fresh feeling": Feminist therapeutic interventions for healthy female embodiment. *Women & Therapy 27* (3/4), 5–21. doi:10.1300/J015v27n03_02

Romeo, R.D. (2003). Puberty: A period of both organizational and activational effects of steroid hormones on neurobehavioural development. *Journal of Neuroendocrinology 15*, 1185–92.

Romeo, R.D., & McEwan, B.S. (2006). Stress and the adolescent brain. *Annals of the New York Academy of Sciences 1094*, 202–14.

Romeo, R.D, Richardson, H.N., & Sisk, C.L. (2002). Puberty and the maturation of the male brain and sexual behavior: Recasting a behavioral potential. *Neuroscience and Behavioral Reviews 26*, 381–91. doi: 10.1016/S0149-7634(02)00009-X

Rosenbaum, J.E. (2009). Patient teenagers? A comparison of the sexual behavior of virginity pledgers and matched non-pledgers. *Pediatrics 123*, e110–e120. doi: 10.1542/peds.2008-0407

Rosenthal, D.A., Smith, A.M.A., & de Visser, R. (1999). Personal and social factors influencing age at first sexual intercourse. *Archives of Sexual Behavior 28* (4), 310–33.

Ross, S.A. (2001). The bridegroom and the bride: The theological anthropology of John Paul II and its relation to the Bible and homosexuality. In P.B. Jung, with J.A. Coray (Eds.), *Sexual diversity and Catholicism: Toward the development of moral theology* (pp. 39–59). Collegeville, MN: Liturgical Press.

Rostosky, S.S., Wilcox, B.L., Wright, M.L.C., & Randall, B.A. (2004). The impact of religiosity on adolescent sexual behavior: A review of the evidence. *Journal of Adolescent Research 19* (6), 677–97. doi: 10.1177/0743558403260019

Rousseau, M.F. (2000). John Paul II and theology of the body. *Chicago Studies* 39 (Sum 2000), 162–75.

Rudy, K. (1994). Thinking through the ethics of abortion. *Theology Today 51,* 235–48.

Ruether, R.R. (1983). *Sexism and God-talk: Toward a feminist theology.* Boston, MA: Beacon Press.

Sabo, D.F., Miller, K.E., Farrell, M.P., Melnick, M.J., & Barnes, G.M. (1999). High school athletic participation, sexual behavior and adolescent pregnancy: A regional study. *Journal of Adolescent Health 25,* 207–16.

Salzman, T.A. (2003). *What are they saying about Catholic ethical method?* Mahwah, NJ: Paulist Press.

Salzman, T.A., & Lawler, M.G. (2008). *The sexual person: Toward a renewed Catholic anthropology.* Washington, DC: Georgetown University Press.

Santelli, J.S., Kaiser, J., Hirsch, L., Radosh, A., Simkin, L., & Middlestadt, S. (2004). Initiation of sexual intercourse among middle school adolescents: The influence of psychosocial factors. *Journal of Adolescent Health 34,* 200–208. doi:10.1016/j.jadohealth.2003.06.004

Savage, M.P., & Holcomb, D.R. (1999). Adolescent female athletes' sexual risk-taking behaviors. *Journal of Youth and Adolescence 28* (5), 595–602.

Schneiders, S.M. (1991). *Beyond patching: Faith and feminism in the Catholic Church.* Mahwah, NJ: Paulist Press.

Schooler, D., Kim, J.L., & Sorsoli, L. (2006). Setting rules or sitting down: Parental mediation of television consumption and adolescent self-esteem, body image, and sexuality. *Sexuality Research and Social Policy 3* (4), 49–62.

Schreck, L. (1999). Adolescent sexual activity is affected more by mothers' attitudes and behavior than by family structure. *Family Planning Perspectives 31* (4), 200–201.

Schussler Fiorenza, E. (1990). *In memory of her: A feminist theological reconstruction of Christian origins.* New York: Crossroad. (Originally published in 1983).

Schvaneveldt, P.L., Miller, B.C., Berry, E.H., & Lee, T.R. (2001). Academic goals, achievement, and age at first sexual intercourse: Longitudinal, bidirectional influences. *Adolescence 36* (144), 767–87.

Second Vatican Council (1965a). *Gaudium et spes* [Pastoral constitution of the Church in the modern world]. Retrieved from http://www.vatican.va/archive/hist_councils/ii_vatican_council/documents/vat-ii_cons_19651207_gaudium-et-spes_en.html

Sercombe, H. (2010). The gift and the trap: Working the "teen brain" into our concept of youth. *Journal of Adolescent Research 25* (1), 31–47. doi: 10.1177/0743558409353065

Shivanandan, M. (2001). John Paul II's theology of the body. *Living Light 37* (3), 67–74.

Sibley, C.G., & Wilson, M.S. (2004). Differentiating hostile and benevolent sexist attitudes toward positive and negative sexual female subtypes. *Sex Roles 51* (11/12), 687–696. doi: 10.1007/s11199-004-0718-x

Sieg, E. (2007). 'What you want, or what you get?' Young women talking about the gap between desired and lived heterosexual relationships in the twenty-first century. *Women's Studies International Forum 30,* 175–86. doi:10.1016/j.wsif.2007.01.007

Sieving, R.E., McNeely, C.S., & Blum, R.W. (2000). Maternal expectations, mother–child connectedness, and adolescent sexual debut. *Archive of Pediatric and Adolescent Medicine 154,* 809–16.

Silverman, J.G., Raj, A., & Clements, K. (2004). Dating violence and associated sexual risk and pregnancy among adolescent girls in the United States. *Pediatrics 114* (2), e220–e225. Retrieved from http://www.pediatrics.org/cgi/content/full/114/2/e220

Simes, M.R., & Berg, D.H. (2001). Surreptitious learning: Menarche and menstrual product advertisements. *Health Care for Women International 22,* 455–69.

Sinha, J.W., Cnaan, R.A., & Gelles, R.J. (2007). Adolescent risk behaviors and religion: Findings from a national study. *Journal of Adolescence 30,* 231–49. doi:10.1016/j.adolescence.2006.02.005

Sisk, C.L., & Foster, D.L. (2004). The neural basis of puberty and adolescence. *Nature Neuroscience 7* (10), 1040–47. doi:10.1038/nn1326

Skandhan, K.P., Pandya, A.K., Skandhan, S., & Mehta, Y.B. (1988). Menarche: Prior knowledge and experience. *Adolescence 23* (89), 149–54.

Skinner, S.R., Smith, J., Fenwick, J., Fyfe, S., & Hendriks, J. (2008). Perceptions and experiences of first sexual intercourse in Australian adolescent females. *Journal of Adolescent Health 43,* 593–99. doi: 10.1016/j.jadohealth.2008.04.017

Slater, A., & Tiggeman, M. (2002). A test of objectification theory in adolescent girls. *Sex Roles 46* (9/10), 343–49.

Smiler, A.P., Ward, L.M., Caruthers, A., & Merriwether, A. (2005). Pleasure, empowerment, and love: Factors associated with a positive first coitus. *Sexuality Research & Social Policy 2* (3), 41–55. doi: http://dx.doi.org/10.1525/srsp.2005.2.3.41

Smith, T.E., & Leaper, C. (2005). Self-perceived gender typicality and the peer context during adolescence. *Journal of Research on Adolescence 16* (1), 91–103. doi: 10.1111/j.1532-7795.2006.00123.x

Somerville, L.H., Jones, R.M., & Casey, B.J. (2010). A time of change: Behavioral and neural correlates of adolescent sensitivity to appetitive and aversive environmental cues. *Brain and Cognition 72,* 124–33. doi:10.1016/j.bandc.2009.07.003

Song, A.V., & Halpern-Felsher, B.L. (2011). Predictive relationship between adolescent oral and vaginal sex: Results from a prospective, longitudinal study. *Archives of Pediatrics and Adolescent Medicine 165* (3), 243–49. doi: 10.1001/archpediatrics.2010.214

Sorsoli, C.L., Porche, M.V., & Tolman, D.L. (2005). "He left her for the alien": Girls, television, and sex. In E. Cole & J.H. Daniel (Eds.), *Featuring females:*

Feminist analyses of media (pp. 25–39). Washington, DC: American Psychological Association.

Spear, L.P. (2000). The adolescent brain and age-related behavioral manifestations. *Neuroscience and Behavioral Reviews 24,* 417–463.

Stavans, I. (Ed.). (2010). *Quinceanera.* Santa Barbara, CA: ABC-CLIO, LLC.

Stayton, W.R. (1996). A theology of sexual pleasure. In E. Stuart & A. Thatcher (Eds.). *Christian perspectives on sexuality and pleasure* (pp. 332–46). Grand Rapids, MI: Wm. B. Eerdmans.

Steensma, T.D., Kreukels, B.P.C., de Vries, A.L.C., & Cohen-Kettenis, P.T. (2013). Gender identity development in adolescence. *Hormones and Behaviour 64,* 288–97. doi: http:dx.doi.org/10.1016/j.yhbeh.2013.02.020

Stein, E., & Kim, S. (2009). *Flow: The cultural story of menstruation.* New York: St. Martin's Griffin.

Steinberg, L. (2008). A social neuroscience perspective on adolescent risk-taking. *Developmental Review 28,* 78–106. doi: 10.1016/j.dr.2007.08.002

Steinberg, L. (2010). A behavioral scientist looks at the science of adolescent brain development. *Brain and Cognition 72,* 160–64. doi: 10.1016/j.bandc.2009.11.003

Strasburger, V.C. (2005). Adolescents, sex, and the media: Ooooo, baby, baby—a Q & A. *Adolescent Medicine 16,* 269–88. doi:10.1016/j.admecli.2005.02.009

Striegel-Moore, R.H., & Cachlin, F.M. (1999). Body image concerns and disordered eating in adolescent girls: Risk and protective factors. In N.G. Johnson, M.C. Roberts, & J. Worell (Eds.), *Beyond appearance: A new look at adolescent girls* (pp. 85–108). Washington, DC: American Psychological Association.

Sweeny, K.C. (2006). The perfection of women as maternal and the anthropology of Karol Wojtyla. *Logos 9* (2), 129–53. doi: 10.1353/log.2006.0020

Swenson, I.E., Foster, B., & Asay, M. (1995). Menstruation, menarche, and sexuality in the public school curriculum: School nurses' perceptions. *Adolescence 30,* 677–83.

Taylor, C.R., & Dell'Oro, R. (Eds.) (2006). *Health and human flourishing: Religion, medicine, and moral anthropology.* Washington, DC: Georgetown University Press.

Teevan, D. (2003). Challenges to the role of theological anthropology in feminist theologies. *Theological Studies 64,* 582–97.

Teitelman, A.M. (2004). Adolescent girls' perspectives of family interactions related to menarche and sexual health. *Qualitative Health Research 14* (9), 1292–308. doi: 10.1177/1049732304268794

Thistlethwaite, S.B. (1989). Every two minutes: Battered women and feminist interpretation. In J. Plaskow & C.P. Christ (Eds.), *Weaving the visions* (pp. 302–13). New York: HarperCollins.

Thompson, S. (1990). Putting a big thing into a little hole: Teenage girls' accounts of sexual initiation. *Journal of Sex Research 27* (3), 341–61.

Thompson, S. (1995). *Going all the way: Teenage girls' tales of sex, romance & pregnancy.* New York: Hill and Wang.

Tolman, D.L. (1994). Doing desire: Adolescent girls' struggles for/with sexuality. *Gender & Society 8* (3), 324–42.

Tolman, D.L. (1999). Female adolescent sexuality in relational context: Beyond sexual decision making. In N.G. Johnson, M.C. Roberts, & J. Worrell (Eds.), *Beyond appearance: A new look at adolescent girls* (pp. 227–46). Washington, DC: American Psychological Association.

Tolman, D.L. (2000). Object lessons: Romance, violation, and female adolescent sexual desire. *Journal of Sex Education and Therapy 25* (1), 70–79.

Tolman, D.L. (2002a). *Dilemmas of desire: Teenage girls talk about sexuality.* Cambridge, MA: Harvard University Press.

Tolman, D.L. (2002b). Femininity as a barrier to positive sexual health for adolescent girls. In A.E. Hunter & C. Forden (Eds.), *Readings in the psychology of gender: Exploring our differences and commonalities* (pp. 196–207). Boston, MA: Allyn & Bacon.

Tolman, D.L. (2005). Founding discourses of desire: Unfettering female adolescent sexuality. *Feminism & Psychology 15* (1), 5–9. doi: 10.1177/0959 -353505049696

Tolman, D.L. (2006). In a different position: Conceptualizing female adolescent sexuality development within compulsory heterosexuality. In R.W. Larson & L.A. Jensen (Series Eds.) & L. Diamond (Vol. Ed.), *New directions for child and adolescent development: No. 112. Rethinking positive adolescent female sexual development* (pp. 71–89). San Francisco: Jossey-Bass.

Tolman, D.L., Impett, E.A., Tracy, A.J., & Michael, A. (2006). Looking good, sounding good: Femininity ideology and adolescent girls' mental health. *Psychology of Women Quarterly 30,* 85–95.

Tolman, D.L, Striepe, M.I., & Harmon, T. (2003). Gender matters: Constructing a model of adolescent sexual health. *Journal of Sex Research 40* (1), 4–12.

Tolman, D.L., & Szalacha (1999). Dimensions of desire: Bridging qualitative and quantitative methods in a study of female adolescent sexuality. *Psychology of Women Quarterly 23,* 7–39.

Traina, C.L.H. (1997). Oh, Susanna: The new absolutism and natural law. *Journal of the American Academy of Religion 65* (2), 371–401.

Traina, C.L.H. (1999). *Feminist ethics and natural law: The end of anathemas.* Washington, DC: Georgetown University Press.

Traina, C.L.H. (2006). Under pressure: Sexual discipleship in the real world. In L.S. Cahill, J. Garvey, & T.F. Kennedy (Eds.), *Sexuality and the U.S. Catholic Church: Crisis and renewal* (pp. 68–93, 210–14). New York: Crossroad Publishing Company.

Trible, P. (1978). *God and the rhetoric of sexuality.* Philadelphia, PA: Fortress Press.

Uecker, J.E., Angotti, N., & Regnerus, M.D. (2008). Going most of the way: "Technical virginity" among American adolescents. *Social Science Research 37,* 1200–1215. doi: 10.1016/j.ssresearch.2007.09.006

Vigil, P., Ceric, F., Cortes, M.E., & Klaus, H. (2006). Usefulness of monitoring fertility from menarche. *Journal of Pediatric and Adolescent Gynecology 19*, 173–79. doi: 10.1016/j.jpag.2006.02.003

Wade, L.D., Kremer, E.C., & Brown, J. (2005). The incidental orgasm: The presence of clitoral knowledge and the absence of orgasm for women. *Women and Health 42* (1), 117–38. doi: 10.1300/J013v42n01_07

Wang, Y., Adamson, C., Yuan, W., Altaye, M., Rajagopal, A., Byars, A.W., & Holland, S.K. (2012). Sex differences in white matter development during adolescence: A DTI study. *Brain Research 1478*, 1–15. doi: 10.1016/j.brainres.2012.08.038

Ward, L.M. (2003). Understanding the role of entertainment media in the sexual socialization of American youth: A review of empirical research. *Developmental Review 23*, 347–88. doi:10.1016/S0273-2297(03)00013-3

Ward, L.M., Day, K.M., & Epstein, M. (2006). Uncommonly good: Exploring how mass media may be a positive influence on young women's sexual health and development. In R.W. Larson & L.A. Jensen (Series Eds.) & L. Diamond (Vol. Ed.) *New directions for child and adolescent development: No. 112. Rethinking positive adolescent female sexual development* (pp. 57–70). San Francisco: Jossey-Bass.

Ward, L.M., & Friedman, K. (2006). Using TV as a guide: Associations between television viewing and adolescents' sexual attitudes and behavior. *Journal of Research on Adolescence 16* (1), 133–56. doi: 10.1111/j.1532-7795.2006.00125.x

West, C. (1998). John Paul's distinctive contribution. Retrieved from http://www3.nd.edu/~afreddos/courses/264/west1.htm

West, C. (2003). *Theology of the body explained: A commentary on John Paul II's "Gospel of the Body."* Leominster, England: Gracewing.

West, C. (2004). *Theology of the body for beginners: A basic introduction to Pope John Paul II's sexual revolution.* West Chester, PA: Ascension Press.

West, C. (2005). A response to Luke Timothy Johnson's critique of John Paul II's "disembodied" theology of the body. Retrieved from http://www.evangelizationstation.com/htm_html/moral%20theology/Sexuality/a_response_to_luke_timothy_johns.htm

Wheelwright, P., & MacInnes, T. (Producers) & MacInnes, T. (Director) (1996). *Under wraps: A film about going with the flow.* [Video]. Montreal, QC: National Film Board of Canada.

Whitaker, D.J., Miller, K.S., May, D.C., & Levin, M.L. (1999). Teenage partners' communication about sexual risk and condom use: The importance of parent–teenager discussions. *Family Planning Perspectives 31* (3), 117–21.

White, L.R. (2013). The function of ethnicity, income level, and menstrual taboos in postmenarcheal adolescents' understanding of menarche and menstruation. *Sex Roles 68*, 65–76. doi: 10.1007/s11199-012-0166-y

Wight, D., Parkes, A., Strange, V., Allen, E., Bonell C., & Henderson, M. (2008). The quality of young people's heterosexual relationships: A longitudinal analysis of characteristics shaping subjective experience. *Perspectives on Sexual and Reproductive Health 40* (4), 226–37. doi: 10.1363/4022608

Williams, D.S. (1993). *Sisters in the wilderness: The challenge of womanist Godtalk.* Maryknoll, NY: Orbis Books.

Williams, J.M., & Currie, C. (2000). Self-esteem and physical development in early adolescence: Pubertal timing and body image. *Journal of Early Adolescence 20,* 129–49. doi: 10.1177/0272431600020002002

Wojtyla, K. (Pope John Paul II) (1981). *Love and responsibility* (H.T. Willetts, Trans.). New York: Farrar, Straus, Giroux. (Original work published 1960).

Wong, D.B. (1988). On flourishing and finding one's identity in community. *Midwest Studies in Philosophy 13* (1), 324–41.

Yurgelun-Todd, D. (2007). Emotional and cognitive changes during adolescence. *Current Opinion in Neurobiology 17,* 251–57. doi: 10.1016/j.conb.2007.03.009

Zosuls, K.M., Miller, C.F., Ruble, D.N., Martin, C.L., & Fabes, R.A. (2011). Gender development research in *Sex Roles:* Historical trends and future directions. *Sex Roles 64,* 826–42. doi: 10.1007/s11199-010-9902-3

INDEX